A Farmhouse in Tuscany

Victoria Springfield inherited a passion for Italy from her father who loved visiting Tuscany, particularly the tiny village of Gioviano which helped inspire *A Farmhouse in Tuscany*. Victoria grew up in Upminster, Essex. After many years in London, she now lives in Kent with her husband in a house by the river. She likes to write in the garden with a neighbour's cat by her feet or whilst drinking cappuccino in her favourite café. Then she types up her scribblings in silence whilst her mind drifts away to Italy. Victoria's debut novel, *The Italian Holiday*, set on the Amalfi Coast, is also published by Orion Dash.

Twitter: @VictoriaSWrites
Facebook: @VictoriaSpringfieldAuthor.

Also by Victoria Springfield

The Italian Holiday

A FARMHOUSE
IN TUSCANY

Victoria Springfield

This paperback first published in Great Britain in 2022 by Orion Dash,
an imprint of The Orion Publishing Group Ltd.,
Carmelite House, 50 Victoria Embankment
London EC4Y 0DZ

An Hachette UK Company

A CIP catalogue record for this book is
available from the British Library.

ISBN (Paperback) 978 1 3987 0894 5
ISBN (eBook) 978 1 3987 0370 4

www.orionbooks.co.uk

In memory of Marjorie and Kenneth Russell
and their 'palace' in Gioviano.

Prologue

Luigi was leaning out of the church tower using a long wooden stick to adjust the hands on the village clock. It was months since it had told the right time. Donna waved but Luigi was too engrossed in his task to notice her.

Donna rode on. It was a fine, June morning and from her vantage point on Caesar's back she could see across the village rooftops to the lush green valley and the hills beyond. Swifts were screeching as they circled overhead; the scent of wild thyme was in the air; the sun was warm on the back of her neck. On a day like this she could almost believe that she was living the life she had chosen.

She crossed over the road to the scrubby old bit of land that lay alongside the vineyard. Caesar threw his head around, blowing loudly through his nostrils.

'Steady,' Donna admonished. She let out a little rein. The horse responded with a small buck of excitement.

No matter how many times she cantered along this route Donna still felt a surge of adrenalin. At the top of the vineyard she eased Caesar back to a walk and although she continued to use her legs and reins to guide him, the old horse needed no instructions to find his way home.

Donna's thoughts returned to the time she had ridden far away from the village, not knowing where she was going, not caring if she ever returned. When she finally came to her senses, Caesar had found the shortest route back whilst she, half blinded by tears, could hardly see the road in front of them.

Nearly ten years had passed. Daniela and Marco were all grown up, and Bella Vista riding centre was flourishing. Donna had lived too long in the shadow of the past. She would look to the future. And if she ever saw Giovanni Ginistrelli again, she would walk right on by.

Chapter One

Harriet sat on the thin rubber mat, her knees apart and the soles of her feet pressed together.

Savita's soothing voice drifted across the meeting room: 'Your body is still; your mind still. The thoughts and stresses of the day melting away.'

If only. Harriet sneaked a look at the clock behind her manager's head. Savita gave one of her serene smiles. Harriet tried to smile back in a calm, zen type of way, but the tension in her jaw produced a crazed rictus grin. A brief flicker of alarm crossed Savita's line-free forehead.

'Now, slowly stand up,' Savita said.

Harriet scrambled to her feet, adjusted her glasses – which had been slipping down her nose – and rolled up her mat with indecent haste.

'Thank you, everybody. Same time Monday.'

Harriet sneaked back to her desk. She gripped her computer mouse and dragged some data into a new column. She peered at the screen through her silver-rimmed glasses and twisted a piece of her pale blonde hair around her index finger.

Harriet liked figures; they had their own set of rules. If you understood those, everything added up. What was right one day was right the next. If only relationships were as simple as that. Harriet frowned; she didn't want to think about Peter right now. Or anyone else. It was easier to stay late in the office than go out, meet someone new and get her heart broken all over again.

Harriet felt a hand on her shoulder. She turned suddenly, knocking the dregs of a cup of cold coffee across the desk. Brown liquid splashed on to her hastily discarded yoga hoody.

'What are you still doing here?' Savita said. *I could say the same to you*, Harriet thought. By now her boss was usually heading home to cook a well-balanced, nutritious meal for her two impossibly gorgeous big-eyed children and handsome lawyer husband. Whilst Savita sat on the train, no doubt using the time to brush up on her language skills, Harriet was invariably shifting through the piles of documents that seemed to breed in the corner of her desk.

'Just finishing off these figures. I'll only be five minutes,' Harriet lied.

Savita snatched up Harriet's mouse.

'What are you doing?' Harriet shrieked.

'Saving your work and shutting you down. You're going home.'

'I know, I know. "Work-life balance" and all that.' Harriet tried to keep her voice light, but she could feel the panic rising. 'I guess I'll be fine to get this done on Monday.' She tried to fake a smile.

'You're not coming in next week and I don't want to see you the week after either.'

Harriet swallowed hard. She could feel her face glowing and her armpits began to feel sticky and damp. Surely Savita couldn't be letting her go. No, she'd have to go through HR. There were procedures for this sort of thing weren't there? And there was a huge project coming up in three weeks' time. They couldn't manage without her – could they?

'What do you mean?' She could hear her voice trembling. 'You're not . . . not . . . getting rid of me. I mean I know I made that mistake on the spreadsheet last week.'

'Don't be so daft. Look, Harriet, you're one of my best team members but I need you fresh and focused. We've all got to pull together on the new project but right now your mind's all over the place. There's no point trying to deny it. I carried over some of your holiday allowance last year and I've no intention of doing the same again. I want you out of this office to rest and recharge. I've already pre-approved your days off so you'll have no problem booking them.'

Harriet stared at her.

'Don't look at me like that. If I waited for you to get round to taking time off we'd be here 'til Christmas.'

'But what will I do by myself?' Oh dear, that did sound a bit pathetic but wandering around some historic town or sitting on the beach alone didn't really appeal. It was such short notice she would never find a friend to go with her, besides everyone seemed to have plans with their boyfriends this year. It was okay for Savita: she was the sort of person who could instantly throw together a fortnight's holiday and end up in an impossibly perfect, Instagrammable location without a cloud in the sky.

'I have the perfect idea for you.' Savita smiled. Of course, she did. 'I know how much you've been enjoying the yoga classes since I launched the "Employee Wellness Initiative" but it seems that whilst your body is willing your mind isn't quite in the zone.'

'I love yoga, but it's hard to relax in the office.'

'Which is exactly why you need to go on a yoga holiday. And I know just the place: Italy.'

Harriet hesitated, imagining a minimalist studio full of impossibly thin women in designer gear and huge sunglasses.

Well, maybe they took the sunglasses off when they lay on the mats, but they were bound to be chic and intimidating.

'A place called Bella Vista. My sister went there for a week last autumn. It's an old farmhouse out in the countryside run by a couple of English women so you won't have to worry about the language barrier. Wonderful classes, rolling Tuscan hills, home-grown vegetables, pasta.'

This was sounding good.

'Sitting on the terrace with a big glass of wine.'

This was sounding even better.

'Sunshine,' Savita added. 'Lots of sunshine. I'll write down the name of the website.' She picked up a pad of Post-it notes.

'*Bella Vista*?'

'Beautiful view. Think about it – but remember you've got two weeks off. Don't waste them.'

Harriet pushed open the front door, chucked her mac on the cascading pile of coats on the chair in the hallway and put on the kettle. She carried the steaming mug through to the sitting room. Turmeric infusion – very virtuous; it would make up for the supper of frozen pizza with a side order of crisps she was planning to eat later. It looked as though her housemates Vikki and Matt had gone down the pub; they probably wouldn't be back until late. She had a rare opportunity to stretch out on the whole length of the couch and take full charge of the remote control. Luxury. Who needed a Tuscan terrace when you could lounge on a saggy, old velveteen sofa in Streatham?

There was no need to go jetting off anywhere; she would use the time off to stay in London, meet a few friends, go to the yoga classes at the council gym, perhaps try something new like salsa or tap-dancing – she quite fancied herself as a modern-day Ginger Rogers. Or maybe not – she was bound to look silly.

Harriet put down her mug and propped her feet up on a pile of old cushions. She heard Matt's bedroom door open. She turned her head in surprise. A pale, shirtless bloke in grey jogging bottoms was standing there. Harriet let out a rather girly scream.

'Hey! You woke me up when you came in. Didn't mean to startle you. You must be Harriet. I'm Jez.'

'Jez?' she repeated faintly.

'Yeah. I'm a friend of Matt's. Well, a friend of a friend. He said I could crash here whilst I'm over from Oz. Fancy a beer? Might as well preload before the gang arrive.'

'Sorry?'

'No need.' He grinned. 'Got a couple of mates coming over for a few days. Looks like you've got plenty of space. Told them I could fit one in with me and Matt and the other one could bed down in here. They're not fussy. This is great, this stuff, brewed by monks.' He handed Harriet a can.

'Umm, thanks. I'll be back in a few minutes.' Harriet fled to the sanctuary of her bedroom. She sat down on the narrow single bed, reached for her laptop, and typed in the address Savita had given her. A picture of an olive grove filled the screen. The words *Bella Vista* were written across the blue horizon. In the top right corner was an old farmhouse as pretty as a picture-postcard. There were two strange brown triangular patches at the bottom of the screen. She zoomed in. Ears. Hairy, brown pointed ears. Someone must have taken the photo from the back of a horse.

The fridge door slammed; Jez must be going back for some more beer already. She could hear him talking loudly on the phone: 'Sure, mate, tomorrow's great. More the merrier.'

Harriet clicked on the icon in the centre of the screen. *This website is under construction.* Well, that was that. Then she saw another icon at the bottom: *Book here.* There was a room available.

Jez was lolling across the green couch. There was golf on the television. He took a great swig of beer.

'So, Harriet. Got any plans for the weekend?'

Chapter Two

Harriet lifted her baby-blue holdall up onto the train and made her way through the packed compartment. She glanced around looking for a spare seat.

'Hey, this one's free.' The girl sitting by the window moved her denim jacket and red suede shoulder bag out of the way. 'Sorry, I didn't mean to hog two seats.'

'Thanks,' Harriet said. She hesitated, unsure of where to put her bag.

'Here, let me help you put that up on the rack with mine.' The girl stood up and took Harriet's holdall. Harriet tried to hide her surprise.

The girl grinned. 'It's okay to look shocked. I know you want to ask how tall I am; everybody does. I'm exactly six foot. Fortunately, I've never been too keen on heels – or maybe I just never learnt to walk in them.'

'Me, neither.' Harriet laughed.

'First time in Italy?' the tall girl asked.

'Yes.' Harriet smiled; it would be nice to have someone to chat to after the silence of the plane journey and the fretful business of purchasing her train ticket. She rooted in her shoulder bag and fished out the twin-pack of chocolate-covered wafers she had picked up at the station. 'Would you like some?'

'No, I'm okay, thanks. I couldn't stop eating on the plane.' The girl laughed. She propped her elbow on the pull-out table and twisted the end of her long, curly red hair.

Harriet bit into the first wafer; there was a layer of creamy hazelnut filling in the middle. It was delicious but it didn't take long to discover that chocolate and Italian sunshine weren't exactly a match made in heaven. She rubbed ineffectually at her sticky fingers with a torn piece of tissue.

'You look like you could use one of these.' A boy of around Harriet's age was leaning across the aisle holding out a small plastic package.

'Wet wipes? Wow, you're organised. Thanks!' Harriet plucked one out and handed the packet back.

'I started carrying these when I met my next-door neighbour's little boy. You wouldn't want to see the mess he can make with a bar of chocolate.' The boy smiled; dimples formed at the corner of his mouth. His cropped hair was the colour of honey and he wore a blue short-sleeved shirt that showed off his muscular arms. His hazel eyes were framed by indecently long lashes. Harriet tried not to stare.

The tall girl said something Harriet didn't catch. She reluctantly turned to face her.

'Sorry?' Harriet said.

'I was just saying how much I love Italy,' the girl said.

'Have you been here often?' Harriet asked. The girl chatted away but Harriet found it hard to concentrate; her eyes kept straying to the seat on the other side of the aisle. The boy's face was partially obscured by the novel he was reading. Elena Ferrante's *My Brilliant Friend*. Harriet had a copy on the pile of unread books by her bed. By the time she got back from the office and double-checked her work emails she was usually too tired to do anything other than lounge in front of the TV.

The boy caught her eye. Harriet felt herself blush. He put down his book and leant forward slightly as though he was about to say something but instead he frowned and picked up his book again. She could not help noticing that he was not turning the pages.

The train pulled into the next station. The boy stood up. He hauled his bag down from the luggage rack and stepped towards the door at the end of the compartment. For some inexplicable reason Harriet's heart sank.

He glanced over his shoulder and smiled that lovely smile again. Harriet's stomach did a little flip. She raised her hand in a half-wave.

The boy did the same. He stepped down from the train.

The tall girl leant forward. 'He certainly liked the look of you.'

'Don't be daft.'

'Come on! He couldn't keep his eyes off you; he might as well have been holding that book upside down,' the girl joked. 'Look, he's watching you now.'

The boy was still standing on the platform. He did not seem to be in a hurry to go anywhere. Harriet watched him become smaller and smaller as the train pulled away.

'So where are you going?' the girl said. 'I've been talking so much I forgot to ask. I'm Jess, by the way.'

'Harriet. I'm heading for an old farmhouse called Bella Vista. I'm not exactly sure where it is. I'm hoping there will be a taxi rank at the station.'

'You're absolutely kidding me! So am I. This is the second time I've been. You won't need to worry about finding your way. Marco will be picking us up. He's the son of Donna who owns the place. He'll be bringing the van; people tend to turn up with so many bags. You've done pretty well to fit all your stuff in that little holdall.'

'It was such a last-minute thing I didn't have chance to overpack. Just a few joggers and hoodies. Oh, and one dress just in case.'

'Well, I guess you can always borrow boots and a hat,' Jess said.

'A hat?' Harriet frowned. Maybe they would be doing their classes out on the terrace. She wondered how hot it got; perhaps she should have brought some sun lotion.

'I know it's nice to feel the wind in your hair, but I don't think your travel insurance will cover you if you fall off and they find out you weren't wearing one.'

'Fall off?' She hadn't thought to ask Savita what sort of yoga they did at the farm; this must be some new trendy version.

'I've come off more times than I can count.' Jess laughed. 'But all their horses are really well schooled so I'm sure you'll be fine.'

'Horses? Oh no, I won't be riding. I've come for the yoga classes,' Harriet said.

'Oh. Donna organised a couple of yoga weeks there last autumn. I didn't realise she was still doing them.'

Harriet swallowed hard. Horses? She'd always found them a bit scary. Great big things. She fervently hoped that Jess had got it wrong. She must have. There was no reason to think that the yoga classes had stopped. But she couldn't help thinking back to the home page on the Bella Vista website: photographs of an olive grove and a quaint old farmhouse under a bright blue sky. There was no sign of yoga mats, nor lithe bodies performing sun salutations or warrior poses. Just a view of the countryside seen from between two great big, hairy brown ears.

'We're here!' Jess leapt up.

Harriet stood on tiptoe, but she still could not reach

the luggage rack. Jess lifted down Harriet's holdall. 'It's okay, I've got it.'

The guard was signalling for the train to pull out. 'Quick, quick,' Harriet said. She grabbed Jess's denim jacket. They dived out of the train doors in a tangle of luggage and laughter.

'There's Marco,' Jess said.

A young man of about twenty was leaning nonchalantly against the bonnet of a white van parked opposite the station's entrance. He was dressed in cut-off denims and a faded green T-shirt that revealed a tattoo of skulls and roses wrapped around one bicep; some sort of big cat prowled across the other. His hair sprung out in wild, jet-black curls. Harriet could not see his eyes because he wore large dark sunglasses but when he spotted the two girls a huge smile spread across his face.

'Jess! So good to see you again!' He stepped forward and gave her a big hug.

'This is Harriet.'

'Marco. Good to meet you.'

'You too,' Harriet replied.

Marco chucked their bags into the back of the van.

'Harriet's here for the yoga,' Jess said.

'Yoga?' He frowned. 'I didn't think Mum was doing that any longer. You can ride, can't you, Harriet? We don't usually take beginners.'

'Oh, Harriet's never ridden, but I've told her not to worry.'

'Looks like it'll be me who has to teach her.' He didn't sound too enthused.

'Maybe Harriet could ride Coco,' said Jess. 'He's the old pony.'

'Will my feet touch the ground?' Harriet tried to make a joke of it. Jess laughed but Marco did not respond. He stared straight at the road ahead.

'Don't worry. You'll be fine,' Jess said.

Harriet nodded dumbly. She wiped her sweaty hands on the front of her jeans. It didn't seem the right time to tell either of them that horses made her nervous. She would enjoy admiring them from a distance, but she had no intention of learning to ride. No intention at all. There must be something else to do at Bella Vista.

A few minutes later Marco turned off the main road. A group of small boys playing football in the road scattered as he sounded his horn. They passed a handsome church with a clock tower and entered a square arranged around a small stone water fountain. Two women, one heavily pregnant, stood gossiping outside the village shop under the shade of a striped awning. A short, round man whose T-shirt did not quite meet his waistband stood nearby, smoking and flicking ash onto the pavement.

Marco parked the van with two wheels on the pavement and helped the man manoeuvre several catering-size tins of tomatoes and a tray of peaches into the back. He reversed into a side street and drove back out of the village and turned up a narrow lane. A simple wooden sign pointed the way to Bella Vista. They slowed right down, but Harriet still had to grab the door handle to steady herself as they bumped over the lane's uneven surface.

Marco jumped out and heaved open a hefty five-bar gate. A large, scruffy grey dog shot straight out, running towards them, barking excitedly. Marco opened the van's other door. He patted the passenger seat. The dog lifted one paw and looked up at him. 'Okay, Lupo, I'll pick you up'. He heaved the dog onto the black leather seat. '*Oof.* You get heavier every time I see you.'

'Lupo's getting too old to jump up,' Jess said.

'And too lazy to walk back to the house,' Marco said.

Marco closed the gate and drove up the dusty farm track and parked the van on a patch of gravel.

'We're here,' Jess said.

'Oh,' said Harriet.

The house was beautiful: deep green shutters, terracotta planters filled with herbs by the back door and a view of rolling hills in the distance. But Harriet's eyes were drawn back to the van from where Marco was unloading the trays of provisions from the village shop. It wasn't the Italian number plate or her reflection in its small back windows that caught Harriet's attention. It was the bright pink design drawn across the doors. An artist's impression of a rearing horse, its mane flying and hooves flailing. And what looked like an evil glint in its eye.

Harriet shuddered.

'Mum and Julia will be out on the terrace,' Marco said.

'Come on,' Jess said. 'Donna and Julia – she's Donna's friend who does all the cooking – are both so nice. You're going to love them.'

Harriet picked up her holdall and followed her. She fervently hoped that Marco's mother would confirm that the yoga classes were going ahead and that Jess and Marco had got it all wrong.

'I am so, so sorry,' Donna said. 'This is all my fault. I've been meaning to sit down with Marco and redo the website. And I usually email my guests to find out their riding ability before they come so that I can match them up with the right horses but we're not going to be more than half-full this week, and there's only the two of you here 'til Franny and Bob arrive . . .'

'And I did book at the very last minute,' Harriet said.

Although Harriet assured Donna that she was quite capable of amusing herself, the woman looked so worried that Harriet found herself agreeing to a trial riding lesson the next day. She could wait until the morning to find a way to get out of it.

Julia poured them all a glass of the local red wine. Harriet took it gratefully. She was determined to relax and enjoy the evening, whatever tomorrow held.

'So, how was your journey?' Donna asked.

'Pretty easy. My flight was on time – for once – though I got in a bit of a muddle buying my ticket at the station,' Harriet said.

'Harriet and I bumped into each other on the train,' Jess said.

'That was lucky. That train is usually pretty busy. Did you both get a seat?'

'Yes – and Harriet almost got herself a date.'

'Really?' Julia said.

'It was nothing – some boy kept staring at me, that's all.'

'A rather handsome boy,' Jess said.

Harriet could not deny it, but it wasn't just his good looks that had attracted her attention. There was something more. But there was no point dwelling on their brief encounter. The moment had been and gone.

Chapter Three

Harriet drew back the thin cotton curtains hanging from the narrow, wrought-iron rod above the bedroom window. She pushed open the shutters. It was broad daylight outside but the hands on the bedside clock confirmed her suspicion that it was far too early for breakfast. Six o'clock – only five o'clock back in England – but she was wide awake. She washed quickly in the small en-suite bathroom and padded quietly down the stairs in her soft pink socks. She slipped silently out of the front door, startling a chicken that was perched on the doorstep. It gave an indignant cluck and stalked off on its skinny legs.

Harriet sat on the step and laced up her trainers. She looked out across the valley; all was calm and still. She could see why Savita's sister had found this to be the perfect place for a yoga holiday. Perhaps she could stay behind and practise her own routines whilst the others went horse riding. Yes, that was a good plan. She could do an hour of yoga twice a day out on the terrace; enjoy the sunshine, the local food and the wine; take a few walks and work her way through a couple of the books that had been left on the shelf on the landing by previous guests. There was absolutely no need to get up close and personal with any of the four-legged inhabitants of Bella Vista.

The bottle-green shutters on the upstairs windows were closed; it seemed that no one else was up and around. She was tempted to walk down to the five-bar gate that led to the village but instead she made her way around to the back of the house. Lupo appeared from under a bench by the back door. The dog sniffed her left trainer with half-hearted interest.

'Hello, old fellow.' Harriet scratched the top of the dog's silky head. *Please don't bark.* She walked past the chicken run to the top of the stable yard. Lupo followed along right behind her, the dog's pointy nose pressing against the back of Harriet's calf. Although she had barely made a sound, inquisitive heads began to look out of the stables, which lined two sides of the yard. Harriet took a step forward, wiping her clammy hands on her jeans. She walked down the row of horses, keeping a safe distance.

A brass name plate was screwed to the half-height door of the first stable: *Caesar.* A huge black head looked out at her. She was glad Caesar was safely shut away; he looked enormous. He might be a gentle giant, but she wasn't going to get near enough to find out.

Just as she was about to go back to the house – she'd braved the yard; that was pretty good wasn't it? – a chocolate-brown head peeked over one of the stables. Soft brown eyes framed by long dark lashes peered out from beneath a thick, black forelock and looked straight at her: *Coco.* His head was a lot smaller than Caesar's. *Come on, Harriet, you can't be scared of him.*

She took a step forward. Coco made a soft, whinnying sound. Would she, could she dare touch him? She reached out slowly and placed her hand on his forehead. Coco dropped his head lower as if encouraging her to explore further. She ran her hand along his neck, surprised by the contrast between his soft coat and his thick wiry mane, which stuck out at odd angles as if he had just got out of bed. He stretched his neck towards her. She scratched behind his ears and stroked his long velvet nose.

'Coco. Hello, Coco,' she said.

He tossed his head as if in answer then snorted loudly, showering her with spray from both his nostrils. Startled, Harriet jumped back. She grabbed the handle of a wheelbarrow to steady herself. A metal fork that had been lying across it clattered to the ground. As if in answer Caesar began to kick and bang on his door, setting off several of the others who sounded like they would break out of their boxes at any moment.

'Caesar!'

Harriet spun round. An old man in well-worn jeans and a checked short-sleeved shirt was coming towards her. The veins in his wiry arms were protruding from the effort of carrying two full water buckets; one leg dragged slightly as he walked. His presence triggered another burst of kicking and banging from Caesar's box.

As he got nearer, she noticed that his brown, weather-beaten face was deeply lined; his bulbous nose patterned with broken veins. A wisp of hay was caught in his thick, grey moustache. He said something in rapid Italian and laughed. Harriet gave him a friendly smile but her confusion must have been evident.

'English?' he said.

Harriet nodded.

'I am Alfredo. *Buongiorno.* Caesar — he want breakfast.' He grinned; a front tooth was missing.

'Harriet.'

'Harriet,' he repeated. 'You wait here. Okay?'

Harriet nodded. Alfredo disappeared, dragging his leg behind him. A few minutes later he returned with a couple of plastic buckets filled with a mixture of chopped hay

19

and some sort of cereal. He went to draw back the bolt on Caesar's stable and gestured for her to stand back. She did not need to be asked twice. He pushed the big, black animal back with the palm of one hand whilst tipping the contents of the bucket into a triangular plastic box in the corner of the stable.

'Look!' he said. Harriet peered in cautiously. Caesar's long neck was bent towards the floor as he munched noisily.

'Hungry. Always he is hungry.' Alfredo smiled. His eyes, beneath his unruly brows, were kind. Harriet waited as he continued to feed and water the horses.

'Finished. Come . . .' Alfredo tipped his head in the direction of a wooden shack with a corrugated-iron roof situated at the far end of the stable yard. Harriet hesitated for a moment. It was still early and there was no one around but she knew instinctively that she would be safe with him.

It took a moment or two for her eyes to adjust to the dim interior after the bright early morning light. The narrow room reminded her of her old school cloakroom but instead of duffel coats and gym bags the shelves and pegs were laden with riding paraphernalia. Saddles rested on wall-mounted racks, head collars made of bright nylon webbing hung from the hooks below. A jumble of riding hats, their soft velvet covers worn away in patches, was piled up on a big wooden chest. A small rickety desk was barely visible under a pile of leather bridles.

Alfredo pulled out one of two small chairs for Harriet to sit down, then fished out a battered old tin from the top drawer of the desk. Harriet didn't normally have a craving for toffees at half past six in the morning, but she felt it rude to refuse. She peeled the green crinkled wrapper from the sticky old sweet with some difficulty and pushed it carefully into the corner of her cheek.

'Now we clean,' Alfredo said. He unscrewed the metal lid from a tub filled with a waxy yellow substance. Then he handed her a bridle and a circular piece of sponge.

Harriet was about to protest; she hadn't come on holiday to scrub horse tack, but Alfredo's smile was so genuine and his welcome so warm, she did not have the heart to walk off and leave him to his chores. The old man probably wanted some company.

Once she got the hang of it, working the saddle soap into the leather was surprisingly therapeutic. And it was satisfying to learn a new skill, albeit one she wasn't likely to need again.

'Oh, there you are!' Marco was standing in the doorway. 'My mother was worried you'd done a runner. But I told her you were hardly likely to have galloped off,' he added sarcastically. He turned to leave, clearly expecting her to jump up and follow him.

'Sorry. I've been helping Alfredo.'

'At least you've been making yourself useful. Come on, you'd better wash your hands before breakfast.' Harriet glanced down; her knuckles were embedded with dirt and her nails were black. Lovely.

She said goodbye to Alfredo and followed Marco back to the house.

'I hope Alfredo's sweets haven't wrecked my appetite,' she quipped. She might as well try and lighten the atmosphere.

'Last time I had one of his toffees I got an eighty-euro bill from the dentist.' Marco cracked a smile and his whole face changed: his tense jaw softened, and his eyes flashed with amusement. Talk about a transformation. He might be quite attractive if he wasn't so moody.

'I'll see you later. I'll be giving you a riding lesson after breakfast,' Marco said.

Harriet hesitated. Visiting the yard and chatting to Alfredo had been fun but riding a horse – no way. Donna would be disappointed, but it was Harriet's holiday and her choice how to spend it. Coco was sweet, unlike that great beast, Caesar, but she was quite happy simply petting the little chap; she had no desire to hop on his back.

'Unless you're scared of Coco. He doesn't usually bite.' Marco smirked.

Harriet felt a surge of annoyance. 'Of course I'm not!' she snapped back.

'See you at ten then.'

'Looking forward to it,' Harriet said. Why, oh why had she let Marco rile her? It was too late to back out now. She went in for breakfast, but she wasn't sure she would manage to eat a thing. Her stomach was fluttering too much.

'Relax!' Marco commanded. But that was impossible. Harriet found it hard enough to relax whilst lying on a yoga mat listening to the soothing sound of Savita's gentle voice. How could she relax when she was sitting on a crazy pony that was careering around the schooling ring at a decidedly unleisurely trot? If Donna hadn't been so kind and clearly so anxious that Harriet's holiday might be ruined before it started, she would never have agreed to give this a go. That and Marco's sarcastic smirk.

If only Coco would respond to her urgings. He was taking no notice of her attempts to bring him back to a steady walk let alone a standstill.

'Whoa! Whoa, Coco! Good boy,' she pleaded. The pony clearly didn't understand English or he was having a good laugh at her expense.

'Sit back! You're leaning forward like a jockey. No wonder he is going so fast.' Marco sounded cross but she could see the corner of his mouth twitching with amusement.

Harriet gradually began to find her balance and Coco slowed down to a walk. She concentrated hard on her posture, keeping her back straight and her heels slightly down. Her elbows were now resting quietly by her sides, her arms no longer flapping like a chicken's wings.

'Good,' Marco said. 'Now that you are more relaxed he is walking better.' She wasn't sure relaxed was the right word but the out-of-control lurching in her stomach had subsided and she began to enjoy the feel of the pony's swaying motion.

'Soften your hands,' Marco continued. 'Hold the reins like two little birds. You don't want the little birds to fly away, but you don't want to kill them by squeezing them too tight. Good. Now ask him to halt.'

Much to her surprise Coco responded immediately.

'That's enough for now. Take your feet out of the stirrups, swing one leg over and gently drop to the ground.'

Harriet followed Marco's instructions, glad that Coco was so small. She landed lightly on her feet.

'You weren't so bad after all,' Marco said rather grudgingly as he led the pony back to its stable. 'Your balance is good – that helps.'

'I did a lot of ballet when I was young.'

'Oh.' He didn't sound at all interested. She tried a different topic: 'It must have been nice to grow up amongst horses.'

'Not really.'

'Can I give him a treat?' Harriet reached into her pocket. There were a few mints left in the packet she'd bought for the aeroplane.

'He doesn't get treats. He's a working animal not a pet.'

Marco turned away and busied himself undoing the pony's girth and removing its saddle. Then he looked round. 'You can go now.'

Harriet did not need telling twice. What an odd character Marco was. Donna seemed like such a warm, friendly person that it was strange she had such a moody son. But Harriet wasn't going to waste her time wondering what was eating him. She was here to enjoy herself. She had survived her first lesson and much to her surprise she found herself looking forward to riding Coco again.

She sat on the bench by the back door and unzipped the jodhpur boots Donna had lent her. A fluffy white cat was lying by the chicken run watching the hens pecking around searching for the last grains from their morning feed.

Marco walked up through the stable yard. He stopped and leant over Coco's box. He seemed to be talking to the pony. Coco's chocolate-brown nose appeared over the door. He stretched his neck out to nuzzle Marco's shoulder. The boy responded by giving him a good scratch behind his ears in return.

Marco reached into the pocket of his cut-off shorts and pulled out a green and white tube. He tipped something into the palm of his hand then offered it to the pony. Coco lunged for the treat then immediately pushed his nose into Marco's arm clearly searching for another titbit. Marco gave the animal an affectionate pat and strode off across the yard. It wasn't just humans he blew hot and cold with.

The bright pink roses planted at the end of each row of vines were in full bloom. Jess crouched forward to take her weight off the saddle as Caesar cantered across the vineyard with his long smooth stride. She had almost forgotten how good it felt to be out on a horse in the

Tuscan countryside, the breeze in her face and the warmth permeating her cotton shirt.

Donna and Jess slowed down and brought their mounts back to a gentle walk. Here, across the top of the vineyard, they were able to walk two abreast although Caesar insisted on keeping just half a step ahead of Donna's horse, Guido, an elegant, dappled grey who was a good three inches shorter.

'How does Caesar feel?' Donna asked.

'Great.' Jess patted the big horse's neck.

'I gave him a ride out yesterday so he wouldn't be too fresh; I knew you would want to ride him.'

The first time Jess visited Bella Vista, Donna had appraised her six-foot frame without wincing and led out Caesar. It was love at first sight. It was such a different experience to her first riding holiday in the South of France where the brittle Marie-Louise looked her up and down with ill-concealed distaste and declared she was far too big for her fine animals. Jess had ended up riding an old, well-built cob from a nearby farm. He looked as sturdy as a bull, but he was a kind and responsive animal and surprisingly fast. Jess still laughed at the memory of Marie-Louise's horrified face as she flew right past her at a barely controlled gallop. The thrill that she felt made up for her hostess's frostiness, but she resolved to find a friendlier establishment for her next riding holiday. And she had found it at Bella Vista.

'I thought we would ride over to the old chapel tomorrow and stop for lunch at Il Carciofo on the way back,' Donna said. 'There's an American couple coming for two nights, Franny and Bob, and though they've both done a fair bit of riding I don't want them tackling something too daunting on their first day. I can take Harriet and Coco on a lead rope if she's survived her lesson with Marco.'

'Sounds perfect,' Jess said.

Jess and Donna rode back to the farm at a walking pace. The sun had burnt the clouds away and it was getting quite warm. As they picked their way through the olive grove the horses began to stride out purposefully, knowing they would soon be home.

They walked up the dusty track to the entrance of Bella Vista. Jess led Caesar into his stable and removed his tack. The horse plunged his head into his water bucket and took a long drink. Jess topped up his water then left the stable and took the steps to her room two at a time. She chucked her riding clothes on the floor and pulled on some jeans and a blue shirt she'd found in Topman. She caught sight of herself in the mirror on the back of the door and frowned. Her friends were forever bemoaning their own stumpy legs, telling her how lucky she was being so tall, but she knew they were only being kind. They didn't struggle with ill-fitting trousers, maxi dresses that turned into midis and short skirts that were positively indecent. Sometimes it was easier just to shop in a men's store, even if the results weren't always terribly flattering.

Through the window Jess could see Harriet lounging on the old wicker recliner on the terrace. Harriet had changed out of Donna's old jodhpurs into a pair of grey marl leggings and a loose striped shirt and had swapped her metal-framed specs for a pair of tortoiseshell sunglasses. Her morning with Coco seemed to have done her the world of good; she looked quite contented.

Jess grabbed her sketchpad and the green metal tin that held her pencils and sticks of charcoal. She made her way back downstairs and out onto the terrace. Back home in Birmingham she could go months without drawing but when she came to Bella Vista she felt inspired to put pencil to paper. She struggled to capture the scenery, but she was pleased with some of the drawings of horses and people she had made on her previous visit. Perhaps this time she would try her hand at sketching Lupo, if Donna's dog sat still for long enough.

Tomorrow they would ride past the old chapel. The place brought back such vivid memories, she flushed pink just thinking about it. Jess loved riding Caesar – but that wasn't the only reason she had returned to Bella Vista.

Chapter Four

'Jeepers, I feel like I'm perched on a pincushion!' Bob flashed a wide smile. His boy-band teeth looked strange in his weather-beaten face.

Harriet laughed. She had been trying to keep a straight face ever since Bob and Franny walked into the stable yard dressed as though they were extras in a John Wayne movie.

Franny stood on the mounting block, put her left foot into the stirrup, swung her right leg over Brando's back and, to Donna's obvious relief, lowered herself down very gently. 'Isn't this just fun! We've never ridden on English saddles before.'

Bob held the end of both reins in a loose loop in his left hand and straightened his shoelace tie with the other. The metal points on his shirt collar glinted in the morning sun.

'You'll need to take one rein in each hand,' Donna said.

Marco led the way with Franny and Bob following – luckily they soon appeared quite at home sitting on the unfamiliar, flat English saddles. Caesar and Jess went next. Harriet and Donna brought up the rear. Donna held the end of a thick plaited lead rope, which was clipped onto Coco's bridle. The two animals had to squeeze quite close together to pick their way between the olive trees. Harriet found it quite tricky; her toes seemed determined to stick out at odd angles. She was relieved when they reached a cluster of fruit trees and the path widened.

'We're going to split into two groups when we get to the end of this orchard,' Donna said. 'You and I will walk the short route and the others will go the long way round past the old chapel; there's a nice path where they can have a bit of a canter. We'll all meet up at Il Carciofo where we're going to stop for lunch.'

'I hope I'm not making it boring for you,' Harriet said.

'Not at all. It's fun to canter but there's so much to see when you walk this way. I won't be missing out at all, I promise you. Come on, Coco. He's a little bit reluctant to separate from the others.'

Donna turned Guido away from the other horses and after a few encouraging clucking noises, Coco consented to follow although his head twisted awkwardly to one side until the rest of the horses vanished behind an old grain store.

'Look. There's a wonderful view from here. See that little village on the horizon – that's not far from Siena. Beautiful isn't it?'

'Wow!' Harriet said.

'The others won't have seen that view today. Siena's a beautiful city. Have you ever been?'

'I've never been to Italy before. But I know I'm going to come back.'

'You know that already?'

'Strange isn't it? I've barely arrived, but I've fallen in love with the countryside here. And I'd like to see Siena and Florence too.'

'Italy gets under your skin,' Donna said.

Harriet was about to reply but there was something in Donna's eyes that stopped her. A faraway look.

'Are you happy to have a short trot? Don't worry if you bounce around a bit; it takes a bit of time to learn to rise up and down with the horse.'

'Sure.' Harriet sounded braver than she felt.

Donna squeezed her legs gently and Guido broke into a trot. Harriet felt a surge of adrenalin as Coco increased his pace to keep up with the bigger horse. She couldn't help breaking into a great big grin. Scared? Not her.

'This is such fun. I'm having just the best time ever. It's a such a shame we're only here for a couple of days. I wish we'd booked for a week.' Franny beamed as Donna helped Bob to secure his horse to one of the iron rings embedded in the side wall of Il Carciofo.

'I really enjoyed the ride,' Harriet said. She was surprised to find she meant it. She gave Coco a pat and followed the others through the brick-edged white arch that led into the trattoria.

'*Buongiorno!*' The owner greeted them effusively. She wiped her flour-covered hands on her floral apron and clasped Donna by the shoulders, kissing her warmly.

'I have made my special pasta with *funghi* and Filippo he makes the *crespelle* with the spinach – I know how you like those – and the *spaghetti al pomodoro*.'

'Mushroom pasta, spinach crepes and spaghetti with tomato sauce,' Donna translated. 'Wonderful. But I can smell something else.'

'*Brava!* You have a good nose. I have a big pot of *coniglio con peperoni*.'

'Rabbit with peppers! Goodness, Maria, will the horses be able to carry us home?' Donna drew the shape of a huge belly with her hands.

The older lady chuckled. 'Sit, please. In the garden if you like. I will fetch water.' She bustled off.

'Every time we come here I tell her we want a light lunch but she cannot help herself. I just hope you're all hungry,' Donna said as they took their seats under a flower-draped pergola.

'Starving,' Jess said.

'I can fit in plenty.' Bob patted the front of his denim shirt.

'Here.' Maria put down two water jugs. She was accompanied by a man in chef's whites who looked briefly startled at the sight of Bob's full-length fringed suede chaps but composed himself quickly. He placed a cotton drawstring bag filled with chunks of fresh bread at each end of the table.

'*Ciao*, Donna,' the man said quietly. His deeply lined face was red and damp with sweat.

'This is Filippo,' Donna said.

The man smiled shyly and scuttled back to his duties. Harriet cut into her *crespelle*. Chopped spinach and ricotta oozed out. Perfect. Too perfect. By the time she had sampled the other pasta dishes and eaten a heaped ladle of rabbit stew, Harriet was feeling full to bursting. She laid down her cutlery and dug out her phone.

'I know it's a bit unsociable, but I couldn't get a signal earlier on,' she said.

'Oh, I should have told you before, there's not much point trying to get a signal out on the terrace; the best place is round the back of the house by the chicken run,' Jess said.

'Thanks, I'll remember that.' Harriet scrolled down her messages. There was one from Savita: *Office just surviving without you!! So sorry about the yoga. I can't believe you've been learning to ride! Glad Donna is as nice as my sister said she was. Have you met her son yet? I hear he's rather handsome.* She had added a winking emoji.

Harriet sighed. She didn't know why she should be surprised; people were forever trying to fix her up. But surely Savita could come up with someone more suitable. She was nearly thirty and Marco looked barely twenty.

31

Besides, Harriet had only been single for eighteen months – it wasn't that long, was it? She dashed off a non-committal reply and pressed *send*.

'Everyone ready to go?' Donna asked.

Harriet took Coco's reins in one hand.

'Always check your girth is fastened properly before you set off – we don't want the saddle slipping,' Donna said. 'Lift up the saddle flap, that's right . . . perfect. Now I'll give you a leg-up.'

Harriet adjusted the reins; she almost felt as though she knew what she was doing. They picked their way along dusty tracks and through vineyards until they came to the olive grove on the outskirts of the village. Coco pricked his ears and marched forward, knowing he would be home very soon.

Harriet helped Marco to settle him in his stable. Afterwards everyone sat out on the terrace chatting, eating yet more food that Julia had prepared and drinking wine until no one could stay up any longer.

Harriet stood in her small bathroom brushing her teeth in front of the rectangular mirror that hung by a chain over the basin. She was about to get undressed and hop into bed, but she could not resist checking her phone. Of course: no signal. She should have popped round to the chicken run before she came indoors. No matter, it was unlikely there would be anything that couldn't wait for the morning. But it was an ingrained habit to check her work emails before she went to bed. She still needed to know what was going on in the office whether she was on holiday or not. And now that she knew the best place to stand it was just too tempting.

She made her way quietly back down the stairs and slid back the bolt on the front door. The village beyond Bella

Vista was in total darkness. There were no streetlights in this sleepy place. She scanned the inky sky but there was no sign of the moon. Fortunately, there was one outside lantern casting a soft glow on the terrace. She stepped carefully around to the back of the house using the torch on her mobile to guide her.

A long shaft of light came from the boot room door; she wasn't the only person up and around. Marco was standing with his back to the open doorway.

'Damn Harriet!' Marco exclaimed.

Harriet froze.

Chapter Five

Harriet stood rooted to the spot. She held her phone tight against her body so that it no longer cast any light.

'Can't she have a cookery lesson or something,' Marco said.

'I could have asked Julia to change her day off, but I know she's already arranged to meet Luigi.' It was Donna's voice.

'Can't stand in the way of true love,' Marco said sarcastically.

'No, I can't,' said Donna. She sounded frustrated.

'So, I don't have a choice,' Marco said.

Harriet held her breath. She wished she could go back inside but she dared not risk taking a misstep and crunching on the white gravel border.

'You've always got a choice. I'm just hoping you can help me out. Jess won't mind what we do tomorrow, but I promised the two Americans we'd ride through the chestnut woods to the ruined castle. They're surprisingly good riders once you can see past that cowboy garb. Harriet's not bad at all for a beginner but I can't take the chance with her, not with that steep descent and those two long canters.'

'Even Coco goes hell for leather when he gets on that second stretch,' Marco said.

'You know I wouldn't ask you to skip your trip to Siena . . .'

'It's okay,' Marco interrupted. 'I'll stay behind with Harriet and give her another lesson. I'll get those toes up and heels down if it kills me.' His laugh had an edge to it.

Harriet's face was burning. She could have sworn she could hear Marco's laugh still echoing long after the boot room door slammed shut. She slunk back around the house; checking her phone could wait until the morning.

She pulled the heavy front door shut behind her. The metal bolt closed with a snap. A woman gasped. Harriet swung around, praying it wasn't Donna standing there. She didn't want Donna to have any inkling that she had overheard her conversation with her son. She couldn't care less what Marco thought of her but she had taken an immediate liking to the owner of Bella Vista. The last thing she wanted to do was make Donna feel awkward.

In the second it took for Harriet's eyes to accustom themselves to the brightness she realised the figure in the hallway was Julia, the cook.

'Harriet, are you okay? You gave me quite a shock.' Julia bent down and dabbed at the worn Persian rug where some tea had sloshed out of the half-pint mug she was carrying.

'I . . . umm . . . just popped out for some air,' Harriet stammered. She took a step towards the foot of the stairs. Julia put out a restraining hand.

'No, don't go up yet. Come and have some tea with me. You look like you need it. You were as white as a sheet when you walked in.'

Harriet hesitated.

'There's plenty more in the pot. I should have just made a cup for myself but I can't seem to get out of the habit of brewing up gallons of the stuff.'

Harriet nodded. She wasn't nearly tired enough to go to sleep. Talking to this friendly woman was more appealing than going back to the silence of her own little room and lying on her single bed with Donna and Marco's conversation going round and round in her head. She followed Julia into the large farmhouse kitchen and sat in one of the chairs in the corner of the room.

'Miu Miu, get off, *vai!*' Julia shooed a fluffy white cat off a small tapestry-topped footstool and set down a red enamel tray with two mugs. She opened a round metal tin and tipped some lemon-scented biscuits onto a floral plate.

'Some of my *ricciarelli* in case you're still hungry,' she joked.

'I don't think I'm ever going to go hungry here. I haven't quite got my head round having a bowl of pasta before my main course.'

'I've got used to that now, though I still eat too much of it,' Julia said. She pinched at a bit of flesh above the waistband of her chinos and shrugged. 'I should go on a diet really. I used to ride a lot when I first came out here but now cooking and organising the kitchen is a full-time job. I can't remember when I last went out for a hack.'

'Have you worked here long?' Harriet was genuinely curious.

'More than nine years now. Nearly ten. I always wanted to cook. I did okay at school but I was always happiest up to my elbows in flour. I didn't bother trying for university; I went straight to catering college. I spent a few years doing private events for wealthy folk in North London, but my goodness some people were so demanding. They wanted to dictate every little detail. It quite took the fun out of it. Then one of my old customers took over a disused pub in the countryside, by the river, not far from Cambridge. Lovely kitchen they had, huge great range cooker, big marble slab for rolling out pastry. I could devise my own menus and I lived on site in a couple of rooms carved out of the old stable block. Turned out I didn't miss London at all.'

Harriet nodded. She could quite imagine rosy-cheeked Julia, in her lavender ditsy-print blouse, rolling out pastry in the English countryside, her cornflower-blue cotton scarf knotted in her curly brown hair.

'Then Donna called me. Of course, I didn't hesitate to come; she's my oldest friend. It was only going to be for a couple of weeks, a month at most, just to help her get back on her feet, to get over the shock, you know.'

'The shock?' Harriet sat up a little straighter. She set down her mug of tea although there was still half left.

Julia glanced around and lowered her voice. 'Perhaps I shouldn't say any more, but if you're here for a while you're bound to find out. It's not as though it's a secret.'

Harriet waited for Julia to continue. She was dying to know what had happened, but she didn't want Julia to think she had a prurient interest in Donna's life. But if some momentous event had occurred in the past perhaps it might shed some light on what lay behind Marco's contrary character.

Julia took a sip of tea. The hot, comforting liquid seemed to do the trick. She tweaked a tendril of hair that had escaped from her blue cotton scarf and tucked it behind her ear.

'Donna and I met at school. It must be more than thirty years ago, now. There was a school disco at the end of the first term. She lent me her crushed-velvet dress and Impulse body spray and I lent her my Dolcis shoes. Can you imagine?

'Despite the dodgy dress sense I was a bit of a Miss Sensible, my catering career all planned out. But Donna, she didn't know what she wanted to do. Her parents were desperately keen for her to go to university. They were so proud when she went off to study Spanish and Italian. She had to spend a year in Italy as part of her course. Florence was where she went. Three days after she arrived, she met Giovanni. He was a few years older than her, a postgraduate student researching English literature. By Christmas she was pregnant with Marco's older sister, Daniela.

'Donna's parents put on a brave face and flew out for the wedding. Giovanni's sister and I were the two bridesmaids. We all thought they would carry on with their studies, but they cooked up a plan to restore this old farmhouse and that was the end of university for both of them. They left Florence and moved here. Of course, everyone told them it was a crazy idea. But I knew Donna better than anyone. Everyone has dreams but most people let them drift away. Donna was always going to reach for the stars. And they were so in love back then.' Julia gave a small sigh.

'It was a huge task, restoring this old place, and before Daniela was two, Marco came along. Giovanni doted on both children, but Donna had her hands full trying to look after the place whilst Giovanni took the clients out on their rides. The business grew steadily and when Marco was around eight or nine they employed a local man, Francesco, as a sort of part-groom, part-handyman, a jack of all trades, if you like. He helped with everything from feeding the horses to fixing the guttering. Giovanni became less and less involved with the everyday tasks. He started writing a novel. He was determined to get it published – and eventually he succeeded. But the hours he spent scribbling away took their toll. Donna came to rely on Francesco more and more. Giovanni didn't like them being so close. He started to get jealous. He somehow got it into his head that they were having an affair.'

'Were they?' Harriet couldn't help asking.

'Of course not!' Julia snapped. Then seeing the look on Harriet's face, her voice softened. 'I'm sorry. Why shouldn't you ask? It's just that when you know someone as well as I know Donna . . .' Her voice tailed away. She reached for the teapot. 'Top-up?'

'Yes please.' Harriet held out her mug. She didn't really want any more but she was desperately keen to keep Julia talking.

'It was just before Marco's eleventh birthday. Giovanni was telling everyone in the village bar that he was going to have it out with Francesco. The next day Francesco didn't turn up for work. Nor the next. Well, that was enough for Giovanni. He was sure it was proof of his guilt and that he was a coward too. Nothing Donna said could convince him otherwise. Giovanni walked out. He's stayed a sleeping partner in the business here, but he hasn't set foot in Bella Vista since that awful day.'

'And Francesco?' Harriet couldn't help asking.

'No one's seen him since. A week later Donna employed Alfredo to take Francesco's place.'

Harriet was silent. Maybe Julia was wrong. It seemed so strange that Francesco had left so suddenly.

'Of course, Donna didn't think Giovanni would be gone for long. She knew how impetuous he could be. They were both quite feisty; if they had any sort of disagreement sparks would fly. Giovanni would storm out, but he would always be back after an hour or two begging her forgiveness.

'When she rang me he'd been gone for twenty-four hours. She told the children he had gone to visit some friends. She said that she was probably being silly, that he would be back in a few days. But there was something in her voice; I knew she didn't believe it.

'I booked a flight out as soon as I put down the phone, rang her back, told her I was coming out for a couple of weeks whether she liked it or not, and that the moment Giovanni reappeared I would take myself off for a trip around Tuscany to go and see all the little towns and villages I'd never visited. That was nearly ten years ago. Giovanni never came back so I never left. And after a while I had another reason to stay.'

'You met someone?' Harriet didn't really need to ask. It was obvious from the way Julia's voice softened.

'Luigi. He's the local farrier; he's lived here in the village all his life. He came to shoe the horses a few weeks after I arrived. I liked him immediately. We were just friends for a long time, then one day . . .' Julia smiled.

'You're really happy with him, aren't you.'

'Yes, I've been really lucky. He's a great guy.'

'But what about Daniela and Marco?' Marco hadn't exactly endeared himself to Harriet but no little boy deserved to be abandoned by his adored father.

'Daniela seemed to sail through it all unscathed; she was a very inward-looking child, always lost in a book, and much closer to Donna than she was to Giovanni. But I've no doubt it must have affected her more than we know. Marco took it very badly; he always worshipped his father.

'Giovanni rented a place in Siena. He was wrapped up in his writing, but he always found time to see his children. He knew what it was like to grow up without a father; his own papa died when he was just six years old. At first, he would meet the children down in the village. Bianca, the old lady who lives at the corner house with the cherry tree, would fetch them from Bella Vista and drop them back when Giovanni had gone. But Bianca never felt comfortable about it. She has always been so fond of Donna, you see. She was one of the first people Donna got to know in the village. So, after a few months had gone by, one of us would see them safely onto a train and Giovanni would meet them on the platform in Siena.'

'That must have been hard on them, even so,' Harriet said.

'Something changed in Marco the day he realised Giovanni wasn't coming home. You should have seen him when he was young. He was the happiest little boy you could ever meet. He had such a wonderful, sunny nature; his smile lit up the room.'

Harriet nodded. She could imagine that was true. She had seen Marco's flashes of humour, the easy laugh when something tickled him.

'As soon as he realised his papa wasn't coming home Marco withdrew into himself. He had always been top of the class but he lost interest in his schooling. That bothered Donna, of course it did, but it was his lack of interest in his hobbies that tore her apart. Coco was his pride and joy, but he didn't want to go near him, let alone ride him. It was like he wanted to punish his father, to hurt him as much as he had been hurt.

'Giovanni's grandfather was a brilliant horseman. He took part in the *Palio*, the famous horse race in Siena. Giovanni had wanted to buy Marco a pony when he was much younger but they never had the money. When Coco arrived Marco was a natural rider from the start. Giovanni was so proud. He hoped that one day Marco would follow in his great-grandfather's footsteps.

'When Marco found out that his papa had gone he hurled his little whip to the ground. He insisted that he would never ride again. He had that same stubborn, self-destructive streak Giovanni has. Marco told Donna to sell Coco but of course Donna knew it would break his heart.'

41

Much to her surprise, Harriet had a lump in her throat. She took a sip of tea, but it had long grown cold. 'But Marco started riding again,' she said.

'That was Bianca's doing. Many people in the village say she has special powers because of the herbal remedies she mixes up. She told Marco that I had a special power too: that I could communicate with animals and read their minds. Marco asked me if it was true. I don't like to lie to children but I realised at once what Bianca was up to. I told him that I spoke to the old cat we used to have here, the one before Miu Miu. A couple of days later he crept into the kitchen. Stood there so quiet and solemn it tugged my heart. Asked me if I had spoken to Coco. So, I told him I had and that Coco was very sad. He had lost his friend and didn't know what he had done wrong.

'After lunch we heard hooves crunching on the gravel. Marco was riding Coco round and round the house. There were hoof prints all over Donna's prize herbaceous border but she would have gladly dug the whole thing up to see him back on that little pony. Later on, when it was time for bed, she found him sitting in the tack room with Alfredo, sponging Coco's bridle and guzzling his way through that tin of sweets Alfredo keeps.'

Harriet smiled. 'So, does Marco still see his father?'

'Oh yes. And he's forgiven him for leaving. It may be a cliché but time's a great healer. I'm sure if Marco asked him to, Giovanni would even visit him here. But he won't. They're two of a kind, both as stubborn as each other.'

'I can well believe that,' Harriet said. 'I'm having more trouble imagining Marco as a sweet little boy.'

'Oh, I know Marco can be difficult but deep down he's a lovely lad. Talking of which, how have your riding lessons gone?'

'He's a good teacher but I'm finding him hard to please. But I'm loving it and at least Coco's always happy to see me.'

'Don't take anything Marco says too much to heart. I think seeing you learning to ride on Coco is stirring up all sorts of memories – things he doesn't like to dwell on.'

'I won't,' Harriet promised. 'And what about Donna? Does she ever speak to her ex-husband?'

'Oh, Giovanni's not her ex-husband. He and Donna have never got round to getting divorced. Now, can I make you more tea?' Julia said.

'No, no I couldn't.'

Julia looked up at the clock on the kitchen wall. 'Goodness, have you seen the time?'

'I've kept you up talking far too long.' Harriet gathered up her hoody and stood up.

'Nonsense. It's been a pleasure. But, Harriet, when I saw you in the hallway you looked shaken. I've been so wrapped up talking about the past I quite forgot to ask why. Are you okay?'

'It was nothing, honestly. But I was just wondering – do you think Donna would mind if I skipped tomorrow's ride and went sightseeing in Siena?'

Chapter Six

Any sympathy Harriet felt for Marco had vanished. He hunched over the steering wheel, eyes on the road ahead, her attempts to chat dismissed with one-word answers. What was wrong with him? He'd got what he wanted hadn't he? He could spend his day in Siena, instead of staying at Bella Vista grudgingly helping his mother out by giving Harriet another lesson on his childhood pony. Harriet's ex, Peter, had had his faults but at least being moody hadn't been one of them.

'I heard you talking last night.' Harriet did not know why she said it. For a moment she thought he wasn't going to reply, but at least he had the grace to look embarrassed.

'To my mother?' he said.

'I walked round to the chicken run last night to try and get a signal on my phone. I didn't want you to give me a lesson today if it was such a bother for you. So now I'll get to see Siena and you can do whatever it is you wanted to do.'

'It's too late now.'

'I didn't think it was far away.'

'It's not that.' He sighed dramatically.

'Well, what is it then?' Harriet snapped.

'If you must know, I'll tell you. I got a call from the radio station, where I work, yesterday night. They're going to be interviewing Addolorata Di Marzio. You won't have heard of her. She's a local model and blogger. Not exactly my speciality but rumour has it she's tipped to play Ingrid Bergman's role in an Italian remake of *Casablanca*. The guy who does the hour-long lunch slot has been taken ill and her people won't reschedule.'

'Jess told me you had a temporary contract on the production side.'

Marco's lip curled; his eyes narrowed. 'I do.'

Suddenly it all became clear. 'So, this was your big opportunity,' Harriet said.

'Yes, and I'm not likely to get another one.'

'But it's not even ten o'clock,' Harriet said.

'You don't honestly think they were going to hang around and wait for me to make up my mind, do you? They gave the interview to another guy on the team, Nico. That guy's so full of himself I'm never going to hear the last of it.'

'But your mother . . .' Harriet started to speak.

'My mother thinks I wanted to come into Siena to buy some new shirts. I was going to sit her down and get her to listen to the catch-up show online and surprise her. Besides, as soon as I knew she needed me to look after you I couldn't tell her the truth; she would have insisted I came here, even if it meant leaving her in the lurch. But I would never do that. I would never do anything to cause a problem for my mother. She's the most important person in my life.' His eyes blazed.

'And what are you going to do now?' she said.

'Go shopping I suppose.' He tweaked the edge of his faded cotton shirt. 'I could do with smartening myself up a bit, don't you think?'

Harriet shrugged; she wasn't going to be drawn into commenting on Marco's wardrobe.

'But thank you,' he said suddenly. 'You tried to help me out by pretending you wanted to see Siena. But you won't regret spending the day here – it's one of the most beautiful cities in Italy. Though I'm biased I guess.'

'You have a fault!' Harriet couldn't help quipping.

He raised an eyebrow. 'I have may have one or two. And being terrible at parking is one of them. When we get around the corner you're going to have to jump out and guide me in.' It was the nearest he was going to get to calling a truce.

Harriet somehow directed Marco into the tiniest of parking spaces.

'Follow me,' he said.

Harriet looked around. 'Wow!'

'This is Piazza del Campo, known as The Campo. The heart of Siena.' There was pride in Marco's voice. He threw out an arm in a gesture that took in the sweeping panorama in front of them. 'Probably the most impressive town square in the world. Though as you can see, it's not shaped like a square, it's more like a shell. It was a built as a meeting place where all the people could come together. In medieval times the whole population could assemble here. In the height of the summer season it sometimes feels like they still do.' He smiled but as he was sporting a completely unnecessary pair of black-framed sunglasses Harriet could not tell if his smile reached his eyes.

'Right. I'll leave you here.' Marco had quickly lost interest in playing the tour guide. 'It's a pity it's such a grey day; it looks like it's going to rain any minute. I'll meet you at four back at the Torre del Mangia.' He pointed to an impressive brick clock tower looming over The Campo.

Harriet looked up. She could just make out the tiny people right at the very top who had presumably climbed up to get the most Instagrammable view of the city. 'Okay,' she said.

'I presume you can find your way back to the tower.'

'Oh, I might just manage to spot it.' She echoed his obvious sarcasm.

He smirked, turned on his heel and walked briskly across The Campo. She watched him until he ducked through an archway and the top of his curly hair disappeared down a flight of steps.

Harriet was left staring up at the tower. How tall was it? Three hundred feet, perhaps. Marco was right: this had to be one of the most impressive town squares in the world.

She looked around. A large middle-aged lady, with carefully coiffed hair dyed an improbable shade of blonde, was carefully picking her way past a group of denim-clad twenty-somethings sprawled across the piazza. They were eating toasted paninis, their grubby rucksacks piled in a heap. A bald man in tassel loafers was clinging onto the lead of a large black dog, which was trying to pull him in the direction of the delicious smells emanating from the backpackers' rapidly disappearing snacks. Two women in smart, shiny-buttoned blazers crossed in front of Harriet, talking rapidly. How chic they were; she could happily spend all day here, people-watching.

She opened the guidebook that Donna had lent her. A fat splash of rain landed on the page. She hurried towards the row of smart cafés at the top of The Campo. The seats shaded by the wine-coloured awnings were all taken; she would have to sit inside – or risk getting soaked. She chose a café at random and heaved herself up onto one of the stools tucked under a wooden ledge at the back. Her legs dangled comically in the air. She nudged a slim navy-blue

47

leather folder to one side – it was definitely too early for wine – and ordered a coffee.

She reopened the guidebook, but she was soon distracted by the display of black and white photographs of Siena covering most of the exposed brick wall.

'Cappuccino.' The waiter placed the white cup and saucer down in front of her and pushed a square glass jar filled with twists of sugar towards her.

Harriet tore her eyes away from the photographs. 'Thank you. *Grazie.*'

'You know *Il Palio*?' The waiter tapped a finger on the glass frame protecting the display.

'I've heard of it, but I don't know anything about it,' Harriet said.

'The most famous horse race in Italy. It is held twice a year, right here. Look at the crowds.'

Harriet studied the photograph he was pointing at: a chaotic-looking bareback horse race taking place right in the heart of The Campo. The square was packed to the hilt with spectators, most of whom had no chance of seeing the action; the lucky ones were jammed onto balconies or leaning out of the windows of the elegant buildings surrounding the makeshift racetrack. She could almost hear the jeers and shouts of the thousands of people greeting the winning rider as he crossed the finish line waving his flag.

'When I worked in London, we went to Royal Ascot to watch the racing. Everyone dressed up and drank champagne. That was fun. But *Il Palio*, it is more than a horse race. It means everything. The honour of your own district, your *contrada*, depends on it.' The waiter's eyes were shining.

'Siena is divided into seventeen *contrade* or districts,' he continued. 'When you are baptised here you are baptised twice – once into the church, once into your *contrada*. This

48

great city unites us all but on the day of *Il Palio*, there is no unity. Only rivalry.'

'Oh.' Harriet bit her lip. The intensity of the waiter's gaze was a little unnerving.

'When the race starts, anything can happen. The horse that passes the line first wins whether he has a jockey on board or not. In the past it was like the Wild West; some riders were dragged from their horses and trampled underfoot.'

'Really? And what are those flags with the pictures of animals on them?' Harriet could see a goose, a giraffe, a panther and what looked like an elephant with a tower perched on its back.

'Each one is the symbol of a *contrada*. When you walk around Siena, look at the streetlamps and signs and fountains. You can find these little symbols of the different districts. You are sightseeing today? This rain will stop very soon; it's only a shower.'

'Roberto!' a man called, his voice sharp and high.

The waiter sighed. 'I must go. Enjoy your cappuccino.'

Harriet sipped her drink, still studying the photographs. This one was taken in the 1950s, judging by the men's artfully styled quiffs and the women's flared skirts and tiny waists. Was that a small dog that elegant woman was carrying, or an unusual handbag? Harriet leant forward. The three-legged stool rocked alarmingly. She grabbed at the wooden ledge to steady herself. The stool shot back out from under her and crashed to the floor. Somehow, she landed on her feet.

The waiter was beside her in an instant, but she waved him away, hot with embarrassment. She righted the stool and scrabbled around picking up the pages of the wine list, which were now fanned out across the chequered floor tiles. She hauled herself back into her seat and resolved to leave as soon as she had finished her cappuccino. But as she shuffled the pages back into the navy leather case, a line of bold type written in English caught her eye: *The Pigeon Smuggler.*

The Pigeon Smuggler – it brought back the funniest memory. Harriet let out a loud laugh, which she quickly tried to change into a cough. A man at a table nearby raised a well-groomed black eyebrow. She felt her cheeks flush and looked away. She really didn't want to attract any more attention; she had caused enough of a commotion falling off her stool.

She scanned the dozen typed paragraphs on the simple sheet of white paper: this clearly wasn't the wine list she'd assumed it to be. But wait, it wasn't just the title that reminded her of that school outing to Trafalgar Square all those years ago. This anonymous writer had written her story. Hers and Zoe's. Harriet's throat was dry. She took a swig of coffee, but she could barely swallow it. The cup clattered as she replaced it on the saucer.

The air in the café felt like a damp, cloying blanket wrapped around her. A shaft of sunlight was highlighting the smears and fingerprints on the glass-fronted photographs. The rain had stopped. She was desperate to be outside in the sunshine. She hastily shoved the papers back in the navy-blue folder and tucked her stool under the wooden ledge.

The chatty waiter called out *ciao!* and raised his hand. As she paused to return his gesture, she was almost knocked flying by a man rushing in.

The man had clearly got caught in the earlier downpour; dark blotches were splattered over the shoulders and lapels of his light-blue cotton jacket. He was good-looking, for a man who was probably in his late forties, with strong features and a rather regal nose.

He pushed his damp, dark curls out of his eyes and strode across the café's chequerboard floor, straight towards the stool where she had been perching, snatched up the navy-blue leather case from the ledge, turned on his heel and walked out.

Instinctively Harriet followed him outside. He was striding briskly towards the imposing buildings at the bottom end of the square. He was easy to spot, his jacket a flash of blue, his bearing proud and upright. Harriet hesitated. She could hardly run after this stranger and quiz him about the story in his folder, but she couldn't let him disappear out of sight. The man was getting further away. It was now or never. She set off after him.

Chapter Seven

The man walked across the downward slope of The Campo. He was heading towards an exit in the bottom right-hand corner. It led to a road that was wide and busy enough for Harriet to follow at a discreet distance.

The man paused. Harriet tried to blend into a crowd of teenagers taking selfies. Her heart was pounding. The man did not look round. He made a sudden right turn into a steep, narrow road. Harriet made a mental note of the road sign high up on the wall. She did not want to get lost in a maze of twisting streets. The man's blue jacket was rapidly disappearing up the flight of steep steps that ran up one side of the road. She grabbed the thin iron handrail and began to climb. Puffing slightly, she reached the top of the steps. The road stretched away to the left. She hurried along but there was no sign of the man. He had disappeared into thin air.

That was that. She would retrace her steps to The Campo and buy a ticket for the Palazzo Pubblico; she would visit the black and white striped cathedral; perhaps she would even climb all the steps to the top of the Torre del Mangia.

As she retraced her steps she spotted another exit at the other end of the narrow road; what appeared to be a dead end led to a dim passageway. She broke into a jog.

Harriet found herself on a much wider and busier street lined with shops selling handbags and jewellery, clothes and books. She stepped into the road to avoid a tour group shuffling along, four abreast. She hurried past a shop window filled with handmade marbled paper and decorative stationery. Just ahead of her a light-blue jacket was bobbing and weaving through the crowds.

By the time the man had crossed a small piazza she had almost caught up with him. He adjusted the sleeve of his jacket, perhaps checking the time on his watch and increased his speed. A moment later he turned into another small square. Harriet ducked into a nearby doorway, aware that she must look ridiculous.

The man walked purposefully up to the front door of an imposing building flanked by two miniature bay trees in square terracotta pots. He rapped the brass knocker against the scarlet paintwork. The door was opened immediately. Harriet caught a glimpse of a dark-haired woman in a teal silk blouse. The door slammed shut behind him.

Harriet looked around. She was standing in a small residential square. A scruffy white dog, some sort of terrier, was sniffing around the base of a black bicycle with an old-fashioned wicker shopping basket that was leaning up against the wall. The dog soon became bored. It trotted over and cocked its leg against the base of a granite fountain topped with a sculpture of a pouncing panther. She must be in the district of the panther *contrada*. It seemed rather appropriate. With his dark hair, stealthy tread and proud look there was certainly something rather panther-like about the man from the café. She pulled out her phone and snapped a photo of the panther on its plinth. It was really rather beautiful.

She stood and waited for a few minutes but there was no sign that the man would reappear. She couldn't even say why she had followed him. The story in the folder was probably some bizarre coincidence. After all there were billions of people in the world. Some of them must have done the same crazy things that she and Zoe had. She would try and get it out of her mind, take the waiter's advice and explore some of the further reaches of the city.

Harriet turned into a street decked with bright blue and yellow wall lamps, signifying she was in another *contrada*, no doubt. This road was deserted. The only person she passed was a woman with a pushchair who had her hands full trying to control a child of about two or three and a lively puppy.

Soon she could walk no further, her progress blocked by a low stone wall. She had come to the edge of the city. Beyond the wall, a young woman in pink dungarees wielding a pair of secateurs was tending the neat herb garden surrounding three sides of a pale apricot-coloured house; its rough terracotta roof tiles and neat shutters gave it a picture-postcard appearance. A row of deep-green cypress trees partially obscured a cluster of soft-yellow buildings in the distance. The countryside stretched as far as she could see. This was the Tuscany Harriet was falling in love with. She took a deep breath, unfurled her pocket map and spread it out on the lichen-covered wall. She polished her glasses on the edge of her shirt and looked for the best route back into the centre.

She passed a small café with metal chairs taking over half the pavement and sidestepped a white Fiat that was half-on, half-off the road, jammed sideways into a non-existent parking place. An elderly gent nodded a greeting as she passed. She acknowledged him with a smile. The distinctive black and white marble stripes of Siena cathedral were visible in the distance. It had turned into a beautiful sunny day. There was plenty of time before she was due to meet Marco. She would forget all about panther-man, as she now thought of him, and his folder full of stories. She was off to see the sights.

Harriet waited by the entrance to the Torre del Mangia just as Marco had instructed. She hoped his shopping trip had been successful, though no number of new shirts was going to make up for missing the radio interview that would have been such a boost to his career. She wasn't looking forward to his sarcastic comments on the drive home. At least she was sharing a riding lesson with Jess tomorrow; there was a limit to how grumpy he would be if there was someone else present.

Marco walked towards her carrying two substantial, glossy red carrier bags. It was difficult to make out his expression as he was still wearing his sunglasses. She wondered if he had taken them off during the morning's rain showers. He raised his hand in greeting. As he got nearer, she could not miss his wide smile.

'Harriet, hi! Had a good day?' For a moment she thought he was going to hug her.

'Yes, great.' What had got into him? She could almost believe he was glad to see her. He really was a Jekyll and Hyde.

'And you?' She gestured to the carrier bags.

He smiled ruefully. 'An expensive one. I got a bit carried away.' He opened one of the bags, which looked to hold half a dozen cellophane-wrapped shirts.

'So not a total disaster,' she ventured.

'Not at all. All thanks to you. Don't look so puzzled. I'll tell you all about it whilst we're driving back.'

They drove in silence until Harriet could bear it no longer.

'What happened?' she asked.

'What didn't!' He laughed.

'Was the interview with Addolorata cancelled?' Perhaps it had been rescheduled and Marco had got the gig after all.

'No, but I know a few people who wished it had been.' He slowed to let a car out of a side road. 'I just spoke to a mate in production. Addolorata turned up too late to rehearse then dashed off to the loos and came back sniffing. She wouldn't stop talking and wasn't making much sense. She kept swigging out of a can of iced tea, at least that's what she said it was, but Nico had his suspicions when she started slurring and swearing.

'They managed to beep out the worst words but when Nico apologised on her behalf she went crazy, ranting and raving. He should have just switched off her mic straightaway, but I think he was in a state of shock. Eventually he came to his senses and cut to an ad break. The afternoon's phone-in show was jammed with people calling to complain and the website has crashed. And believe you me, our boss is not at all happy about it.'

'So, you had a lucky escape,' Harriet said.

'Harriet, I honestly think you just saved my career.'

'Does that mean you'll be gentle with me in the lesson tomorrow?' Harriet quipped.

'Quite the opposite. I want to make you into the good rider you deserve to be. I'll be cracking the whip – only metaphorically of course.'

Behind his sunglasses, Harriet was sure she detected a wink.

Julia handed Luigi the rasp. He lifted the grey horse's front leg and carefully placed it on the tripod. 'Not long now,' he said.

Julia nodded. She knew all the elements of Luigi's shoeing routine off by heart now, but she never ceased to wonder at the way a tall, heavy horse – like this grey one – stood so quietly whilst her slight, wiry partner went about his work.

'At last!' Luigi stowed his tools and anvil in the back of his white van. He pushed the farmer's dog, who was nosing around the back wheels, out of the way before slamming the double doors. 'Damn dog,' he murmured, then bent to ruffle the spaniel's head. They drove out of the farm, Julia hopping out to bolt the five-bar gate behind them.

'Sorry about that,' Luigi said.

'Nonsense. There's no rush – it's just a picnic,' Julia said.

'But I hate to make you wait around for me when it's your day off.'

'I like to watch you work,' she said.

'You're crazy!' He grinned, his eyes crinkling.

They stopped at the edge of an olive grove that belonged to one of Luigi's cousins. All his family lived within a few miles of the village. Julia spread out a fringed tartan blanket on the grass. She unwrapped some fennel salami and *prosciutto crudo* and arranged them on a blue-rimmed tin plate. Julia liked to make her picnics look as pretty as possible. Maybe it was a hangover from her old catering days, but somehow a little effort made the food taste better.

She tore a piece off the rough *pane toscana* loaf. It was pleasantly chewy. Luigi was munching on some baked onion and spinach flan with an expression of rapture. Julia loved to watch him eat; he devoured her food with such evident pleasure. And it was true, she loved to watch him work, to see that blend of strength and gentleness which made his work as a farrier look so simple despite the years of training needed to do the job. Maybe she was crazy, but it was a nice kind of crazy. The homemade bread, the cold meats, the tangy pecorino cheese, the quiet of the olive grove, Luigi sitting beside her. Who knew the secret to happiness was so simple?

If only she had realised, when she was younger, how undemanding and uncomplicated love could be when you found the right person. That might have put her mind at rest through all those lonely years.

Julia had never been one of those young girls that the boys seemed to like with their flirty, flicky hair and soft laughs. She was blessed with wild, curly locks with a tendency to frizz into a crazy fright wig and although she had enviably long legs her knees were invariably covered with cuts and bruises. She couldn't really see the point of fussing around with make-up and as for heels – she wanted to run, not hobble about. She didn't bother with hanging around the recreation ground where the other girls met up with the local lads. She spent her weekends at the local riding school with Donna.

Donna had always been pony-mad. Even as a little girl she was galloping and snorting around the playground, pigtails flying. Julia would have been content to play with her two guinea pigs, but she tagged along with Donna to the stables where they spent hours sweeping the yard and cleaning tack in exchange for the chance of a free riding lesson when somebody cancelled. No one there cared if she was cute or pretty. No one judged her.

Julia felt the same the first time she walked into a professional kitchen. Her parents lacked the contacts to find her a nice smart office job for her school's compulsory work experience week. Instead her French teacher found her a spot helping in the kitchen of her friend's local brasserie. When the time came to leave school she had no doubt where her future lay.

She would have happily spent her whole working life rolling out dough, poaching and braising, working evenings and weekends, going home late and shattered to her quiet, empty flat. She had a good group of friends, a few men amongst them, but she wasn't as close to any of them as she'd been to Donna – and by the time they were in their twenties, Donna was in Italy living her dream life. Julia visited occasionally and she became godmother to Daniela. She hadn't been desperate to have children herself but when she saw Donna and Giovanni together, she couldn't help feeling it would be nice to have someone to come home to.

Luigi dabbed at the last crumbs on his plate with a damp finger. 'Mmm, that was delicious, as always.'

Julia tidied up the remnants of the picnic; there wasn't much left. She had meant to save a piece of the *torta di mele* for Donna, but Luigi had eaten his way through three pieces of the scrumptious apple cake. Still, she didn't mind; she suspected he probably wouldn't bother cooking for himself that evening.

Luigi fetched a pack of cards from the glove compartment in his van and dealt them out whilst she poured the last of the coffee from the tartan thermos flask. He shuffled the pack. His palms were rough and calloused from years of work and the cuticles around his battered nails were ragged. His tanned arms, visible below his rolled-up shirt sleeves, were strong and wiry. He looked at her with his dark eyes. 'Shall I deal?'

Sometimes Julia felt guilty that it was Donna's bad luck that had led to her good fortune. When Giovanni walked out and Donna called in such a state, Julia had set off for Italy straight away. She had never expected that Bella Vista would become her home. And she certainly never imagined falling in love.

Chapter Eight

Alfredo could hear Marco's voice calling out instructions and peals of laughter drifting over from the schooling ring. It sounded as though Jess and Harriet were having a good time whilst Marco put Coco and Brando through their paces. Jess had been more than happy to switch to the smaller piebald horse; Caesar's big stride was far more suited to cantering through the countryside than to trotting around in a figure of eight.

Alfredo strung up Coco's hay net and fastened the quick-release knot. He rubbed the small of his back. Lugging around bales of hay and buckets of water was a young man's job. But he would not be defeated. He loved his work and if one day he dropped down dead in the yard, he would die happy. Besides, he would never let Donna down the way that Francesco and Giovanni had. He owed her too much.

For many years Alfredo had worked as a private groom to Luca di Robilant, the eccentric industrialist who owned Villa Susino, the big house on the far side of the village. His employer's death had changed everything. Luca's two sons had no intention of leaving Milan to come and live in the middle of nowhere so his six horses were rehomed on a farm in Umbria. The house was sold to Vittoria and Vincenzo, who turned Villa Susino into the village guest house.

Alfredo and his wife, Benedetta, were barely surviving on the seasonal work he could find at the vineyards and the olive press. They were talking of leaving the village and moving to the outskirts of Florence where he might find some factory work. Alfredo knew that when he left the village he would be leaving part of his soul behind, but he had no choice.

The week after both Francesco and Giovanni vanished, he was employed as groom and handyman at Bella Vista. Donna could have found a younger man, a fitter man, but she had thrown him a lifeline. And after Benedetta passed away, Bella Vista gave him a reason to carry on.

What a fool Giovanni was to walk out on a woman like Donna! Alfredo had no doubt it was nothing but stubbornness and pride that kept him from coming home. As for Francesco, Alfredo had his own theory about his disappearance. He had no doubt at all that Donna and Francesco had never been more than friends. Not one person in the village had truly believed in their so-called affair. Donna was innocent. He just wished he had some proof.

Only Jess and Harriet were riding today now that Franny and Bob had gone. It was the perfect opportunity to catch up on all those odd jobs he'd been meaning to do. He would go through the drawers of the heavy wooden chest in the corner, sorting out the spare quilted saddle pads, horse bandages and travel boots – all the paraphernalia that had accumulated over the years. Then he would tackle the job he had been putting off for a long, long time: cleaning and repairing Caesar's old saddle.

The saddle lay on a high shelf, sharing its dusty, neglected home with a pile of old jute horse rugs and rough blankets – long replaced by modern, breathable, easy-clean versions – but kept in case of some unforeseen and unlikely eventuality. Caesar had no use for the saddle. He was ridden in the beautiful custom-made black leather replacement that Donna had bought as a surprise for Giovanni's birthday. The birthday present he never opened.

Alfredo had managed to lift the saddle down once before, many years ago, by standing on his desk, balancing on one leg and stretching as far as he could. He wasn't going to try that again. But when he had mentioned the necessary repairs to Donna, her eyes filled with tears and he had been unwilling to broach the subject again. But nearly ten years had passed since Giovanni had left. The old saddle had stayed up on that shelf ever since, unused and unwanted. Something needed to be done with it. It was time.

Alfredo worked methodically through the wooden chest, emptying it drawer by drawer. He prised the lid off his tin of sweets and unwrapped the cellophane from one of his favourite strawberry bonbons. He would be getting through plenty of those before today's tasks were finished.

'Alfredo! Can we come in?' It was Jess. Alfredo glanced at the clock in surprise. He didn't seem to have got very far.

'*Certo*, certainly. Come, come.' He stood up slowly.

Jess and Harriet hesitated in the doorway.

'Where shall we . . .' Jess began. She was holding two bridles and had Brando's saddle over her forearm. Harriet was clutching the other saddle and the riding hat she had borrowed.

Alfredo looked around. 'Here, is okay for now.' He pointed to the pile of horse rugs on the floor. Harriet popped her hat and saddle down. Alfredo smiled. She was such a dainty little thing, she reminded him of his daughter, a long, long time ago. Jess on the other hand – he didn't think he had ever seen a woman so tall. Of course! Why hadn't he thought of it before?

'You help?' Alfredo pointed to the top shelf.

'Of course,' Jess said.

'Is old saddle, green cover.'

Jess climbed onto Alfredo's desk. She stood on tiptoes, but Caesar's old saddle was just out of reach. The desk was wobbling too, despite Harriet and Alfredo holding on to it.

'Okay. You try. Is no problem.' Alfredo sighed.

'Wait a minute,' Harriet said. 'What about standing on that chest?'

'Let me take a look.' Jess scrambled down from her precarious position. She rapped her knuckles on the top of the chest. 'It's solid and it looks tall enough. We could try and move it.'

'It very heavy,' Alfredo protested. He did not want anyone getting hurt.

'We could lift the drawers out,' Harriet said.

Jess pulled open the top drawer. 'Oh, this is empty.'

'Yes. I tidy everything,' Alfredo said. He looked at the tack and equipment piled all over the room. Why did tidying up make a place so untidy?

'Oh, I wondered where all this stuff had come from,' Jess said. She began yanking out the empty drawers and stacking them in the corner.

'Ready?' With Jess pulling and Alfredo and Harriet pushing, bit by bit they slowly manoeuvred the old chest across the room. It made a horrible scraping sound as it dragged across the floor.

'Just here,' Harriet said.

Alfredo straightened up. He would need to soak in a hot bath tonight.

'Much easier!' Jess climbed up onto the chest and lifted down the saddle.

'*Brava!*' Alfredo spluttered through a cloud of dust.

Jess climbed down and wiped the back of her grimy hand across her forehead. She handed the saddle to Alfredo. He peeled back the faded pea-green saddle cover. It was just as he remembered it.

'*Grazie*. Thank you,' he said.

'Ready to move that chest back, Harriet?' Jess said.

Harriet was struggling. 'I can't seem to get it to shift.' She redoubled her efforts.

'Wait a minute, I think there's something caught under the back corner that's making it stick. Yes, there's a bit of paper.'

Jess bent down and handed Harriet a piece of lined notepaper folded in half. The corner had been torn off and was still stuck to the chest. Harriet looked around for a bin.

'Wait!' Alfredo reached for the piece of paper with trembling hands. He swept the pile of saddlecloths from his chair and sat down heavily. He unfolded the paper and placed it on the table. He traced the words with his index finger. His lips were moving, but he did not utter a sound.

'What is it?' Harriet looked alarmed. She glanced at Jess.

Alfredo refolded the note. 'Jess, get Marco,' he said in a voice barely louder than a whisper. 'But please be quiet. Donna – she must not know.' He pressed a finger to his lips.

Jess was only gone for a minute, but it felt like ten.

'What on earth have you guys been doing?' Marco surveyed the tack room.

'Alfredo's been tidying up,' Harriet said.

Marco raised an eyebrow. 'Is that what you call it? Anyway, what's the problem? It had better not take long. Julia's making *pollo alle olive* for lunch and I'm starving. And what on earth is that doing there?' He gestured at Caesar's old saddle.

64

'The girls they find something. Something important.'
Alfredo handed Marco the note. He read it quickly.

'I can't believe it! After all this time,' Marco said.

'What?' Harriet could not bear the suspense any longer.

'It is a note for my mother. From Francesco. Written nearly ten years ago.'

Harriet was shocked. A love note. After all this time. Giovanni had been right all along.

Chapter Nine

'We'd better go,' Harriet said. They should leave Marco alone with Alfredo. He would need some time to digest the news.

'You two aren't going anywhere. Not until I've come up with a plan.' Marco's eyes were steely, his jaw clenched.

'A plan?' What on earth did he mean? Whatever the rights and wrongs of Donna's behaviour all those years ago, Harriet had grown very fond of her. There was no way she was going to get involved with any revenge Marco might be planning.

'It could be a misunderstanding,' Jess suggested.

'It couldn't be clearer.' Marco handed her the note.

Jess's eyes widened as she read in silence. 'I can't make out all of it. My Italian's not that good – but this is incredible.'

'My bloody stupid, stubborn father!' Marco exclaimed.

Harriet felt lost. One minute they had proof of Francesco and Donna's affair. The next minute Marco was cursing his father.

Jess caught sight of Harriet's bemused expression and turned to Marco. 'Will you tell us exactly what it says?'

Marco nodded. '*My dear Donna,*' he read aloud. '*I apologise for this rushed note, but I must leave at once. My mother has been taken gravely ill. I have managed to get a seat on tonight's flight from Pisa. Then tomorrow I have a long journey ahead of me to my parents' cottage in Oban. I hope that it will not be too late.*

66

Although I feel great loyalty to you and Bella Vista, my father is now quite frail and will need my help. Family must come first; you will understand. I don't know when, or if, I will return. I know Giovanni has not been very happy with our friendship so I will leave it to you to decide if you want to contact me. I wish he understood the innocence of my feelings for you. I think, perhaps, you know the reason why it is so. I wish you all good fortune, my dear, dear friend. Yours affectionately, Francesco.'

'I always knew it,' Marco said. 'Even though I was very young. How could my father believe my mother was unfaithful to him?'

'Your father is a great man. But also, how you say, hot-headed like his father, your grandfather,' Alfredo said.

'Deep down he must have doubts. He had no proof that Francesco was my mother's lover.' Marco shook his head.

'Giovanni: he is proud, stubborn,' Alfredo said. *Like father, like son*, Harriet thought.

'But now we have proof that nothing went on between them,' Jess said.

'We tell Donna?' Alfredo said hesitantly.

'No. We tell no one. Not Mum, not Julia. We must get my mother and Papa together and confront them with the truth. I will think of a way, but until then no one must say anything. Now, quick, we must join the others on the terrace for lunch before they wonder what is going on. Alfredo, put the letter away safely. Yes, slip it between a couple of winter rugs. No one will look there. Harriet, Jess: you must promise you won't breathe a word.'

'We promise,' they both said at once.

Julia's *pollo alle olive* was one of Alfredo's favourites but despite the tantalising smell of chicken and garlic he had no appetite. His mind was racing. He was sure his face must betray Jess and Harriet's discovery. He half-heartedly ate a couple of the green olives. Donna was looking at him with concern, so he hastily gulped down everything else on his plate. The chicken felt like a brick wedged in his stomach.

At last, lunch was over. He had never been gladder to be alone in the tack room. Well, almost alone – he could feel Miu Miu rubbing her soft head against his trouser leg. Alfredo was exhausted by the morning's events, but he was too restless to take his usual afternoon siesta. Instead he unravelled and re-rolled every stable bandage. The rhythm of the task seemed to calm him and distracted his whirling mind from the letter hidden in the pile of winter horse rugs.

Gradually he worked his way through the piles of clutter until everything was back in its place. The drawers and cubbyholes seemed as jam-packed as ever. Caesar's saddle, stored in its protective green bag, was still perched on top of the chest like a giant, squatting toad. He carefully lifted it onto his desk and removed the cotton cover.

It seemed like yesterday that Giovanni was riding Caesar through the village, out to the olive trees and the vineyards beyond. Caesar had been a young horse then; he was just six years old when he arrived at Bella Vista. A handsome, black horse. Now his mane and tail were streaked with grey. They were all younger then; Giovanni's hair had been a mass of coal-black curls, like Marco's.

Alfredo ran his hand over the curve of the saddle. The seat was made from a cheap, artificial leather; no wonder Donna had ordered the beautiful custom-made saddle for Giovanni's birthday. But the wipe-clean surface had its advantages. A damp sponge and soft cloth were all that Alfredo needed.

He unscrewed the lid from the orange tin of metal polish and buffed the small metal name plate until he could see that the raised letters once more spelt *Caesar*. So far, so good. But beneath the saddle flap the leather girth straps were worn and split where they had been buckled and rebuckled umpteen times, and the years of neglect had caused the leather to dry out and crack. Alfredo rubbed in some saddle soap and sighed. It was no use: the straps would have to be replaced and the stitching on the webbing where they were affixed was coming adrift. The saddle was far too dangerous to use in its current condition. He slid it back into its pea-green cover and placed it on top of the chest. Right now, there was nothing more he could do.

Jess pressed the last piece of pasta dough gently into shape, pinching the four corners between her thumb and fore-finger. The kitchen's humidity had caused her red hair to frizz out in all directions. There was a smear of flour across the end of her nose. She screwed up her face and studied her handiwork. Her pasta shapes looked nothing like the regimented rows of *tortellini* lined up on Julia's side of the kitchen counter.

'Hmm. They're a bit wonky.'

'Look at mine,' said Harriet. Her *tortellini* were piled up on the olive wood board in front of her.

'I thought they were supposed to be square,' Jess said.

'They are square – well sort of . . . maybe,' Harriet said. Her lips began to twitch and she gave a snort of laughter.

'And they're supposed to be the same size . . .' Jess said.

'They do seem to, umm, vary a little bit,' Julia said. She was obviously trying not to be too discouraging.

Jess began to arrange the two girls' pasta shapes in a row – the littlest at one end, the largest at the other. Harriet clapped a hand over her mouth in a vain attempt to stem a fit of the giggles. The kitchen door opened. It was Donna.

'How are you getting on?' she said but no one could answer her. Jess was doubled up, clutching her stomach. How could laughing hurt so much? She tried to form a sensible reply, but the words would not come. Instead, she silently pointed at Julia's neat pasta shapes then the two girls' own endeavours.

'I'm sure they'll still taste great,' Donna said. Then she was laughing too, the four of them setting each other off.

'Sorry about the mess, Julia. Once we've cleared up, we'll get out from under your feet before we cause any more chaos in here,' Jess said. 'Whenever I do any cooking it looks like there's been an explosion in the kitchen.'

'I never cook at home. I usually live on takeaways and things on toast,' Harriet said.

'You don't cook?' Julia sounded incredulous.

'By the time I get in from work I don't have much time for cooking – or anything else.'

'You must really need this holiday. I'll help Julia clear up in here, it's really no bother. Why don't you both go and sit on the terrace for a bit?' Donna said.

'If you're sure you don't mind. I'd love to go and catch some more sun. I'll just go and fetch my sketchpad,' Jess said.

'May I have a look?' Harriet flicked quickly through the rough, white pages, past sketches of the view across the valley and the shapes of the Chianti hills. She seemed to find the portraits more interesting: studying Jess's sketches of Julia, her hands in a mixing bowl; Alfredo polishing the buckles on a bridle; and several pages taken up with drawings of Marco. Marco had been happy to pose for Jess, but she was too embarrassed to ask him too often. Sometimes it was easier to sketch from the photographs she had taken. She never tired of drawing him; it gave her the perfect excuse to look at his handsome face.

'These are really good. I love the one of Alfredo. What are you going to draw now?' Harriet said.

'I was hoping I might sketch you but only if you're sure you don't mind.' Jess felt a little awkward asking Harriet to pose.

'Mind? Not at all. Now, where shall I sit?' Harriet said.

Jess wheeled the wicker lounger right to the edge of the terrace by the low grey stone wall. She knew if Harriet was comfortable she would make a better subject.

'Could you turn a bit further that way?' Jess said.

'Like this?' Harriet wiggled into a different position.

'Perfect.' Jess held a pencil at arm's length to help her get the right perspective.

'I've never had anyone draw me before,' said Harriet.

'Just relax. You can close your eyes if you like. I won't be drawing in any details for a while.'

Jess settled back into one of the wooden seats and adjusted the position of a plump rose-coloured cushion so that it nestled against the small of her back. Harriet was beautifully positioned on the lounger with a view of the valley behind her. The scent of rosemary drifted over from a terracotta planter. Jess closed her eyes for a second and took a deep breath. She picked up her stick of charcoal. Before long she was thoroughly absorbed.

Harriet shot upright.

'What is it?' Jess said.

'I felt something touch my leg. Oh, it's the cat. Miu Miu, where on earth did you creep up from? You can't sit here.'

'Oh, it's okay, let her curl up on the end of the lounger. I can put her in the drawing. She was probably escaping from all that mess in the tack room,' Jess said.

71

'Fancy finding that letter from Francesco. I can't stop thinking about it.'

'Me, too. I was terrified of catching Donna's eye during lunch and blurting it all out. I'm so glad we had that cookery lesson with Julia straight afterwards,' said Jess.

'Even if your *tortellini* came out a bit wonky,' Harriet quipped.

'Speak for yourself!' Jess said. She let out a giggle. 'Quick, change the subject. I can't have you cracking up when you're meant to be posing.'

'What do you think Marco's dad is like?' Harriet asked.

'I don't know. He must be very stubborn. What sort of person storms out of a marriage without any proof?'

'Someone moody and a bit scary. I can see where Marco gets it from.'

'Marco? Maybe he can be a little bit moody, but you can't think he's scary. He's lovely,' Jess said.

'That's because you already know how to ride. Try getting him to teach you from scratch,' Harriet said.

'Hold still a moment. All done.' Jess put down her stick of charcoal.

'Hey, let me see.' Harriet reached over.

'Okay. Don't hate me if you don't like it,' Jess said in a jokey voice, but she bit her bottom lip as she handed over the sketchbook.

'Miu Miu looks good,' Harriet said.

Jess looked away. A small green lizard was scuttling along the mortar between two rows of bricks at the edge of the wall. 'Oh, don't you like it?'

'I love it. It's just that you've made me look so pretty.' Harriet was blushing.

'You are. You're so dainty and blonde.'

'Really? I just think of myself as short. And kind of

ordinary.' Harriet pushed up her glasses to rub the bridge of her nose. 'I'd love to be tall like you.'

'Funny, isn't it? If we've got straight hair, we want curls; if we've got curly hair, we want it poker-straight. I've never liked being tall. Though I guess it's useful sometimes.' *Though not when you're trying to get a date.*

'It came in pretty useful today. We would never have found Francesco's note if you hadn't got that saddle down,' Harriet said.

'Do you think Marco can pull this off?'

'I don't know. I guess we're going to have to wait and find out.'

'What was Marco like when you drove to Siena?' Jess said. She had been dying to ask; she had thought about it often enough. Marco was only supposed to give Harriet a lift, but what if they had spent the day together? She was probably being silly. Harriet was nearly ten years older than Marco, but didn't everyone love a blonde, especially a pale creamy blonde with clear grey eyes like Harriet?

'Okay . . . you know,' Harriet said vaguely.

Harriet's face betrayed nothing. She definitely didn't sound like she had fallen for Marco. And why would she? Harriet and Marco hadn't even liked each other when they first met. But wasn't that how all the best romcoms began?

'Did you spend much time together?' Jess had to know. She had to be sure.

'No. He showed me The Campo then went off. But something really strange happened after he left. I was going to tell you straight after our riding lesson but then we found Francesco's note and I didn't get the chance.'

'What happened? No, wait. Let's grab a couple of glasses of wine to bring out here and you can tell me.'

They perched side by side on the wicker lounger as Harriet recounted her tale.

'That's so weird,' Jess said. She picked up her wine glass. She had not touched a drop whilst Harriet had been talking. 'That building by the panther fountain. Do you think that's where he lives?'

'I don't know. To be honest the whole thing freaked me out. I'm going to try to forget all about it.'

'You're right. You and Zoe can't be the only two schoolkids who've tried to smuggle a pigeon out of Trafalgar Square. It's just a weird coincidence. It must be.'

'You're probably right,' said Harriet. But she did not sound very convinced.

Donna walked through to the kitchen. Julia was frying onions. It was not that long since lunch but the smell made Donna feel hungry all over again.

'Can I help?' Donna asked although she knew the answer already. The kitchen was Julia's own kingdom. After Jess and Harriet's escapades with the *tortellini in brodo* she had probably had enough of other people under her feet today.

'No, but you can do me a favour. Try a glass of this wine. Vittoria recommended it to me. They've been serving it down at their guest house. I've given some to Jess and Harriet. I think we might drink it at dinner tonight.' Julia poured out a generous glass. 'Now go and sit on the terrace with the girls and let me get on with my work. Go on, out with you!'

Donna retreated, laughing. Harriet and Jess were deep in conversation so she chose one of the wooden garden chairs at the other end of the terrace. She drew her legs up under her, inhaled the aroma of the red wine and took her first sip. Heavenly.

Donna let out a sigh of relief. She hadn't realised she was tense. Everything was working out well but the sooner they sorted out the website the better. There could have been six yoga-seeking Harriets all turning up at once. It didn't bear thinking about. Thank goodness Harriet had been persuaded to ride Coco. For a complete beginner, she had done pretty well, especially as Marco wasn't likely to be the most forgiving of teachers.

Donna would never forget the day little Coco arrived. The look on Marco's face when he threw his arms around the pony's neck and declared it his 'best birthday ever' would stay with her forever. How sweet Marco had been back then: a small wiry child, full of energy, running around the farm, chasing the chickens despite her scolding, and playing with their new puppy, Lupo. He had been the happiest little boy in the world. She hadn't imagined that anything could change Marco's sunny nature. Then Giovanni upped and left them. His adored father. Gone. Just like that.

No wonder Marco could be a little difficult, but perhaps it was inevitable he would turn out that way; Giovanni hadn't been the easiest of men. Daniela, Marco's older sister, was content with her quiet life working behind the scenes at Siena's civic museum; she had her grandmother's looks and gentle ways, but Marco had inherited his father's temperament along with his strong features and untameable hair.

Donna was glad her two children had been able to salvage a good relationship with their father but sometimes she couldn't help wishing that he had disappeared without a trace.

Over the last ten years she had experienced every emotion: anguish, denial, despair, rage and hopelessness, all punctuated by moments when she couldn't help believing that one day he would see sense and come back home. On the rare occasions he phoned the house, her hopes soared, but it was always the same: a cursory exchange of practical information and the click of the receiver before she even had a chance to ask: 'How are you?'

Giovanni's absence had dominated her life as much as his presence had. She often wished she could parcel all her feelings up in a box and throw away the key.

It would be so much simpler if Giovanni had moved further away, up to Milan or to somewhere in the south. It would be easier to move on with her life. But Giovanni would never leave Tuscany. Siena had been his family's home for generations. It was in his blood.

Chapter Ten

'Yes please,' Harriet said. She held out her mug. Julia steadied the huge brown teapot with both hands and poured her a top-up. Harriet took a sip of tea. She looked over at Marco who was helping himself from a bowl of soft, velvety peaches in the centre of the breakfast table. She wondered if he had managed to devise a plan to bring Donna and Giovanni together. His face gave nothing away.

'I hope it's not a problem, but I've invited someone to dinner tonight,' Marco said. He took a bite of his peach.

'Oh.' Donna frowned slightly.

'I know I'm celebrating with my friends at the weekend but I thought it would be nice to have a meal here this week, to mark my birthday. A real family meal.'

'Who have you invited? Your cousin Paolo?' Donna asked.

Harriet busied herself spreading honey on her bread, aware that Jess had stopped midway through her peach; a drizzle of juice was running down her chin.

'It's not Paolo, Mum. It's Daniela.'

'Oh, that's fantastic, darling! Why didn't you tell me before?'

'I couldn't. I only messaged her yesterday and she texted me back this morning. It was so lucky she could come. And I know she'll get on with both of you,' he said, looking at Jess and Harriet.

'My daughter, Daniela, works at the civic museum in Siena. She's a quiet girl but she does enjoy meeting new people,' Donna said.

'I'll make *arista con patate* and your favourite fennel gratin. I'll phone the butcher straight away to make sure he has enough pork. And I can easily pop to the shop and pick up a few extra bits,' said Julia. She took a jotter pad from the pocket of her apron and started scribbling down a list of ingredients.

'I'm going to wear one of my new shirts. I thought we might dress up a bit, make it a real occasion,' Marco said.

'I'll have to put on a nice blouse,' Donna said.

'No, Mum. Wear your high heels and that new blue dress of yours. The one that you wore for Bianca's birthday.' Marco picked up a knife and started spreading a thick layer of chocolate and hazelnut spread on a hunk of *pane toscana*.

'Of course, if you like.' Donna laughed. She reached out and ruffled her son's hair.

'Get off, Mum!' Marco scowled. He bolted down the rest of his breakfast with indecent haste and pushed back his chair. 'I'll go and help Alfredo to tack up. I'll see you in the yard.'

Harriet forced herself to linger at the breakfast table a little while longer even though she was dying to speak to Marco. She was pretty sure it wasn't Marco's big sister, Daniela, who was coming to dinner. But there was no chance of speaking to Marco before they set off; Donna always seemed to be somewhere within earshot. Harriet could only guess what Marco had planned.

It was the first time Harriet had ridden outside the farm without the security of knowing that Donna was holding the end of Coco's lead rope. Harriet was starting to feel that she had some sort of control over the little pony though she suspected her ability to get him to walk and trot to order was mainly down to Coco's desire to follow close behind Donna's horse, Guido.

They picked their way through the olive grove, skirted the edge of the vineyard and cantered across a meadow of wildflowers. It now seemed incredible that Harriet had lived for twenty-eight years without riding a horse. She felt as though she could ride all day, though she might need to build up a bit more strength in her legs. Her thighs still ached after a few hours in the saddle. There must be somewhere near London where she could ride after she got back home. She had never had time for hobbies before unless she counted drinking with her colleagues in the bar after work. She was beginning to think that there might be life outside the office if she just raised her head from her computer screen long enough to take a look.

Harriet removed Coco's saddle and bridle; the morning's ride was over. She lingered over removing her jodhpur boots and lacing up her trainers, willing Donna to go inside so that she and Jess could find out what Marco was planning.

'I'll take that.' Marco nodded towards Donna's saddle, which was resting against the stable door, as she carefully pulled the headpiece on Guido's bridle up and over his big grey ears.

'Thanks, love.' Donna wiped her hands on her dark brown jodhpurs. 'I'll go and see if Julia needs a hand in the kitchen. I think she's got quite a feast planned for tonight. I'm so glad I persuaded her we only needed to take some *panini* with us for lunch.'

'There were enough of those to feed an army.' Marco grinned. 'Ready, Harriet? Jess? Let's get all these things back to the tack room.'

Marco pushed the wooden door shut behind them. Butterflies danced in Harriet's stomach. Alfredo was chopping up an apple with a Swiss penknife. His rickety wooden desk was covered with discarded sweet wrappers. He pushed the tin towards them.

'I am nervous, I eat.' He shrugged.

'When I'm nervous I can't. I don't know how I'm going to get through dinner tonight,' Harriet said.

'Oh, my sister's not that bad,' Marco quipped.

'It's not really your sister who's coming, is it?' Jess said.

'Daniela *is* coming, thank goodness. I'm so lucky she can make it. My father is picking her up on the way. There's engineering work on the railway line today, which gave her the perfect excuse to ask for a lift. We don't want Papa changing his mind at the last minute. And he's much less likely to start an argument if Daniela's around. She's a very calm person. She takes after my granny on Mum's side, I suppose.'

'How on earth did you get your father to agree to come here?' Harriet said.

Marco smiled. 'I asked him.'

'You just asked him? But Julia said he hasn't been here for nearly ten years. Not since . . .' Harriet's voice tailed off. She did not want Marco to think that she and Julia had been gossiping about him.

'You are right. I was just a young boy when Papa left. I vowed I would never ask him to come back. I would never beg for my father to visit me here, in my own home.' Marco's eyes flashed with anger.

'And now . . .' Alfredo began to speak, but instead he stopped and picked at the skin around his left thumbnail.

'And now, I am not doing this for me. I am doing it for my mother. Papa has been asking me what I want for my twenty-first birthday and I hadn't thought of anything. So, I told him I had decided at last: that it has been my dearest wish for him to come and eat here, at Bella Vista with me and Daniela and my mother. To have a meal as a family this one time.'

'So, he agreed, just like that,' Harriet said.

'He knows how much it took to ask him,' Marco said. His arms hung by his sides, but his fists were clenched.

'Does Julia know?' Jess asked.

Marco glanced around the tack room. 'No, I think it would be unfair on Julia to have to keep our secret.'

'So, she's only expecting five for dinner, unless Alfredo is staying,' Harriet said.

'Harriet, are you seriously worrying that Julia might not make enough food?' Marco said.

Harriet thought of the huge loin of pork, and the mountain of potatoes Julia had been peeling. 'I guess not.' She laughed.

'Roll on half past seven,' Marco said. 'See you later.'

Harriet hugged her grey hoody around her. The warmth had gone out of the day, and the sky was no longer blue, but she was reluctant to leave the comfortable wicker lounger, which had become her favourite spot since she had arrived at the farm.

Jess laid down her sketchpad. 'I don't know how Marco's keeping so calm. I usually lose myself when I'm drawing but I can't stop thinking about this evening. It feels like we shouldn't really be here. It doesn't really seem right that we're going to be slap, bang in the middle of someone else's family drama.'

'I've been thinking that too, but Marco says having some outsiders here should make it less intense. Giovanni is more likely to sit and read Francesco's note calmly if there are other people around.'

'It's a pity Alfredo couldn't be persuaded to stay for dinner,' Jess said.

'He said he was far too nervous. He's really worried about how Donna is going to react. She and Giovanni have spoken on the phone occasionally about Daniela and Marco, but Donna hasn't set eyes on him since the day he left,' said Harriet. 'What if she doesn't want to see him? Maybe she's happy with the way things are.'

'I hadn't thought of that, but I've got the strong impression from Julia that despite everything, Donna still loves him. Talking of Julia, I think I'll go and get changed then see if she needs any help. I'm too jumpy to sit out here. I'd rather keep out of the way for a bit, and she's promised to show me how to make her *polpette* – they're some sort of meatball and they're seriously delicious.'

'Yep. I think we should both make ourselves scarce. I'll go and check Alfredo's okay then I might join you.' Harriet pushed her hands into the opposite cuffs of her hoody and set off towards the tack room.

'Alfredo!' Harriet rapped on the door. A flurry of barks answered her. She pushed the door open. Lupo leapt up, his two big paws landing on Harriet's knees, almost knocking her flying. 'Hey, Lupo. Did you get shut in? Where's Alfredo?'

Alfredo appeared in the doorway. His shoulders were sagging with the weight of the bulging hay nets he carried in each hand. 'Last hay. Then home.'

'Can I help?' Harriet asked.

'No, no need. But maybe, walk Lupo.'

'Where?'

'Anywhere . . . in village.'

'Okay, sure.' Harriet zipped up her hoody. Lupo reached up his front paw and whined. 'Okay, old boy, we'll go for a walk.'

Alfredo pointed towards a brown leather lead that lay coiled on the table. 'You forget something!' He laughed but she noticed the old man's hand was trembling as he handed it to her.

'Are you okay?' Harriet asked.

'I worry, I worry for Donna. Today, a black cat, he walk through the yard.'

'But that's lucky,' said Harriet.

'In Italy, very unlucky.' Alfredo shook his head.

'Donna is English. It will be lucky for her.'

'I hope so, *tocca ferro*.' He touched an iron ring embedded in the wall.

'In England we say: touch wood.'

Alfredo gripped the doorframe with his calloused brown fingers. 'Touch wood, touch iron. Now is okay.' He bent down to scratch Lupo's grey head. 'I hope.'

Harriet set off down the path, Lupo looking back over his shoulder every few yards as if surprised that Harriet was the one holding the lead. Their pace was slow; it seemed that Lupo found something to sniff at the base of every plant and tree. By the time Harriet turned to replace the latch on the gate she could see Alfredo beginning to make his way across the yard. He held his back stiffly, one leg dragging slightly behind him. She wondered how long it would take him to reach his small cottage.

She walked down the main street towards the bobbing, red balloon tied to the cherry tree that marked the corner house where Bianca lived. The old woman was, as always, sitting on the bench outside her cottage. She looked up as Harriet passed, called out a cheery *buonasera* then went back to stitching an old linen cloth that looked as though it had seen many previous repairs.

Harriet passed the clock tower. The swifts were circling overhead; she could still hear their screeches as she made her way past the village shop and Beppe's Bar. Enticing smells of garlic and fresh herbs were wafting from Beppe's kitchen. Somewhere in the distance a cuckoo was calling.

Harriet carried on down towards the old guest house. Despite its slightly unkempt state, the place looked welcoming. The front door was painted a warm sunshine-yellow and surrounded by pots of bright red geraniums. A straggly white jasmine had spread beyond its trellis fixed to the property's stone wall. Three bicycles, one with a wicker front basket, leant against the wall of the garage where an old Vespa that had seen better days was propped up against a chest freezer. A metal sign decorated with a painted plum tree swung in the breeze, declaring that she had arrived at Villa Susino.

Although it was still light, a lamp was glowing in one of the downstairs rooms, illuminating a short, middle-aged woman carefully placing a wine bottle and tumblers on a sturdy table surrounded by mismatched chairs. Lupo stopped and lifted his leg right by the front door. Harriet realised what the dog was doing a second too late. She clapped her hand to her mouth.

'Lupo. No!' Harriet took a firm hold on the leash and pulled him away before there was a chance the woman might look out and spot them.

They walked back through the village but instead of heading straight to Bella Vista, Harriet took the path that led to the olive grove. She was in no hurry to get back to the house. She was happy to meet Marco's sister, Daniela, but she was in two minds about encountering the mercurial Giovanni.

Alfredo was right to worry; so many things could go wrong tonight, black cat or no black cat. Marco was so pleased with his plan that Harriet could not bring herself to express any doubts. At last, he believed he had the proof of his mother's innocence, which would bring his parents back together. Of course, he was expecting there to be a happy ending. But maybe Donna was happy with her life. Maybe Giovanni was the last person she wanted to see.

Harriet reached out and touched the rough bark on a twisted branch. There was something magical about this place. There was so much history here. The old trees with their gnarled trunks and silvery green leaves produced their fruit generation after generation. The workers now had smartphones in their pockets, but the fruit was still harvested by hand in the time-honoured way.

Lupo sniffed at the base of a tree.

'Okay, you can run about. There's no one around.' Harriet bent down and unclipped the lead.

She looked up. A cyclist was approaching from the direction of Villa Susino. As the bicycle drew nearer, she could see the rider was a man in his fifties. A navy sweater was knotted around his waist and his blue shirt collar was open, revealing a jaunty red and blue spotted scarf tucked into the neckline.

Lupo started to bark. Harriet bent down to reassure him. It was too late. Lupo was off, heading straight into the path of the oncoming bike.

The man skidded to a halt.

'I'm sorry!' Harriet shouted. But the man had dismounted and was crouched down petting the errant dog.

'It's no problem,' he replied in English. 'Lupo. Is it really you?' He smiled up at Harriet. 'It is Lupo isn't it?'

His accent was hard to place. Italian mixed with something else. Irish? Scottish perhaps.

'Yes, it's Lupo. I'm walking him for Alfredo. I'm staying at Bella Vista.'

'Alfredo, from the village? He works there now?'

'Yes. I believe he's been there for some years.'

'And Donna. Is she well?' There was genuine concern in his voice.

'Oh yes.'

Lupo was now lying on his back, all four legs in the air. The man bent down and stroked his soft stomach.

'He likes you,' Harriet said.

'I have not seen him for ten long years. He was just a puppy back then. But see, he still remembers.'

'He's eleven now, I believe.' Harriet tried to keep her voice level.

'We all get older.' He shrugged. 'Donna – she is at home today? I am on my way to pay her a visit – a surprise. I hope it's a nice one.'

So, this *was* Giovanni. But where was Daniela? Perhaps they were travelling separately after all. Harriet had so many unanswered questions, but she responded with a simple nod.

'Good. I have been thinking about today for a long, long time,' he said.

Giovanni was not at all like the stern, handsome character she imagined. This man's brown, weather-beaten face was etched with lines and a cluster of broken veins fanned out from the sides of his nose. But his dark brown eyes, which crinkled when he smiled, were kind. He exuded a calm air, a million miles from the temperamental, impetuous person Julia had described. Giovanni had obviously mellowed. Harriet was no longer dreading the evening.

'If you are staying at Bella Vista then I will be seeing you later . . .' He swung a leg over his bicycle.

'Pleased to meet you. I'm Harriet,' she said and held out her hand. He grasped her hand in his and shook it firmly.

'Pleased to meet you, Harriet. I am Francesco.'

Chapter Eleven

Harriet stood open-mouthed. Francesco was back – and pedalling off in the direction of Bella Vista. She had to stop him.

'Francesco!' she called but he did not turn around. Her voice must have been carried away on the wind. She had to catch him before it was too late. She reached down to clip the lead back onto Lupo's collar. Out of the corner of her eye she saw a movement in the grass, a flash of white tail. But Lupo had seen it first. The rabbit shot across the olive grove with Lupo in hot pursuit.

Francesco's bicycle was getting smaller and smaller as he headed for the path leading to Bella Vista. If she ran as fast as she could, there was still a tiny chance that she could catch him up, but she couldn't risk anything happening to Lupo. Her heart was thumping in her chest as she tried in vain to catch the dog.

'Lupo! Come here!' she shouted but Lupo was darting through the trees. The dog's old legs were no match for the rabbit but Lupo had found a new game: as soon as Harriet got close, he turned and ran a few paces in the opposite direction.

Harriet dodged through the trees. She misjudged a low branch, smacking her face on the rough bark.

Lupo trotted over and jumped up, his paws making muddy marks on Harriet's jeans. 'Lupo, you're a menace.' Harriet sighed and clipped on the lead.

It was too late. Francesco must have reached Bella Vista by now. There was nothing Harriet could do. She led Lupo up the lane, unfastened the latch on the five-bar gate and walked up to the house.

Donna picked up her eyeshadow palette; there were eight shades, seven untouched. On an impulse she ignored the hollowed-out rectangle of beige and loaded the little sponge-tipped applicator with a silvery green. Then she picked up her eyeliner, closed an eye and drew carefully along the edge of her upper eyelid, blinked and studied her reflection in the oval mirror. It was strange to be making such an effort but if it was going to make Marco happy, then why not?

She stepped into the blue dress Marco had insisted she wore. She could just reach around far enough to pull up the zip. She glanced in the mirror. She squeezed an inch of flesh critically. She wasn't as slim as she used to be, but the bias-cut skirt skimmed over her hips and stopped above her still-neat ankles and the V-neck provided just a hint of cleavage. She should wear it more often. But when did she ever go out? It was the sort of dress you could wear on a first date and when was she going to go on one of those?

She could not help thinking back to her first proper date with Giovanni. Florence was so romantic. They had gone for a walk along the River Arno, then for a picnic in the Boboli Gardens. No dresses for her back then. She had worn cargo pants and a cut-off T-shirt. She had worn a lot of crop tops in those days. She had even toyed with the idea of a belly button ring. Imagine that!

She smoothed down her skirt then fastened the blue topaz pendant that Giovanni had given her to celebrate Marco's birth. She hardly ever wore it, but it seemed appropriate tonight. It was hard to believe her little boy was turning twenty-one in a couple of days. She couldn't wait to surprise him with his present: a rail pass that would take him all over Europe when his contract at the radio station ended. To her surprise she felt a tear pricking the corner of her eye. Twenty-one and twenty-three: soon Marco and his sister wouldn't need her at all. Soon she really would be alone.

She blew her nose, crossly. She shouldn't wallow like this. She still had Bella Vista – she had made a home here with the house and the horses that she loved. And she had Julia too, her very best friend. But Julia had Luigi.

Of course, Donna was thrilled to see how love had blossomed for her oldest friend. But while Julia and Luigi were getting together what had Donna done? No matter how many times she'd vowed to sort out her life, she'd avoided meeting another man. She had toyed with the idea of setting up an online dating profile. She knew she was putting it off. She couldn't imagine she could ever feel again the way she had felt about Giovanni. But she would never know if she didn't try. Tomorrow she would sign up to a dating website. And this time she meant it. The next time she wore this blue dress she would be going on a proper date. She had wasted more than enough of her life.

She fastened the delicate ankle straps on her rarely worn high-heeled shoes. Daniela was already at the door. She was banging the knocker much more forcefully than usual.

'I'll get it!' Marco shouted.

Donna put her hand on the smooth wooden bannister as she made her way slowly down the stairs. Her shoes weren't made for running no matter how keen she was to see Daniela.

'Mum!' Daniela stepped forward. Donna pulled her into a warm embrace, feeling Daniela's cool cheek against her own and inhaling the familiar fragrance of her daughter's clean, freshly washed hair. But as she did so, her senses quickened at the subtle smell of leather and woodsmoke that reached her nostrils. She dropped her arms to her sides, released Daniela from her embrace and looked up.

Giovanni. Standing right there in front of her. How could this be happening after all these years? Had she conjured him up by vowing to forget him? She grabbed the end of the bannister with hot, sweaty hands. She could not rely on her legs to hold her upright. Perhaps she was seeing things, perhaps this was some kind of mirage. She put out a hand as if her arm might pass right through him but her fingers alighted on the smooth weave of his jacket sleeve. He was real. Her heart thumped against her chest.

'Hello, Donna,' he said. His voice had not lost its deep, honeyed richness.

She looked up. Her eyes flitted across his face. His full lips and his strong, Roman nose were unchanged, but his high forehead was etched with new lines, and some of the stray curls falling above his strong black eyebrows were streaked with grey. His eyes roamed across her face, his expression inscrutable. She hoped her own face was just as unreadable, but she feared her eyes might give away the emotional turmoil his arrival had unleashed.

She was standing face to face with the man she had loved to the exclusion of any other. The man she had sworn to love for eternity. Just a few minutes ago she had vowed to forget him. Now she knew that was impossible. At last, she managed to speak.

'Hello, Giovanni. What are you doing here?' Her voice sounded as if it was coming from somewhere far away.

'You haven't seen me for nearly ten years and this is how you greet me?' His voice was stern, but his golden eyes danced with amusement. 'You really didn't know I was coming? So, you always look like . . .'

'Like what?' Donna said. Her cheeks burnt under the warmth of Giovanni's intense gaze.

'You look . . . well, never mind.' He reached out as if to touch the blue topaz charm around her neck. Donna's heart was pounding. She held her breath. 'You are wearing this . . .' he murmured.

'We are celebrating Marco's birthday,' Donna said. She was surprised how calm her voice sounded.

'Of course. I thought perhaps . . .'

He thought she had worn it for him. Donna struggled to think of something to say.

The door from the kitchen swung open. Julia let out a gasp but after a moment's hesitation she took charge of the situation.

'Daniela . . . and, umm, Giovanni . . . how lovely to see you both,' Julia said. 'Please come through to the sitting room. Daniela, why don't you hang up your dad's jacket on one of the hooks by the front door. And, Marco, could you pour some wine? I've put the bottle and some glasses out on the dresser.'

'I brought this, seeing as it's a special occasion.' Giovanni handed Julia the bottle he was clutching.

'*Brunello di Montalcino*. Very nice,' Julia said.

'It's good to see you, Julia; it's been a long time,' Giovanni said.

'Yes, too long.'

Donna caught the slight edge to Julia's voice. This was awkward. She bit her lip and glanced at Giovanni, but he did not seem to have noticed anything amiss.

'And this is Jess,' Julia said. 'Jess, this is Giovanni, Marco's father.'

'Pleased to meet you.' Jess held out her hand.

Giovanni shook her hand. He seemed to be suppressing a smile.

'Do sit down, everybody,' Julia said.

Donna perched awkwardly on the edge of a small hard chair by the door. Her legs felt so weak she feared she might not get up again if she sank into one of the comfortable sofas. She accepted a glass of wine gratefully. How she needed it. She took a sip, savouring the rich berry flavour.

'This is delicious. Thank you, Giovanni.' How formal she sounded. And how disconcerting it was to see that Giovanni had automatically sat down in the same corner armchair, where he had once sat night after night, as if he had never been away.

'Jess has stayed with us before. We just have her and Harriet staying here at the moment,' Julia explained.

'Though I'm not sure where Harriet is right now,' Donna added. Her voice sounded more normal now the wine was beginning to relax her. Thank goodness the two girls were staying at Bella Vista. Their presence would make the evening less intense.

'I saw Harriet heading down towards the village with Lupo. Alfredo is getting her earning her keep.' Marco grinned.

'I expect the old man needs all the help he can get these days. He must be well past seventy,' Giovanni said.

'He's still good at his job,' Donna said abruptly. She sometimes wondered how Alfredo kept going but Giovanni had no right to imply the old man might be struggling.

'That must be Harriet at the door now. I wonder why she didn't just come round the back. She knows the spare key is under the basil pot,' Marco said.

'I'll go.' Donna jumped up quickly.

'I'll fetch some more wine glasses and a jug of water,' Julia said. She disappeared in the direction of the kitchen.

Donna strode across the hallway, pulled back the bolt and opened the heavy wooden door. It took her a second or two to recognise the lined, weather-beaten face in front of her.

'Francesco,' she gasped.

Marco had invited Giovanni to Bella Vista behind her back. And now he had somehow magicked up Francesco too. Giovanni would go crazy. Her foolish, foolish son. Did he have any idea what he had done?

Chapter Twelve

'Donna!' Francesco's brown eyes softened. 'I hoped and prayed you would still be here. You look wonderful.'

'And you too. You look so well.' Francesco's hair had turned quite silver and his deeply lined complexion spoke of a man who spent a great deal of time outside but the slightly haunted look she had sometimes discerned in his eyes had vanished. The jaunty spotted scarf tied in the neck of his blue shirt seemed to emphasise his cheerful demeanour.

Donna was delighted to see her old friend looking so content, but she was engulfed by an overwhelming sense of panic.

'Donna. What is it? Was I wrong to come?' Francesco touched her arm, his eyes full of concern.

'Marco did not tell me . . .' she began.

'Marco? Marco knows nothing about this.' Francesco's brow creased. 'The only person who knows I'm here is Harriet.'

Harriet. What could she possibly have to do with Francesco's arrival? Donna's mind was spinning. But before she had time to reply, the door from the sitting room swung open.

'Come on, Donna. Julia has rustled up some amazing . . .' Giovanni's voice tailed off.

'Good evening.' Francesco stepped forward, his face wreathed in genuine smiles.

'What the heck is going on?' Giovanni flung his arms out, knocking an ornamental horse off the mantelpiece. It crashed to the floor, scattering tiny pieces of glass in all directions. The crash sent Marco rushing into the hall.

'Papa!'

Giovanni did not even turn around. He advanced on Francesco, his smart leather brogues crunching over the debris. 'What the hell are you doing here?'

Francesco physically recoiled. He backed away until he was pressed flat against the front door.

'It's okay, Mum.' Donna felt the soft pressure of Marco's hand on her shoulder.

'Don't worry. I'm not going to hit him; he's just not worth it,' Giovanni said. 'But you, Marco! You think you can lure me here and trick me like this? What is this game you are playing?' His eyes were blazing.

'We had no idea . . .' Marco began.

'No idea?' Giovanni bellowed. 'I am your father. You take me as a fool.' He turned towards Donna. 'And you! I have not seen you for ten whole years. And if another ten go by it will be too soon.'

Donna's hand flew to her mouth. Her other hand gripped Marco's arm.

Giovanni brushed past them both into the kitchen. His elbow caught the edge of the long work surface as he stormed past. Julia dived across the room just in time to grab her lovingly prepared tray of *bruschette* as it wobbled mere inches from disaster. Giovanni disappeared through the back door in the direction of the chicken coop. It appeared there would be one less for dinner tonight.

'I will go. It was wrong of me to come,' Francesco said quietly.

'No!' Marco spoke so loudly that Donna jumped. 'You're not going anywhere. Tonight was the first time my father has been in this house for almost a decade. And he's left because of you. The least you can do is give us a proper explanation of why you're here.'

'Marco!' Donna gave him a look.

'No, don't tell the lad off. He's right. I've turned up so unexpectedly it is only right I explain myself.'

'Papa will be back soon enough,' Daniela added. She touched Donna's arm.

'I wouldn't be so sure,' Marco muttered.

'Well he won't get very far without these.' Daniela held up a set of car keys.

'You stole them!' Marco looked as surprised as Donna felt. Her placid daughter had a rebellious streak after all.

'I pocketed them as soon as we arrived. I didn't want to risk Papa running off.' Daniela shrugged.

'And he's left his jacket on a peg in the hall,' Julia said. She slid her hand into the pocket and pulled out Giovanni's mobile phone. 'Now he'll have to come back. Why don't I bring out the *bruschette* and some more wine to keep us going?'

'Wait a moment. I heard something outside. Do you think he's back already? If everyone else goes through to the sitting room, I'll try and talk some sense into him,' said Daniela.

Donna nodded. Her calm, quiet daughter was the only one likely to get through to Giovanni in his present state of mind.

Donna perched on the edge of the wooden chair, her fingers tightly clutching the stem of her wine glass. Her body tensed as she heard Daniela open the front door. She strained to hear the quiet voices in the hall – female voices.

The door to the sitting room was pushed open. Harriet walked in. 'Hi, everyone,' she said.

'Here, Harriet. Have some wine.' Julia held out a glass.

Harriet accepted the glass. She looked across at Francesco. 'Hello again,' she said.

Donna looked at Harriet, waiting for some sort of explanation.

'Francesco and I met in the olive grove. Lupo recognised him at once,' Harriet said.

'And he's about to tell us all what he's doing here,' Marco interrupted. He glared at Francesco.

'Well, take a *bruschetta*, Marco, and let the man speak,' Julia said.

'Okay,' Marco muttered. He leant against the wall, noisily crunching his way through the toasted bread. Lupo sat at his feet, nose twitching, waiting hopefully.

'Go on, Francesco,' Donna said.

Francesco took a slurp of wine and swallowed it with a noisy gulp. He set down his glass and pulled out a large cotton handkerchief to wipe the beads of sweat from his forehead.

'It is a long story, but I shall make it as short as I can. Believe me, I had no idea that your father would be here tonight. Until a few weeks ago I did not even know if the riding stables were still here. Of course, I have thought about Bella Vista many times over the years. It was a nice memory, nothing more. I knew Giovanni, your father, had become suspicious of my friendship with Donna and I thought once I had gone that perhaps things might be easier for you all if I stayed away. And then life rolled on and my time at Bella Vista seemed further and further away.'

'But you left so suddenly.' Donna could not help interrupting.

'My mother was taken ill so abruptly there was no time to do anything but pack up and go. I took the first plane I could. When I got to Scotland she was so weak I could not hide the shock on my face. But we had a few days together and I was with her when she passed away. She looked so peaceful . . .'

'And you stayed . . .' Julia prompted gently.

'Yes. My father needed me. He wasn't in the best of health himself, but he was determined to honour my mother's memory by not giving up. He used to say he could imagine her looking down from heaven and ticking him off if he tried to get away with grabbing a slice of toast for dinner. I helped him with the shopping and keeping the place clean and tidy. He was still making his legendary *pollo alla diavola* until the end.' Francesco paused. He wiped away the tear that was glistening in the corner of his eye.

'Your parents ran an Italian restaurant in Oban, in the highlands of Scotland, didn't they?' Donna said.

'Yes, you are right. My parents emigrated to Scotland in the 1960s. We visited Italy a handful of times when my nonna was still alive, but I was just a little boy and I don't remember much except sitting on the edge of a fountain eating what seemed like the biggest ice-cream in the world. Then in my early twenties I came out to Italy to work in my uncle's restaurant in Bagni di Lucca; my parents thought it would be a good experience for me.

'I flew out here, not knowing what to expect. I fell in love with Italy almost at once. I couldn't imagine what had possessed my parents to leave this beautiful sunny place for cold, damp Scotland. For the next twenty years I went back to the UK just once a year. I no longer thought of Oban as home. It was only when I was sitting in my parents' restaurant with the smell of my mother's bean stew bubbling on the stove that I felt that I still belonged.

'I hoped that when my parents retired and sold up that they might return to Tuscany but they had made so many friends in Scotland they did not want to leave, and now I, too, feel the same way. A few months before my father died I met my partner, and one day – just like that – I realised my heart was no longer here in Tuscany. We've been married three years now and still live in Oban, in a little stone cottage by the water.'

'So, what brought you here?' Donna asked.

'Nothing but idle curiosity. I was delayed at the dentist, flicking through some old magazines when a photograph caught my eye. I looked again and realised it was a picture of the old house at the end of the village, the one that was turned into a guest house.'

'Villa Susino?' Harriet said.

'Yes, that's right. The journalist was exploring the local vineyards and had stayed a night or two there. It made me curious, so I booked two nights on a whim. So much time had passed I wasn't even sure if Donna and Giovanni were still running Bella Vista. When I arrived, Vittoria told me that Giovanni was now living in Siena, but Donna was still running the riding centre here. Of course, now I wish I had called before I came. It was crazy to come and knock on your door. I have caused nothing but trouble.'

'It's not your fault, Francesco. It should have been a lovely surprise. But you came by yourself? Your wife, did she not want to see the village where you once lived?' Donna said.

'It was something I wanted to do alone. I never had the chance to say goodbye to you properly. Unfinished business I suppose. Alasdair, my husband, is flying out the day after tomorrow to join me in Florence for a few days.'

'Your husband . . .' Marco began.

'Yes. He's an artist, a watercolour painter. As soon as I met him, at an exhibition of his work, everything fell into place. Of course, deep down I always knew. That's why I spent so many years by myself. So, you see, Marco, there was never any truth in the rumours that I was involved with your mother.'

Donna felt stunned; if only Francesco had been more open about his feelings Giovanni might never have left.

'But why didn't you just say?' Marco echoed her thoughts.

'The older I get the more I ask myself the same thing. No one has been anything but welcoming to Alasdair and me since we got together. But times are different now, even compared to ten years ago. And in a small place like this, you know, it is not always so easy.'

'I don't remember too much about Papa leaving. But I do know one thing: he's a bloody idiot!' Marco's eyes were blazing. 'He wrecked our family for nothing. But I'm not going to let him ruin tonight. I've been looking forward to this evening and we're going to have a good time. Mum, why don't you and Francesco go and sit in the kitchen – you've got a lot of catching up to do. Julia, stay here with the rest of us for a bit, I'm sure you've got everything under control.'

'I've just got to take the pork out to rest later on. We can always eat it cold tomorrow.'

'Tomorrow? No way. We'll eat at eight like we planned, Papa or no Papa. But now we're going to have a good time. Jess, grab that pile of CDs on the shelf. There's no point trying to stream anything in here; the internet's bound to cut out. Yep, that's great. Oh good, *Spice Girls*. I thought I'd lost that one.'

'The Spice Girls?' Harriet giggled.

'What's so funny?' Marco demanded.

'Err, nothing.'

'Let's turn it up loud. Harriet, you can be Baby Spice.'

'I'll be Sporty,' Jess said.

'And Julia can be Posh Spice,' Marco said.

'Well, I did take a cordon bleu cookery course once.' Julia grinned.

'But what if your dad comes back? We won't be able to hear him,' Jess said.

'You don't know my father. If he wants to come in he'll make a commotion that would raise the dead. And anyway, he can always come in through the boot room or the kitchen. Now, Jess, are you going to dance?'

Donna looked at Francesco. 'It's definitely time to get out of here,' she said.

Jess feared she was grinning like an idiot as Marco led her around the makeshift dance floor. Marco had a huge smile on his face too as they spun around. Julia and Harriet were gyrating beside them. Harriet looked so cute in her primrose-yellow top; Jess wished she had chosen something more feminine than her usual old jeans and checked man's shirt.

There was a sudden change of key. Jess recognised the opening bars of 'Two Become One' almost at once; she had forgotten that the band had recorded this ballad. Marco let go of her hands. Her heart sank. It was too much to hope that they would dance together to this smoochy song.

Jess went to step backwards, hoping her face did not betray her disappointment, but Marco wrapped his arms around her waist. He pulled her close; their cheeks were almost touching. She tipped her head so that it rested in the crook of his neck and inhaled the scent of his warm skin and freshly washed hair. But she would not have cared if he still smelt of hay and horse manure, it felt so good to be near him.

Over his shoulder, Julia and Harriet were swaying together in time to the music and laughing. How Jess wished that she and Marco were alone together. He pulled her closer. Every part of her body was quivering. How good it felt. How she longed to kiss him. She looked into his soft brown eyes. He did not look away.

Under any other circumstances Donna would have been thrilled to sit down with Francesco and catch up over a bottle of wine but all she could think about was Giovanni. No matter what he had done she did not like the thought of him wandering around outside in his shirtsleeves. The rain was still only drizzling but the sky looked ominous and the wind was beginning to get up. She shivered and wrapped her arms around herself. A branch knocked against the window. Donna's heart lurched; she was a bag of nerves.

Francesco stopped talking. 'I think I can hear something,' he said.

All Donna could hear was Marco's music blaring out. She jumped up and flung open the sitting room door. Her son and Jess were dancing together.

'Turn down that racket!' she yelled.

Marco let go of Jess. He snapped off the switch on the CD player. Above the sound of the wind howling and the rain spattering against the window the sound of pounding on the front door was unmistakable.

'Papa's back. I knew he wouldn't stay out for long,' Marco said.

'Hold on a minute, Marco. I can hear someone's voice, and it doesn't sound like Papa,' said Daniela.

'I'll go and see who it is,' Donna said.

'We'll all go together.' Marco's voice faltered. He had gone quite pale despite his earlier bravado.

Daniela pulled back the latch. Alfredo was standing on the front doorstep. He was red in the face with exertion and his grey hair was sticking out in every direction. Rain was dripping down his face; droplets clung to his eyebrows and moustache.

'Alfredo! What is it? Quick, come inside,' Donna said.

Alfredo staggered through the door and collapsed onto the carved wooden bench in the hallway, panting heavily.

'Wrap this round you.' Daniela grabbed the tartan mohair throw from the back of the chair in the corner. 'Marco, fetch some grappa.'

'Caesar . . . Caesar . . .' Alfredo wheezed.

'What is it, Alfredo?' Donna asked. She tried to keep her voice calm despite her rising panic.

Alfredo took a sip of grappa and coughed. 'Caesar,' he spluttered. 'Caesar . . . he gone.'

'Marco, Jess, can you help Alfredo through to the sitting room where it's warmer? I'll go and get Francesco from the kitchen. If Caesar is missing we will need his help,' Donna said.

Marco helped Alfredo without a murmur. He seemed content to let Donna take charge.

Alfredo slumped on the couch in the corner, the tartan throw clutched tightly around him. Propped up amongst the worn velvet cushions he looked every one of his seventy-six years.

'Donna, Donna. He gone . . . Caesar he gone.' Alfredo threw his arms wide apart.

'It's okay, Alfredo, take your time,' Donna said. First Giovanni, then Francesco turning up out of the blue. And now this. Her head was spinning.

'I am home, making supper. I heat up the *ribollita*. I hear noise: hooves. Sound like Caesar. It cannot be. Caesar . . . I know he is in stable. I check doors and gates three times, always.'

Donna nodded. She knew how superstitious Alfredo was. He never deviated from his daily routine.

'I say to myself: "Alfredo, you imagine." Still, I hear him. I open door. Caesar, he there on road. And then I see him.' Alfredo lifted the glass tumbler of grappa to his lips with trembling hands.

'Who did you see?' Donna asked although she was certain she already knew the answer.

'Was little bit dark. At first, I think I see ghost. Then I see Giovanni.'

'Did he see you? Did he say anything?' Donna's voice rose an octave.

Alfredo nodded.

'What did he say?' Marco snapped.

'He say: "I ride. I ride to Siena."'

Siena. Donna felt the bile rise in her throat. She jumped up, ran from the room and burst into the downstairs cloakroom. Her stomach was heaving. She leant over the toilet bowl. Siena was miles away. Steep wooded paths, unlit roads, a storm brewing. She pressed her forehead against the tiles on the wall behind the cistern. How cool they felt.

'Mum, Mum. Are you okay?' Daniela was banging on the door.

Donna opened it reluctantly. 'Sorry, darling. I thought I was going to be sick. But I'm okay now.' She let Daniela lead her back into the sitting room, holding her hand as if she was the small child and Daniela was the mother.

'Can you really ride to Siena from here?' Harriet asked.

Marco glared at her.

'It is possible. We rode there once, many years ago,' Francesco said.

'I remember,' Donna said. They had ridden that route just once, when Francesco had first come to work at Bella Vista. It was too far and too hazardous to risk taking their guests and they were soon too busy to attempt the journey again.

'When I was about thirteen, I tried to ride there on Coco, but Mum got wind of my plans and dragged me back home,' Marco said.

'I'd almost forgotten that. I couldn't have possibly let you go. Not with those roads and traffic to contend with. And there's a steep path where you have to dismount and lead your horse through the woods.'

'But I know the first part of the route and Guido's a lot faster than Caesar.'

'What do you mean?' Donna inhaled sharply.

'I'm going after him. Papa's a brilliant horseman. He'd make it to Siena on a sunny day but it will be dark before too long, and with this storm brewing, only a madman would try. I've got to stop him.'

'I'll go.' Donna stood up.

Daniela grabbed her arm. 'No.'

'Daniela's right, Mum. You're staying here. There's no time to waste arguing. If it wasn't for me and my stupid schemes, Papa would never have come here. I've got to reach him before this storm sets in. And I'm a better rider than you – you know it.'

'Marco, please . . .' But Donna knew she was wasting her breath. Her son was as stubborn as his father. Once one of them made up his mind, no one had a chance of changing it. All she could do was sit and wait. And pray.

'I'll saddle the horse for you whilst you get some water-proofs and a torch. I guess the key to the tack room padlock is still in the same place,' Francesco said.

'I keep everything the same as before,' Alfredo said.

'Thanks, Francesco,' Marco muttered.

'It's okay, Mum. Everything will be okay,' Daniela said.

Donna looked at her daughter. Daniela had better be right. Despite her earlier promises in front of the mirror, she knew that she had never stopped loving Giovanni. But if anything happened to Marco, she would never forgive him.

Francesco led Guido out into the yard. If the horse was surprised to be taken from his stable at such a late hour, he did not show it. He stood patiently whilst Marco quickly checked his tack. Guido's grey coat seemed to fade into the ebbing light so Francesco had added a fluorescent yellow exercise sheet. He had clipped a spare lead rope to the front of the saddle.

'All set. Do you want a leg-up? I remember that mounting block gets slippery in the rain,' Francesco said.

'Alfredo nailed a strip of rubber tyre onto those steps a few years back; but thanks, I won't take any chances tonight.'

Francesco held Guido's reins in one hand whilst Marco put a foot in one stirrup and swung the other over the horse's back. He lifted the saddle flap and adjusted the girth. 'That's tight enough now,' Marco said.

Francesco walked with Marco to the gate. 'Good luck. I'll just make sure everything's locked up.'

'Look after my mother.'

'You can count on that.'

Francesco stood in the deserted stable yard. He took a deep breath, savouring the sweet smell of horses mixed with hay and manure. How long it had been since he had left Bella Vista and yet now it seemed like yesterday. He looked over the door of Coco's stable and called softly. The pony came straight to the door and stuck out his nose. Francesco rubbed his face and scratched behind Coco's ears. He fancied the little chap still recognised him. The horses in the two stables next to Caesar's empty box were newer inmates so he left them munching their hay undisturbed.

Francesco double-checked the bolts on Caesar and Guido's empty stables. He did not want the doors banging to and fro in the wind. He quickly tidied around the tack room where he had emptied two drawers in his quest to find the hi-vis exercise sheet. He glanced around the room. Everything seemed to be in order. High on the wall someone, Alfredo no doubt, had fixed a small, framed picture of the Virgin Mary. Francesco crossed himself. *Please keep them safe.*

As he moved to close the door something made him turn and look at the two neatly labelled rows of saddle racks. Guido's saddle rack was empty but there was a saddle resting on the rack bearing Caesar's name. That didn't make sense. Not even Giovanni was crazy enough to ride off bareback into the night.

Francesco had a strange churning in his stomach. Something wasn't right.

Chapter Thirteen

The silence in the room was unbearable.

'Let's have a cup of tea. I'll put the kettle on,' Julia said. Donna nodded.

'Is very late to drink tea,' Alfredo said. He had stopped shivering and his usual colour had returned. The mohair throw, which was now cast aside, and the nip of grappa had both worked wonders.

'In England we believe everything is better after a cup of tea,' Jess said.

'And in Scotland, though the Scots would argue for the restorative effects of a good malt whisky,' said Francesco.

'Don't worry, Alfredo. I'll put the coffee pot on the stove whilst the tea is brewing,' Julia said. She set down the big brown teapot.

'Please, no coffee.'

Donna looked up. She had never known Alfredo refuse a coffee. Day or night he drank cup after cup accompanied by one of his favourite boiled sweets. Perhaps he was not feeling so good after all.

'Tea, it make everything better?' Alfredo said slowly.

'So they say,' Harriet said.

'My mum always brews a huge pot when there's a family crisis,' Jess added.

'I drink tea,' Alfredo said. His jaw was set firm, his mind made up.

Alfredo watched intently as Julia poured a stream of the steaming brown liquid into the spare mug that Daniela had fetched.

'Milk?' Jess lifted the earthenware jug.

Alfredo looked around for reassurance. 'Okay.'

Alfredo raised the mug to his lips with all the enthusiasm of a prisoner receiving his sentence. He sucked in a long mouthful. He sloshed the tea around his mouth until the movement of his Adam's apple confirmed he had indeed swallowed it. He set down the mug; a few drops of the hot drink clung to his moustache.

'How's your tea?' Julia asked. Her lips were twitching with amusement.

'Maybe it help Giovanni and Marco.' Alfredo raised the mug again and took another long draught of the hot liquid. Clearly, sacrifices had to be made.

'So, what do you do in Oban, Francesco?' Julia asked.

Donna gave Julia a grateful smile. Perhaps Francesco's stories would help entertain Harriet and Jess. Tonight's drama was not fair on her guests. Jess in particular seemed quite shaken up by events; she looked close to tears.

'I help at the art gallery at the weekends when it's busy but the rest of the week I work at the local garden centre,' Francesco said. 'I couldn't work inside every day. There's something about working with my hands out of doors that feels real, if that doesn't sound too pretentious.'

Donna nodded, encouraging Francesco to continue.

He paused and raised a finger in a silencing gesture. The wind was howling, but Donna could just catch another sound above the squall.

'I can hear something, Mum,' Daniela said.

Hooves. Donna shot bolt upright. She walked quickly into the hall, crossed the worn Persian rug and opened the front door. The others gathered around her, silent, straining to hear. The wind dropped. A rhythmic sound floated towards them: the unmistakable sound of hooves. A horse trotting along the road.

'The gate . . .' Donna said.

'It's open. Marco asked me to tie it back. In case . . .' Francesco said.

Donna nodded, her mouth now too dry to speak. Her heart was racing. Her mind was in a whirl of dread and hope. She looked at Julia. Neither of them spoke. She knew they were both thinking the same thing. There was only one horse coming up the road. Marco and Giovanni weren't together.

It took every ounce of Donna's willpower not to run down the road to discover if it was her beloved son or errant husband who was returning. Her anger at Giovanni's ridiculous escape on horseback and Marco's foolish pursuit no longer mattered. All she wanted was to have them come back safe. Both of them. But she knew that if she suddenly appeared out of the gloom, Caesar or Guido might take fright and bolt.

She stood stock-still, her arms hanging uselessly by her sides, hands balled into two tense fists. She felt Daniela move closer, caught the comforting scent of her peachy hair conditioner. She had never felt so relieved to have her undemanding, level-headed daughter by her side.

'Is Caesar,' Alfredo said.

'How do you know?' Daniela asked.

'I know how he trot. He bang the hooves more hard than Guido.'

Donna's stomach lurched with excitement and nerves. Giovanni was returning. But her fears for Marco grew. How long would he ride in search of his father? Marco had inherited all of Giovanni's stubbornness and impulsiveness. He might not return for hours. They could be in for a long, long night.

'I'll keep out of the way 'til Giovanni calms down,' Francesco said.

'Perhaps you could put the coffee pot on. He'll be desperate for a hot drink,' Julia said.

'That's a good idea,' Donna said. Another confrontation between Giovanni and Francesco was the last thing she needed right now. Her nerves were shredded.

The sound of hooves was growing louder, but they were no longer falling on the road in a two-time rhythm. Caesar was no longer trotting steadily; he was galloping towards the house at full pelt.

'*Mamma mia! Che fa?*' Alfredo muttered.

What was Giovanni doing? Even a less experienced horseman would know he must slow down to a gentle walk, not approach the stable yard at a flat-out gallop. If Marco hadn't had the sense to ask Francesco to tie back the gate, Caesar might gallop straight through it. Her impulsive husband might not care about his own wellbeing but he had no right to risk harming Caesar. She could not believe he'd be so selfish.

'He's bound to head straight for the stable yard. We'd better wait there,' Julia said.

They hovered on the edge of the yard. Waiting. A crackle of lightning in the distance added a flash of extra brightness to the light cast by the open kitchen door.

Caesar thundered up the path. He skidded to a halt just shy of the chicken run. The horse tossed his head violently, the whites of his eyes were showing, and he was snorting in fear. His heaving flanks were wet, whether from rain or sweat, it was hard to tell. His saddle had swivelled around and was hanging off one side of his body. A stirrup leather hung down, the nickel stirrup swinging uselessly.

'Where's Papa?' Daniela gasped.

'Get Francesco! We may need his help,' Donna said.

'Caesar!' Alfredo called softly. The horse pricked his ears. The sound of Alfredo's voice and the familiarity of his surroundings seemed to calm him a little. Alfredo stepped towards him. Caesar snorted. He whirled around almost knocking the old groom over.

'*Calma*! Steady!' Alfredo stood quietly. He caught hold of Caesar's reins and handed them to Francesco who helped to hold the frightened animal still. Alfredo carefully undid one girth strap though the task was made difficult by his trembling hands. The broken end of the other girth strap hung from the saddle.

Alfredo removed the saddle and handed it to Daniela.

'I'll lead him in and get a rug on him. I know where everything is kept,' Francesco said. Alfredo nodded. He stroked Caesar's damp neck before Francesco led him away.

'We'd better go inside,' Julia said.

'What, err, yes,' Donna murmured. She let Julia manoeuvre her back into the sitting room. She sunk back down amongst the cushions. She felt light-headed and vague, as if she were in a dream. If only she could wake up and find Marco and Giovanni back safe and sound.

Daniela placed the damaged saddle carefully on the chest in the corner. 'No wonder the saddle came loose. One girth strap's ripped clean away, and the buckle holes on the other are all stretched and worn.'

'Is my fault.' Alfredo looked down at the floor.

'It's not your fault, Alfredo. None of this is. None of us knew that Giovanni was going to take off like that,' Donna said. She tried to keep her voice calm and level, to keep her anger at bay. How could Alfredo have let Caesar's tack get into such poor condition? But, then again, she hadn't noticed anything wrong with the saddle when she had ridden Caesar earlier in the week.

'Is old saddle. I put on the table in tack room and Giovanni he find it,' Alfredo said.

'Let me take another look,' said Daniela. She ran her hand over the seat of the saddle. 'You're right, Alfredo. This isn't Caesar's usual saddle. It's not even real leather. Hang on a minute, there's a small metal name plate on the back. It says *Caesar* – that's odd.'

'Let me see,' Donna said. 'I can't believe it! That's Caesar's old saddle. I forgot we still had it. When we bought Caesar, the previous owner gave us his old rugs and tack. They were in a bit of a sorry state. I ordered a beautiful new saddle not long after. It was supposed to be a surprise present for your papa, but he never . . .' Donna's voice tailed off.

'Your father left before your mum had the chance to give it to him,' Julia said.

'So, Papa must have recognised this old one and picked it up.'

'But why on earth was it lying around? It's been years since anyone used it,' Donna said.

'Alfredo was tidying up the tack room. We lifted it down from the top shelf for him,' Harriet said.

'You lifted it down?' Donna looked at her doubtfully. Harriet was one of the shortest girls she had ever met.

'We dragged the old chest across the room and I stood on it,' Jess said.

'You shouldn't have been moving something like that.' Donna was concerned; she couldn't have guests shifting hefty furniture about.

'Alfredo wanted to take a look to see if he could repair it so we got it down for him. It's got such a distinctive green saddle cover I guess Giovanni must have spotted it straight away,' Harriet said.

'He can't have got very far, Marco will find him soon,' Julia said.

'Marco will have passed Caesar coming back, Mum. He will know that Papa has had a fall,' Daniela said.

Donna felt sick. She had no doubt that Marco would eventually find his father. But would Giovanni be marching towards Siena, cursing his bad luck, or lying on the ground, badly injured? Or worse. The threat of the storm was not over yet. Marco could be in danger too. Donna didn't know how she would bear to sit and wait.

Donna looked at Jess and Harriet's tense faces. It wasn't right that their holiday should be affected by her family's drama.

'We may as well eat,' Donna said. It was the last thing she wanted to do but her guests couldn't go without their dinner.

'I'll bring everything in. There will be plenty left for Marco and Giovanni when they get home. The pork will be just as good at room temperature,' Julia said. She looked glad to have something to do.

Donna forced herself to take a mouthful of the oozing fennel gratin but she could barely taste it. And although the tender slices of pork and Julia's special crispy roast potatoes smelt as good as always, tonight they were as appealing as a plate of old socks.

Daniela distractedly shovelled in forkfuls of food, only pausing every so often to swivel around towards the door as if hoping her impetuous brother might have silently re-appeared. Even Jess seemed to have lost her appetite, managing a portion of meat that would barely feed a six-year-old and not showing any of her customary enthusiasm for dessert. She picked at the *panna cotta con caramello* with all the enthusiasm of a girl tackling a portion of witchetty grubs. Only Francesco, who had been persuaded to stay for dinner, and Alfredo, who was too exhausted by the evening's dramas to think about going back home, seemed to be tackling their food with relish.

Eventually, Donna finished her meal; she could not bear to see good food go to waste. She drank the coffee Julia had made. She didn't want it and she certainly didn't need any more caffeine – all her senses were on high alert – but it gave her something to do with her hands.

Once again, Donna welcomed Julia's solid, calming presence. Her best friend was the ideal person in a crisis: quick to act when something needed to be done and slow to panic. Now Julia was encouraging Daniela to tell Harriet and Jess about the rich history of Siena. Donna was so thankful; the idea of making conversation seemed impossible. How she envied Alfredo snoring gently in the corner with Miu Miu curled up on his lap. If only she could fall asleep too and wake up to discover tonight had been a bad dream.

At last the rain stopped, though the dark clouds promised the lull was only temporary. The wind had died down, no longer howling in the trees.

'Mum, I think I can hear a horse coming,' Daniela said.

'It must be Guido,' Francesco said.

'I'm sure I can hear Papa's voice,' Daniela said.

'Then he must be with Marco.' Donna clutched her daughter's arm.

Francesco stood up. 'Thank you for dinner, Donna. Thank you, Julia. It'll be better if I've gone before they get here. My bike is round the back of the chicken run. I can slip out the little gate up by the schooling ring.'

'Come by for coffee before you go to Florence.' Donna hugged Francesco and kissed him on each cheek. It had been good to see her old friend even though his unannounced arrival had caused such a commotion.

'It's definitely Marco! I can hear him. And Papa too!' Daniela exclaimed.

Harriet looked at Jess. 'I think we'll go up,' she said.

'Please, girls, don't feel you can't stay,' Donna said.

Jess hesitated as though she was about to sit back down. 'No, Harriet's right. We'll go up now and see you in the morning. You need some time together,' Jess said.

Harriet and Jess disappeared up the stairs. The others stood quietly in the half-light cast by the open kitchen door.

'Mum!'

Marco was leading Guido into the stable yard. His legs moved slowly, wearily, but his eyes were shining with triumph. Giovanni was sitting astride Guido, one hand resting on the front of the saddle. He ran the other through his dark hair, which was wet and matted. One trouser leg was torn, his shirt soaked – not with blood, thank goodness – just with rain. Donna's shoulders sagged with relief. They were back: her son and her husband. Tears ran down her face. She wanted to hold them both tight. Forever.

Jess patted her face dry and squirted a blob of moisturiser into the palm of her hand. The face that looked back at her from the mirror was beaming. Marco was safe. If only she could run down the stairs and fling her arms around him. But this was a family moment; hearing his voice floating up through the floorboards would have to do. The dance they had shared tonight, the way he had looked at her, that was enough. He liked her; he really did. Her last day at Bella Vista was going to be so special. She hugged herself in delight.

She opened her case to add her discarded clothes to the pile of dirty washing wedged in next to her emergency packet of biscuits. Surely tonight's drama called for a chocolate biscuit. Just the one. Who cared if she had already cleaned her teeth? She ripped the packet open and took a bite. All of a sudden her appetite returned. She was absolutely starving.

Chapter Fourteen

Marco drew back the check curtains and opened the shutters. Giovanni blinked in the sudden light.

'Coffee. At last! I've been desperate for one.' Giovanni propped himself up amongst the pillows and reached for the cup Marco was holding. 'A couple of these and I'll be gone.'

'You're going nowhere, Papa. For once in your life you're going to sit here and listen to me.'

'Don't be daft, Marco. You can't keep me here like a prisoner. I've got to teach a writing class in Siena at ten. Pass me that old dressing gown from the back of the door and I'll take a shower. Now where have you put my clothes?'

'They're drying downstairs. Mum put them in the wash to get the mud off. You fell off a horse, remember.'

'No need to be sarcastic. I should sue your mother. That saddle must have been in a shocking state for the girth strap and stirrup leather to break like that. I'm surprised she hasn't killed one of her guests yet. What have I always told you about looking after your tack?'

'And what do you say about checking everything before saddling up.'

'Okay, I should have checked but I was so mad I wasn't thinking straight.'

'You can say that again. What the hell did you think you were doing?'

'I was going to drive home but as soon as I walked out I realised that I didn't have my car keys or my phone. The rain had started so I thought I'd sit in the tack room for a while and decide what to do. The key was still in the usual place so I let myself in. I saw Caesar's saddle straight away. I couldn't miss that pea-green cover. Do you remember when you were a little boy we used to say it looked like a toad?'

Marco nodded.

'As soon as I saw it I realised I didn't have to go back to the house after all. It was pure bad luck I didn't make it. When the saddle slipped, I pitched sideways but I landed on my feet and managed to grab hold of Caesar's reins. I could see the girth strap was broken. The saddle was useless but I knew I could ride the rest of the way bareback.

'I found an old tree stump to use as a mounting block but just as I was reaching up to remove the saddle completely, *bang!* a clap of thunder. Caesar whirled around, knocking me off my feet. That's when I fell and hurt my ankle. I tried to grab him, but it was too late. He was off. I only had a couple of kilometres to go.'

'A couple of kilometres? Come on, Papa, Siena's much further away than that.'

'Siena? You thought I was riding home to Siena with that storm brewing? You think your papa is crazy?' Giovanni was incredulous.

Marco shrugged.

'And what did you think I would do with Caesar when I got home? Tie him to a lamppost and feed him a plate of spaghetti?'

'But you told Alfredo . . .'

Giovanni gave a short bark of laughter.

'It's not funny, Papa.'

'Old Alfredo's hearing must be going. I said *Sienna*, not *Siena*. Sienna Bonechi. You remember our old neighbour? She moved just the other side of the old chapel. She's the nearest person I could think of with a spare room and stables. I was sure she wouldn't mind putting me up for the night. You really thought I was heading for Siena? Jeez, Marco, I don't have a death wish. But if you thought I was heading home how on earth did you find me?'

'I saw Caesar coming towards me or rather Guido did. Caesar really spooked him; I was lucky to stay in the saddle. I headed in the direction Caesar had come from.'

'Lucky for me. But now it's time I did go to Siena.' Giovanni pulled the towelling dressing gown around him, threw back the paisley-patterned quilt and stepped out of bed. He staggered back and sat down heavily, his face scrunched up in pain.

'You're going to have to rest that foot, Papa. Julia told you that.'

'Julia – what does she know?' Giovanni grunted.

'She took a first aid course when she worked at that restaurant in Cambridge. You need to take her advice unless you want us to call for a doctor.'

'Doctor – I don't need to be poked about by some doctor. It's only a small sprain. Isn't that what Nurse Julia said?'

'Nurse Julia – she might like that title.' Marco grinned. 'But let's help you get to the shower before she tries to give you a bed bath. Or else I'll have to go and get Mum.'

'Okay,' Giovanni said. He allowed Marco to help him hobble into the bathroom.

'Finished?' Marco put his head round the bathroom door. He could barely make out the shape of a human figure through the clouds of steam. The scent of pine was so pungent it made his eyes tingle; it seemed his father had been making good use of the collection of lotions and potions. 'Lucky Mum had that bathroom made fully accessible. I didn't fancy scrubbing you down with a flannel,' Marco joked.

'Believe me, the feeling's mutual.'

'I've put some clean jeans out and I've got a shirt I can lend you. It's a good thing we're about the same size.'

'Lavender?' Giovanni peered suspiciously at the cellophane-wrapped object on the dressing table.

'I went to Siena last week and got a bit carried away in Casa Giorgio. Thought I might try something other than white or blue for a change.'

'At least it's not floral.'

Giovanni leant against the dressing table, checking his appearance in the oval, oak-framed mirror as he ran a comb through his still-damp hair. 'But tell me, Marco, what the hell were you doing last night? Getting me and Francesco together after all these years? Did you really think I would just forget everything and shake his hand, or were we supposed to roll up our sleeves, go outside and fight a duel?'

'Believe me, Papa, I didn't know Francesco was coming here. Honestly, I swear on my life. Francesco decided to visit quite by chance. He's married now. He lives with his husband in Scotland.'

'His husband?' Giovanni frowned.

'Francesco was never interested in Mum the way you thought he was. None of us knew the reason why until last night. But I had proof of that before he turned up. That's why Daniela and I wanted to bring you here.'

Marco handed Giovanni a small sheet of tattered, lined paper folded in two.

Giovanni unfolded the note. 'What is this? You'd better pass me my reading glasses. They're in my jacket, over there, on the back of the chair; they're in the inside pocket.'

Giovanni scanned the note. He sank back down on the bed with his head in his hands. Marco tensed, waiting for his father to speak. The only sound in the room was the slow tick of the clock on the dressing table.

Giovanni slammed his hand against the wall. 'Dear God. How could I have been such a fool?'

'But why did you do it, Papa? Why did you leave?' It was the question Marco had wanted to ask for so long.

'I told you, Marco: because I was a fool.'

'I know that, Papa, but I want to know what happened that day. Don't you think it's about time you told me?'

Giovanni sighed. He seemed to have aged in the few minutes since he had read Francesco's note. His skin looked pallid against the vivid lavender of Marco's shirt.

'It all seems so ridiculous now. I had been jealous of the closeness between Francesco and your mamma for a long time. We'd had another row about it early that morning and I made your mother cry. I was due to go to a writing course in Florence that day. I set off towards the railway station without apologising but my conscience got the better of me and just as the train was about to pull out, I changed my mind and jumped off. I ran all the way back to the house, but instead of going straight in I went to the stable yard. I thought a few minutes with the horses would calm me down. That's when I saw them, leaning against Caesar's stable door: Francesco and your mother in each other's arms.

'Now I know for certain that he was only comforting her after our row, but at the time it seemed to confirm my worst fears and when Francesco did not turn up for work the next morning I was sure I was right. Perhaps if I had confronted them, Francesco would have made me see how stupid I was being. But instead I went straight to Beppe's

Bar and drank myself into a stupor. I cursed Francesco to anyone who would listen long into the night.

'Beppe tried to persuade me that I had got it all wrong – perhaps he had his suspicions about Francesco's true leanings, who knows? But I wouldn't listen. I was so determined that no woman would make a fool of me again.'

'Again? What do you mean?' Marco sat down next to Giovanni on the bed.

'I swore I'd never say her name again.'

Marco looked him right in the eye. 'Don't you think, Papa, that it's about time you did?'

'Lila. She was in the class below me, the prettiest girl in the school, at least I thought so. I was seventeen . . .' Giovanni paused.

Seventeen! Marco could hardly believe what he was hearing but he knew it was better to keep quiet and let his papa continue.

'My first proper girlfriend. I doted on her, Marco. I even wrote her love poems. Terrible poems, but I poured my heart and soul into them. It was her sixteenth birthday. I had saved up all my money for a pretty little heart-shaped locket. I fancied she would put a picture of me inside, or a lock of my hair, some such nonsense. I arrived at her party . . .'

Giovanni stopped speaking. He seemed to be studying the pattern on the quilt.

'Go on, Papa.'

'She was there with Pietro, the captain of the football team. She had been seeing him behind my back for weeks. He was the school hero; how could I compare? I could have accepted it, Marco. I could have walked away with my head held high, pretending I did not care . . . but all the boys in the team were there, passing around my poems and laughing.'

'That's terrible, Papa,' Marco said softly. 'But that was years before you met Mum.'

'Believe me when something like that happens it stays with you for a long time. I was so humiliated I never told a soul, but now that you know it suddenly does not seem so important at all. I can hardly believe I made your mother suffer because of some stupid schoolgirl who wouldn't be fit to clean her riding boots. And you know the worst of it? Everyone *has* been laughing at me these last ten years. Laughing at me because I was a fool who walked away from the most wonderful woman in the world.'

'No one's laughing at you. Not Bianca, not Beppe or Luigi, not any of your friends in the village.' Marco hoped he was saying the right thing. He had never seen tears in his papa's eyes before.

'Then they pity me for throwing everything away; I don't know which is worse. Tell me, Marco, tell me honestly: is there any chance for me, or have I lost your mother forever?'

'I'm certain Mum still loves you,' Marco said carefully. 'If she didn't love you deep down do you think Daniela and I would have brought you back here? But I can't say if she would ever take you back.'

Giovanni turned to Marco, his eyes shining. 'Then I have a tiny chance. I swear I'll do everything in my power to put things right. I'll shower her with gifts; I'll fill every room with flowers and if I ever get rich, I'll turn this place into a palace.'

Marco frowned. 'I don't think Mum needs any of that, and besides she likes Bella Vista the way it is.'

'Nonsense!' Giovanni sat up a little straighter. 'You've got a lot to learn about women, Marco. I'm going to treat your mother like a queen if I ever win her back.'

Donna was amazed she had slept so well after all the drama of the night before. She dressed quickly in her most comfortable jodhpurs and her favourite old denim shirt, secured her hair in a brass clip, made her way downstairs and out onto the terrace. All was calm, but water pooling around the base of the terracotta planters bore witness to the previous night's storm. She pulled the dark green waterproof cover off the wicker lounger and spread it over the low wall to dry off. Beyond the terrace some of the trees were sparkling as though they were decked out in white fairy lights. The rain had been trapped on the top of the leaves, which were now gently moving in the light morning breeze. A formation of swifts flew past, feeding on the wing. It was going to be a beautiful day.

She walked around to the back of the farmhouse. Miu Miu was languidly stretched out across the back doorstep. The cat wound herself around Donna's ankles, purring noisily. Soon Alfredo would be busy with his chores; Caesar was already kicking his stable door in anticipation of his breakfast and Julia would be baking fresh pastries for the two-legged inhabitants.

It was a morning like so many others, but nothing would be quite the same again. Giovanni was back. All the certainties in Donna's world had been picked up, shaken about and thrown up in the air to land who knows where. Of course, she knew that Giovanni was only there under sufferance. He would drive back home as soon as he could but right now he was struggling to shuffle around on his sprained ankle. Marco had refused to give his father a lift to Siena or even as far as the railway station where Daniela had gone to catch the early morning train, somehow looking as fresh and well groomed as ever in yesterday's clothes.

Marco had taken his father some coffee, thank goodness; Giovanni was notoriously uncommunicative until he had a couple of shots of caffeine inside him. Now she had the chance to confront him in person about his behaviour all those years ago. She was armed with a good reason why Francesco had never dreamt of becoming her lover, let alone acting on such a dream. Whether Giovanni liked it or not, he was going to finally sit down and listen to what she had to say.

Donna wiped her palms on the front of her jeans. It was ridiculous to feel so nervous about speaking to the man who had once been privy to all her secrets, who had shared her every hope and dream, and whose hands had known every inch of her body. She swallowed hard and walked into the sitting room.

Giovanni was propped up in his old armchair looking at yesterday's newspaper through tortoiseshell-rimmed glasses; *they* were a new addition. Of course, they had both aged over the last ten years. What changes must he notice in *her*? Not that she felt much different from the fresh-faced young girl he had first met. Just a little wiser, a little bruised and battered by the years. She tweaked the hem of her denim shirt, glad that she hadn't chosen a close-fitting T-shirt.

Giovanni looked up. He folded the newspaper in half and let it slide off his lap onto the floor.

'I would get up. But . . .' He gestured towards his right ankle that was resting on the tapestry-topped footstool. He shifted slightly in his chair. A flicker of pain crossed his face; the sprain must be worse than he was letting on.

Donna had so much she wanted to say, but she held back. She wasn't going to rush in and break the heavy silence that filled the room. Let him explain himself for once. He owed her an apology for his behaviour last night. And he owed her so many, many words to make up for nearly ten years of silence, broken only by the briefest of exchanges concerning their children's welfare.

Donna settled herself on the nearest chair. 'So . . .' she said.

'So, you're not going to make this easy for me.' Giovanni gave a rueful smile.

'Any reason why I should?' Donna said.

Giovanni's caramel eyes traced the contours of her face, the way they had done a thousand times before. She felt the heat rising in her cheeks. She shifted her gaze to the framed drawing hanging on the wall behind him: a row of horses' heads looking out across the stable yard at Bella Vista. Jess had sketched it on her first visit and given it to Donna. Her horses, her stable yard, her guests. This was her life now. The life she had built for herself and her children since the day that Giovanni left. She must remember that. She didn't dare look back into Giovanni's eyes. If he looked at her the way he had last night before Francesco's untimely arrival she was afraid that all her righteous anger would melt away. She needed to be strong.

'Look at me, Donna, not at that damned wall.'

Reluctantly she met his eyes. They held a look she had never seen before. Was it regret?

'I've been such a fool.' He spoke so softly she wasn't sure she had heard him correctly.

'What did you say?' she said quietly.

'I've been a bloody fool, Donna.' He rubbed his ankle and winced again.

'You couldn't have known the girth straps needed replacing and part of the stirrup leather had rotted away.'

'I'm not talking about the saddle, Donna.'

'Marco told me you weren't trying to get to Siena but riding anywhere with that storm coming was a ridiculous risk.'

'Forget about last night, Donna. I'm talking about the letter.'

'What letter?' Donna tried to keep an edge of irritation from her voice. It was hard enough to keep her emotions in check without Giovanni talking in riddles.

'Francesco's letter. The letter Marco showed me this morning.'

He handed Donna a piece of lined notepaper. It was heavily creased and the corner had been ripped off. 'When did Francesco write this? It looks a bit battered.'

'You really didn't know anything about this did you? Don't just stare at it, read it, for goodness' sake.'

Donna unfolded the note. She scanned the lines of Francesco's distinctive, curly handwriting. Her heart was thumping.

'Francesco mentioned last night that he had left me some sort of note the day he went away but I never saw it. Where on earth has it been all these years?'

'It had fallen down behind that big old chest in the tack room. Harriet and Jess found it when they were helping Alfredo lift Caesar's old saddle down. They shifted the chest over so Jess could stand on it, and there it was.'

Donna shook her head. This letter was all the proof she had needed to convince Giovanni that there was an innocent explanation for Francesco's disappearance. Stuck down the back of the old chest in the tack room for all this time. It was scarcely believable. All that heartbreak. All those wasted years. All for nothing.

Chapter Fifteen

Pinocchio planted all four hooves firmly on the road. He was not going anywhere.

'Come on. It's not scary.' Donna stroked his neck encouragingly. She could hear Jess's horse, Brando, shifting from hoof to hoof behind her, keen to get on with their ride. Coco stood patiently. The little pony wasn't bothered by anything; he really was the perfect ride for Harriet.

Pinocchio took a tentative step forward. His ears flickering back and forth, listening for sounds of danger. Slowly, slowly he inched past the frightening wheelbarrow.

'Good boy,' Donna said. It was the first time Pinocchio had been ridden since a slight bout of lameness had confined him to the stables. Now he was fully recovered – just in time. Neither Caesar nor Guido seemed to have suffered any ill effects from their adventures the night before but Donna wasn't taking any chances; neither of them would be hacking out today.

This morning's ride was a quiet, gentle walk through the village and up into the hills but Pinocchio was proving quite a handful. One minute he was bouncing with freshness, jig-jogging with impatience as they walked along the dusty roads, the next he was snorting and backing away from any object that did not meet with his approval. Having made it past the scary wheelbarrow he veered dramatically across the road at the sight of Bianca's red balloon, though he must have passed it a hundred times before.

Ordinarily, Donna would be frustrated by the horse's antics but today she welcomed them. She had to concentrate hard to keep Pinocchio heading in the right direction – and at a pace of her choosing, not his. It was the perfect distraction for her whirring mind. The last thing she needed right now was a quiet horse plodding along on autopilot whilst she replayed her conversation with Giovanni again and again.

Giovanni had begged her to forgive him. He wanted to put the past behind them; he would do anything to win her back; he had promised her the world. There was no doubt that Giovanni was the love of her life but he was also the man who had broken her heart.

The sunshine on the windscreen made it hard to see the road ahead. Marco reached into the glove compartment and put on his sunglasses. Two politicians were squabbling on the radio. He flicked the radio onto another station. The sound of one of Tchaikovsky's ballets filled the car. Was it *The Nutcracker*? Julia always played that one at Christmas. It wasn't the sort of thing he normally listened to, but he needed a distraction. Even if there was only the tiniest chance that his mother and Papa could be reunited, he was going to do everything in his power to make it happen. He needed to stop Giovanni leaving Bella Vista before he and his mother had a proper chance to talk.

So far, so good. He had got up early – it helped that he had barely gone to sleep in the first place – checked on Caesar and Guido and helped Alfredo with the hay and water. He had even volunteered to muck out, a chore he usually avoided on his visits back home. To his surprise he enjoyed forking through the wood shavings to separate the manure and wet patches from the clean bedding whilst the horses stood quietly pulling sweet-smelling strands of hay from their morning hay nets.

He could not help thinking about Jess and the way she looked at him as they danced last night. He wished he could spend a long, lazy breakfast enjoying her company, but he had no time to linger. He needed to find a way to keep Papa at Bella Vista. He was so near to reuniting his parents; he could not fail now. By the time he wheeled the last barrowload to the muck heap he had a plan.

It took all of Marco's powers of persuasion to convince Papa's secretary to agree. Thankfully, Silvia was an unashamed romantic, and the thought of helping her boss find his Happy Ever After overrode her fear of Giovanni's reaction. Instead of passing on Giovanni's message postponing his writing course, Silvia agreed to contact the four pupils to advise a change of location. With Silvia onside, and Vittoria and Vincenzo more than happy to accommodate four extra guests at Villa Susino, everything was working out beautifully.

If his father's four pupils were surprised to find their tutor's son on the doorstep, they did not show it. They happily grabbed their bags when Marco instructed them to collect their luggage and hop in the van. They did not even ask Marco to prove who he was, but he guessed most kidnappers would not be accompanied by a large, hairy, grey dog, at least not one as friendly as Lupo.

Once they were driving along, Marco found it easy to persuade them that bed and breakfast at the village guest house was a more appealing prospect than the basic apartments with kitchenettes in Siena that his father had rented for their stay. Three of them: a couple of girls around Marco's age, and a young man in his late twenties, enthusiastically agreed that the Tuscan countryside would inspire their writing. The fourth, a tall, thin older fellow with large heavy-framed spectacles and an intense stare declared that when he entered his writing world he was immune to his surroundings. The taller girl with dark eyes and long, black hair braided into cornrows was obviously trying not to laugh. Marco bit his lip and affected a suitably serious expression.

The turning to the village appeared out of nowhere. Marco yanked the steering wheel hard. The driver of a silver Mercedes blasted his horn twice and accelerated away, waving his fist through his open window. Marco could not make out what the man was shouting, but it certainly wasn't a polite *buongiorno*. He gripped the steering wheel with sweaty hands. He needed to keep his eyes on the road and get his passengers back to Bella Vista in one piece.

The guy in the passenger seat seemed unperturbed by their close shave. Marco turned his head to check on the man and two girls in the back. None looked alarmed; they were busy chatting amongst themselves. Perhaps they had been warned that all Italians were crazy drivers.

Marco prayed that he wasn't too late. Papa had read Francesco's letter, but he was so stubborn he might still take it into his head to drag himself to his car and drive off. There was a chance he had left Bella Vista already. Marco put his foot on the accelerator.

Jess perched cross-legged on the wicker recliner. She did not need to pick up her sketchbook; these views from the terrace would stay etched on her memory forever. And no matter how carefully she depicted the way the sunlight made the trees across the valley shimmer and glitter she was not able to bring to life the scent of the herbs Julia had planted by the wall nor the sounds of the birds twittering. She laid down her sketchbook and took a swig of peach iced tea. Miu Miu padded over and jumped up onto the edge of a terracotta planter filled with rosemary, and posed prettily.

'You want me to draw you again? Okay, you're my best model.'

Jess stroked Miu Miu's dense white fur until the cat batted her hand away with her paw. She turned over a page, picked up a softer pencil and captured Miu Miu with a few deft flourishes. She did not have the patience to concentrate for long; her mind was occupied with thoughts of leaving Bella Vista. And leaving Marco. When they sat down for lunch it might be the last time she would ever see him.

Last night, as they danced together, she could have sworn he felt something for her too. She would never forget the look in his eyes before he rode off into the night in pursuit of Giovanni. But this morning he had rushed off to collect his father's pupils with barely a word. She had to face the truth. His interest in her was just an illusion, which had vanished without a trace, as temporary as last night's storm.

She put her pencil and sketchbook aside. Miu Miu jumped off the planter and stalked off, looking insulted.

'Sorry, Miu, Miu,' Jess murmured.

There was no point sitting here, brooding. She might as well go and see if she could give Julia a hand in the kitchen. If Marco succeeded in transporting his father's writing class to the village, Julia was going to have her work cut out for the next few days. Besides, Jess was building up quite a collection of recipes. At least she could take a taste of Bella Vista home with her. She left her sketchbook by the lounger, wandered around the back of the house and in through the kitchen door.

Julia looked up. 'Good timing! I'm making a chocolate tart, *crostata di cioccolato* they call it here. I'm just about to toast a few hazelnuts ready to sprinkle on top. If you could keep an eye on the pan to make sure they don't burn I can tidy up a bit, then I'll talk you through how to make up the filling.'

'Great!' Jess grabbed a spare apron from the back of the kitchen door and rolled up her sleeves. She stood by the stove watching the hazelnuts turn an appetising golden-brown.

Jess followed Julia's instructions but by the time she had finished mixing up the chocolatey filling, it looked like a gang of pre-schoolers had been let loose on her side of the kitchen. She dampened a cloth under the tap and began wiping splatters of chocolate mixture off the wooden counter.

'Sorry . . . I'm supposed to be helping but I seem to be creating a lot of mess again.'

'That can't be helped. Why don't you take this spatula and scrape out the remnants? I know you're not supposed to lick your fingers when you're cooking but I reckon we can make an exception,' Julia said.

Julia took a palette knife and began to smooth over the surface of the *crostata*. 'This is one of Marco's favourites. I thought it would cheer him up after he missed his own birthday meal. He managed a few slices of cold pork when he got back last night but it's not quite the same.'

'Do you think Marco's going to pull this off?' Jess asked.

'Persuading Giovanni's class to come here? Yes, I think so. Marco can be quite charming when he wants to be. He takes after his father that way.'

'How is Giovanni this morning?' Jess said.

'He seemed a bit grumpy when I took him a bit of breakfast, which wasn't surprising – his ankle is really quite painful. But I wouldn't worry about him. Giovanni's bark is worse than his bite,' Julia said.

Outside, the door of the van slammed loudly. Jess tensed. She looked at Julia.

'Sounds like Marco's back.'

Several voices were talking at once. Marco wasn't alone. Lupo burst through the open kitchen door, barking with excitement.

'Here you are! Good boy!' Julia bent down and patted Lupo. 'Drat, now I've got to wash my hands again.'

Marco's head appeared around the kitchen door. 'Come here, Lupo. Stop bothering Julia!'

'Hi, Marco,' Jess said.

A big smile lit up Marco's face. 'Oh hi, Jess, didn't realise you were here too. I don't suppose Harriet's lurking around as well by any chance?'

'No. She's probably talking to Alfredo. I left her by the tack room when we got back from the ride. Sounds like you picked up your dad's pupils okay.'

'Yep, they're all here. I've sent them round to the terrace to say hello to Mum. As soon as I've confessed to Papa, I'm going to disappear. I've promised to give Harriet a short lesson in the school. I'm going to put Coco on the lunge line. That should really help Harriet's seat and give her a bit more confidence. And it's the perfect excuse to keep out of Papa's way. I might be about to trigger a volcanic explosion.'

Jess smiled. She wished she could think of a suitable quip. She shifted from foot to foot awkwardly.

Julia fished a long, thin loaf of bread out of a brown paper bag and placed it on the hefty olive-wood breadboard.

'Jess, I'll slice the *frusta* if you could mash up these tomatoes. We'll need to mix them up with some garlic for the topping for the *crostini rossi*,' she said.

'Sure.' Jess took the bowl of tomatoes, thankful for the distraction. When she looked up Marco had vanished. Why had she been so tongue-tied? He really did like her after all – she was sure it wasn't just her imagination. When she finished in the kitchen she would go down to the schooling ring and watch Harriet's lesson. Then she would wait for Marco in the stable yard. She had to be brave. She could not return to England without letting him know how she felt.

Chapter Sixteen

Harriet put her hands on her hips. Marco flicked the long lunge whip on the ground behind Coco's back feet and the pony took a step forward.

'Harriet, you look terrified!' Marco said.

'I can't believe I'm not holding on.'

'You've got to relax. I'll be controlling Coco's speed and direction with the lunge rope. All you have to do is concentrate on feeling the way Coco is moving. You'll be using your seat and legs to stay in the saddle.'

Harriet inhaled deeply through her nose then breathed out, dropping her shoulders as Marco instructed. She began to relax into the motion of Coco's stride as he walked around the schooling ring.

'Now can you feel the four-time beat his feet make?'

'It feels a bit weird, but I think I can,' Harriet said.

'Good.' Marco gently clicked his tongue to encourage Coco to keep going. After three more circuits he brought the pony to a halt and walked towards Harriet, folding the brown cotton lunge rope into loops as he approached. 'Feeling less nervous?'

Harriet nodded. She stroked Coco's velvety neck.

'We'll get him to walk in the opposite direction now and then we'll have a slow trot.'

'Without holding the reins?' Harriet's voice came out in a squeak.

'You're lucky I haven't asked you to close your eyes – yet!' Marco's eyes sparkled with mischief. He stepped backwards into the centre of the school and deftly switched the lunge rope and schooling whip over. Coco changed direction.

'Don't worry, we won't go any faster until you're ready,' Marco said.

Harriet rose up and down to the rhythm of Coco's short, choppy trot. The warmth of the sun was permeating the back of her T-shirt, birdsong was competing with the sound of the village clock striking twelve. She felt stupidly happy.

'Well done.' Marco unclipped the lunge line from the metal ring in the centre of Coco's nose band. He tucked it under his arm and reached for the rope attached to the pony's leather head collar.

A small brown bird burst through the hedge. Coco spooked, jumping sideways in alarm. Harriet shot forward. Her right foot slipped out of the stirrup. She grabbed the front of the saddle with one hand. Her other hand clawed uselessly at the air before she managed to grab hold of a handful of Coco's mane. Harriet's antics caused the pony to stumble. She lurched sideways. Her glasses were hanging from one ear. The ground rose up to meet her. She let out a strangled yelp.

Marco grabbed her by the elbows and pulled her back into an upright position.

'It's okay. You're all in one piece.'

Marco pushed her glasses back up onto the bridge of her nose and straightened them up. 'Lucky you didn't lose these. Daft pony, it was only a sparrow. Now ask him to walk on.'

'Can I get off?' Harriet said.

Marco rested one hand on her bare arm. He touched her cheek. 'I won't stop you, but if you get down now, you'll probably never get back on a horse again.'

Harriet's stomach was churning with nerves; she had the unpleasant sensation of damp, sweaty patches spreading across her underarms. She had survived the first twenty-eight years of her life without going anywhere near a horse. Would it really matter if she gave up now?

Out of the corner of her eye she saw a flash of kingfisher blue by the persimmon tree. She turned her head. It was Jess, standing there watching them. Maybe it was foolish pride, but she wasn't going to slide off Coco and slink off defeated with Jess looking on.

'I'll walk a couple of laps of the school first,' she said.

'That's my girl! Just use your lower legs to ask him to walk on.' Marco touched her lightly on the arm. Coco walked forward calmly, his earlier fright quite forgotten. As Harriet approached the persimmon tree, she raised her hand in greeting, but Jess had turned away. She was hurrying off in the direction of the farmhouse.

'Are you okay to lead Coco over there for a pick of grass before he goes back in his stable?' Marco asked as Harriet dismounted.

'Sure. He deserves it, don't you, boy?' Harriet took the end of the lead rope, which Marco had clipped to Coco's head collar.

'Alfredo will help you untack and put him away. I'm doing my best to keep out of Papa's way but if I don't turn up for lunch you'll know I've been minced and put in Julia's *polpette*!'

'Is your dad really mad at you?' Harriet said.

'He's pleased that he hasn't had to cancel his class but he's not too happy that I went behind his back and dragged his pupils out here.'

'He probably wonders why you couldn't just drive him back to Siena.'

'Papa's going nowhere. He's not leaving Bella Vista 'til he's sorted things out with Mum.' Marco's eyes blazed. He spun on his heel and set off towards the house. His posture was upright; he seemed to have grown several inches. Julia said Giovanni was a stubborn and determined man. Harriet strongly suspected that Marco was more than a match for him.

Harriet let Coco's lead rope slacken. The pony dropped his head immediately, pulling on the tufts of long grass that grew around the edge of the schooling ring. Harriet felt quite mean when it was time to drag him back to his stable.

Harriet removed Coco's saddle. She pushed open the door of the tack toom. She had grown to love its distinctive smell of leather and horse. Alfredo took the pony's saddle and slid it back on the rack. He opened the lid of a rectangular plastic box. It was brimming with grilled vegetables and slices of yesterday's leftover pork. He pushed it across the table towards her.

'You stay?'

Harriet was sorely tempted but she feared the others would think her terribly rude if she didn't join them for lunch, especially as Jess would be leaving for the airport in a couple of hours. Besides, she was curious to meet the four students Marco had picked up from Siena. But she wasn't sure she wanted to meet Giovanni. He sounded like the sort of difficult, angry character she would rather avoid.

'Thanks, Alfredo, but I had better go,' she said.

She walked through the stable yard, stopped by the chicken run and pulled out her phone. She clicked on her photographs and found one that Jess had taken. Harriet was standing holding Coco's reins in one hand. She looked absurdly proud, like a primary school child displaying a powder-paint masterpiece. She forwarded it to Savita. The photo would convince her boss that all was well. The poor

141

woman had sounded quite mortified to discover she had dispatched Harriet to a phantom yoga course.

Harriet's fingers hovered over her work emails, so many were marked *unread*. It was funny she had forgotten all about checking them these last few days. She no longer felt guilty; there were plenty of other people in the office who could deal with them. She was on holiday after all.

Harriet slipped in the back door and climbed the stairs. She laid Donna's old jodhpurs over the back of the bedroom chair and pulled on her jeans and a green short-sleeved top. She redid her ponytail and made her way out to the terrace.

Donna was standing there talking in Italian to a man who was lying on the wicker lounger looking out across the valley. Harriet could not see his face, but the wild, dark curls and light-blue jacket were unmistakable.

'Oh hi, Harriet. Meet Giovanni,' Donna said.

Giovanni swivelled towards her. 'Hello, Harriet. *Piacere.*'

A shiver ran down her spine. She was face to face with the man she had followed through the streets of Siena.

Marco stepped over Lupo who was lying across the back doorstep. The smell of toasted *frusta* laden with tomato and garlic greeted him as he entered the kitchen. A huge metal pot of rabbit stew bubbled and hissed. Julia took it from the stove and placed it on a wrought-iron trivet.

'I didn't realise how hungry I was until I smelt that,' Marco said.

Julia wiped the back of her hand across her forehead. 'Good. My favourite people are hungry people. I think I've managed to make far too much.'

Right on cue, Lupo trotted in and looked up at Julia. 'That does not mean there's anything for you, sir!' Julia laughed, shooing him away.

Marco's eyes rested on the fluted dish holding the *crostata di cioccolato*. 'That looks fantastic.'

'Jess helped me with it. It's a shame she couldn't stick around to sample it.'

'What do you mean?' Marco said. A cold feeling of dread washed over him. Jess didn't need to leave until at least four o'clock. She wasn't catching a plane until the evening. Julia was wrong. She had to be.

'She came rushing in saying she'd got the time of her plane wrong. Donna dropped her down at the station.'

'When, Julia, when?' Marco could hear the panic in his voice.

'Donna has only just got back so it must have been about fifteen minutes ago. She . . .'

Marco did not wait to hear the rest of what Julia was saying. He was already out of the kitchen door and starting up the van.

Marco drove as fast as he dared. He could not think why Jess had taken it into her head to rush off without saying goodbye. He only knew that he had to find her. Then he would tell her all the things he should have told her before. Last year, by the old chapel, he had messed up the perfect opportunity. He had almost kissed her, but he had lost his nerve. It had been a miracle that she had come back to Bella Vista but he had dithered instead of telling her how he felt. And now he was going to lose her again.

He pulled up opposite the station, jumped out of the van and ran inside. The illuminated board confirmed his worst fears. The train had been due to depart three minutes ago. The tracks were clear. It had already gone.

He stared helplessly up at the board. *Delay: 5 mins.* He still had two minutes to find her and persuade her to stay. He dashed onto the platform. She was there: standing in a patch of sunlight at the furthest end looking down at her phone. Her bag was between her feet; her red hair glowed in the bright sunlight like a halo around her face.

An announcement blared from the tannoy, the train was pulling in. Jess slid her phone into her pocket.

'Jess, Jess,' he shouted.

She turned and looked at him, bent down, picked up her bag and stepped towards the platform edge.

'Jess, wait!' He ran towards her.

She did not look at him.

He grabbed her arm. 'Don't go . . . please . . . stay!'

She shook him off. 'What for?' she muttered. She turned her head away.

All Marco's carefully chosen words deserted him. It wasn't supposed to happen like this. Jess was supposed to fall into his arms.

'I . . .' he tried again.

A railway worker was signalling for the train to depart. There was no time for fine speeches. He flung his arms around her and pressed his lips on hers.

'Get your hands off me!' She gave him an almighty shove.

Marco reeled backwards.

'Flirting with me and Harriet – you make me sick!' Jess picked up her bag and stepped up onto the train.

Marco clambered to his feet. The train was already moving. He jogged along the platform beside it, knocking on the window as it gathered speed, not caring how stupid he looked. Jess stared straight ahead. And then she was gone.

Chapter Seventeen

Harriet stared at Giovanni. His strong Roman nose, his head of wild curls: apart from those strange, golden eyes he was the spitting image of Marco. Why hadn't she noticed the resemblance before? She opened her mouth, but no words came out.

Donna filled the awkward silence. 'Harriet has been riding Coco. She hadn't ridden a horse before she came here.'

'And is this your first time in Tuscany?' Giovanni said.

'Yes, I've never been to Italy before.' Harriet shifted from foot to foot, twiddling with the belt loops on her jodhpurs.

'And yet you look so familiar.'

'I *have* seen you before,' Harriet said.

Giovanni's eyes widened. 'No! How so? You have been staying here at Bella Vista, have you not?'

'Harriet took a trip into Siena. Perhaps she saw you there,' Donna said.

'Yes, it was in a bar in Siena. In The Campo. You had been caught in the rain. You had forgotten your folder.'

'Indeed, I had. Your memory is much better than mine – that's for sure. What did I do next?' Giovanni asked in a teasing tone.

'You walked down a wide street then disappeared into a secret passageway.' Harriet stopped. She was already regretting saying as much as she had. She certainly wasn't going to admit to following Giovanni all the way to the square with the panther fountain.

Giovanni raised an eyebrow. 'A secret passageway? You have a vivid imagination, as well as a remarkable memory. Perhaps you should be joining my writing class. But tell me, Harriet, were you following me for some reason?'

Harriet felt the heat rising in her cheeks, but Giovanni was smiling, his eyes twinkling with amusement.

'Of course she wasn't. Stop teasing her. You're the one with the overactive imagination,' Donna said.

'Sometimes that is a blessing. Sometimes a curse.' He shook his head.

'Harriet was one of the girls who found Francesco's letter,' Donna said.

'Really? Then I owe you a great deal of thanks, Harriet. Now, where is that son of mine? If he doesn't appear in the next five minutes I'm going to start demolishing these *crostini*.'

'There's *crostini neri* to start with as well as these. I saw Julia frying up the chicken livers earlier,' Harriet said.

'*Mamma mia*! I'll weigh as much as Caesar by the time I get back to Siena.' Giovanni grinned. He was so like Marco, Harriet thought. He could look so fierce and unfriendly, but when he smiled his whole face lit up and his features softened.

'I think I can hear Marco now. I'll go and tell him to get a move on.' Donna hurried off.

Harriet and Giovanni were alone. She desperately wanted to ask him about the contents of the blue folder he had mislaid in Siena – to find out how and why her childhood adventure with Zoe had been immortalised in one of his stories, but she had no idea where to begin. How could she ask him without looking as though she had been snooping through his private papers? She wished she could escape the uncomfortable silence between them.

Giovanni winced. He wiggled his shoulders against the back of the lounger to get more comfortable. He tapped the arm of the wooden seat next to him.

'Come, sit down. The others will be here soon enough.'

Harriet perched awkwardly. She felt trapped by Giovanni's intense gaze like a spider in a web. She wished she had gone to the kitchen to fetch the *crostini neri*.

'So, where do you come from?' he said at last.

'London,' she said.

'London . . . a wonderful city,' Giovanni said.

'Have you ever visited?' Harriet asked.

'Two or three times, yes.'

'Did you see the sights? Madame Tussauds, the Changing of the Guard, Trafalgar Square?' Harriet was amazed how natural she sounded.

'I'm afraid I make a very poor tourist. I tend to wander without much rhyme or reason but, yes, I have been to Trafalgar Square. It was a long time ago, when I was a boy, but I remember it well. You could buy those little packets of seed and stand there with your arms stretched out like a statue until the pigeons came. I remember their little claws digging into my skin. One sat on my head; I think it fancied making a nest in my hair.' He laughed at the memory. 'Yes, London is a wonderful city though of course it cannot compare to the great Italian cities: Rome, Venice and Florence. Yes, I think Florence is the greatest of them all. You must go if you have not been before.

'But no city can compare to nature's own creations,' Giovanni continued. 'The countryside here – it is magical. I have been back less than a day and already I wonder how I could be truly happy anywhere else.'

147

'Home is where the heart is.' Harriet spoke before she could stop herself.

Giovanni's features darkened. His fingers drummed on the arm of the wicker lounger. Harriet bit her lip. Giovanni must think her very nosy to speculate on what might have unfolded that morning between him and Donna.

'Are you always so unsubtle?' Giovanni said.

Harriet squirmed. She willed Donna to reappear, or Lupo to bound over and lighten the atmosphere.

'But you are right: home *is* where the heart is. I have been in exile for ten long years. A foolish, self-imposed exile. I must ask you something, Harriet. We have only just met but you have seen more of my wife this last week than I have seen in a decade. Tell me, you are a woman, you must know these things: do you think I have a chance to put things right with Donna? Am I foolish to believe that it isn't too late?'

Instinctively Harriet reached for Giovanni's hand. 'No, I am sure it is not too late.'

Giovanni nodded. He quickly looked away. He blinked a couple of times and sat up straighter.

'Thank you, Harriet. I hope and pray that you are right.'

'I hope so too,' Harriet said.

She meant what she said. Impatient, sarcastic, hot-headed and reckless, but capable of deep, genuine feelings: Giovanni really was a bundle of contradictions. Donna must have spent their marriage riding a rollercoaster of emotions. It wasn't the sort of relationship Harriet wanted for herself but from everything she had seen and heard, Giovanni and Donna belonged together.

'It will all work out,' she added. '*Tocca ferro.*'

It no longer seemed the right time to quiz Giovanni about the story she had found in his navy-blue folder. She now knew that he had been to London himself and fed the pigeons in Trafalgar Square. Maybe the tale of the two schoolgirls had nothing to do with her and Zoe. But there were so many coincidences. She could not believe it was just the product of Giovanni's imagination. She would ask him about it when the time was right. She did not have to ask him today. It looked as though he was planning to stick around for a while.

Chapter Eighteen

'Give my love to Bianca.' Julia broke off from grating lemon zest into her cake mixture and popped a couple of slices of *crostata di cioccolato* into a paper bag. She handed it to Donna. 'It will do you good to get out for a bit.'

'You're right,' Donna said. She needed to get away, just for a little while. No one was going to miss her. Giovanni's writing class had taken over the dining room; Marco had gone to meet a friend at Bar Beppe; Harriet was reading on the terrace and Julia, as always, was juggling six things at once, impatient for Donna to get out from under her feet.

Donna flipped the latch on the gate and hurried down the path to the village. She walked briskly towards the red balloon that hung from Bianca's cherry tree. The old lady swore that it kept the birds from helping themselves.

Bianca wiped her hands on the skirt of her floral smock and brushed a few cat hairs from her thick, home-knitted waistcoat. She made as if to rise from her bench by the front door.

'Please, don't get up.' Donna sat down next to her. 'Look, I have brought a tart from Julia.'

The old lady took the paper bag and laid it aside unopened. She grasped both of Donna's hands in her own small, rough palms. Bianca's brown face was deeply wrinkled but her eyes were shining as bright as diamonds.

'He is back! Praise the Lord. I knew he would return.'

'But who told you . . .' Donna began. News travelled fast in their small village, but even so, she was surprised that Bianca had already heard of Giovanni's return.

'Only you.' Bianca chuckled.

'I haven't said anything.' Donna frowned.

'Donna, my dear. You have told me everything without speaking a word. Your face, your eyes, even the way you walk. The man you love has come home. Tell me I am not mistaken.'

'Yes, he is back.' Donna's voice trembled. Tears filled her eyes. She wiped them away.

'Come here.' Bianca pulled Donna towards her, enveloping her in a comforting cloud of violet perfume and face powder.

'Oh, Bianca, I don't know why I'm crying,' Donna mumbled.

'You're crying for all the times you didn't cry before; for all the times you were afraid to start in case you never stopped; for all the times you were brave and carried on. Now it is safe to cry.'

Bianca fished out a cotton handkerchief from the pocket of her smock. Donna blew her nose loudly.

'Thank you, Bianca. Oh dear, I must look a state.' Donna sniffed.

Bianca patted Donna's arm. She picked up the paper bag she had cast aside earlier, opened it a fraction and peeped inside. '*Crostata di cioccolato* – how wonderful! Come inside. We will have it with a cup of coffee before it melts in the sun.'

Bianca put down her coffee cup, wiped a blob of sticky, chocolatey filling off her chin, then licked her fingers.

'Now tell me all about it. What brought Giovanni back after all this time?'

Bianca could hardly believe her ears when she heard Donna's tale.

'He tried to ride over to Sienna's house, with that storm coming? *Mamma mia* he is as crazy as ever! I remember when he used to tear around on that moped – what a speed he went! But now he has seen sense. He has asked you to take him back hasn't he?'

'Yes. He wants us to put the last ten years behind us. He wants us to start again.'

'And what did you say?' Bianca's dark eyes scanned Donna's face.

'That I couldn't give him an answer yet; that I needed time to think.'

'*Brava*! You have done the right thing. It is good to make him wait a little. A lover is like a fisherman. He appreciates a fish more when it takes a little longer to catch.'

'But I'm so confused, Bianca. I don't know what to do. I can't just pretend the last ten years didn't happen. Giovanni didn't just walk out on me, he walked out on Marco and Daniela too. And it was all over nothing.'

'But Marco and Daniela have forgiven their father. Why else would they have plotted to bring him back? And you still love him, deep down. That is what matters.'

'There's been so much hurt . . . maybe it is just too much to forgive.' Donna sighed.

'No, that is where you are wrong.' Bianca reached out her hand and touched Donna's cheek. 'People think it is hard to forgive but it is easy. You only need to decide to do it and then it is done. To be angry or unforgiving – that is hard. You carry your anger and your resentment with you. It weighs you down every day for the rest of your life.'

'I hadn't thought about it like that. Perhaps you are right. I'm so glad I came to see you. You're so wise.'

'I wish that were true. I've made many mistakes in my life, but hopefully I can help prevent others doing the same. It is one of the compensations of old age, and, believe me, there aren't very many of those.' Bianca let out a soft chuckle. 'Now off you go. I'm sure you have a hundred better things to be doing than sitting here.'

Donna kissed the old lady goodbye on both cheeks. Bianca's words had cut through the confused jumble of thoughts fighting for space in her head. She walked briskly through the village swinging her arms as she went. Her senses were alive to every little thing: the gentle breeze, the smell of wild thyme, the tiny mauve violas growing in the hedgerows. Bianca had helped her enormously. She wouldn't dwell on past hurts; she would look forward. She would give Giovanni a chance to prove his love; she owed that to Daniela and Marco. But if he put a foot wrong, he would be gone for good.

'Donna, thank you for the wine. It's been great to see you, and wonderful to meet you again, Julia,' Francesco said. 'And you too, you funny old thing.' He bent down and ruffled the top of Lupo's head.

Giovanni put out his hand and shook Francesco's firmly. 'Thank you,' he said.

'You have nothing to thank me for.'

'Yes, I do. For coming back here this afternoon after the way I behaved last night. It was incredibly rude of me to storm out like that without even giving you the chance to speak. And I thank you for not holding the past against me. I was foolish and insecure to think you were playing around with my wife. I doubted your integrity and thought the worst of you when I should have appreciated your hard work and loyalty.'

'Yet it all worked out for the best. If you hadn't been so suspicious of me and Donna, I might have returned from Scotland after both my parents passed away. But then I would never have met Alasdair and had the wonderful life I have now. Without Alasdair I'm not sure I would have ever had the courage to be true to myself. I would have thrown myself into my work at Bella Vista, but I might still be living a kind of half-life.'

'Then I am glad to have assisted, even though it was by accident.' Giovanni smiled.

'It's been lovely to have a drink together but are you sure you don't want to stay for supper? One more won't make any difference. We've got the four students from Giovanni's class joining us. They have just gone down to Villa Susino to settle in,' Julia said.

'That's very kind but Vittoria and Vincenzo are expecting me to eat with them tonight.'

'Next time you come to Italy you must come for longer so we can meet Alasdair. You will come back, won't you?' said Donna.

'You can count on it,' Francesco said. 'I'd forgotten how beautiful it is.' His eyes lingered on the view beyond the terrace.

'And you must stay a couple of nights here with us,' Giovanni added.

With us? Julia looked at Donna and raised her eyebrows. But Donna didn't look taken aback by Giovanni's presumptuous comment. She just smiled.

Julia felt a pang of anxiety; she dreaded her friend getting hurt again. Donna had worked so hard to get back on her feet. A casual acquaintance would never have guessed at the heartbreak hidden behind her friend's sunny smile and can-do attitude. Only Julia had been privy to the long evenings, after Daniela and Marco had gone up to bed, when Donna tormented herself going over and over what she had said and done and how if only this and that had occurred, Giovanni would never have left.

In recent years Donna seemed reconciled to her situation, content even, but still, Julia worried about her. She wished her old friend could find the kind of happiness that she had belatedly found with her Luigi. Donna insisted she was happy being single, that she was too busy to go out on a date. But Julia believed she knew the real reason Donna couldn't open her heart to someone new: her heart still belonged to Giovanni.

Julia's memories of the day that Donna first met Giovanni were as vivid as yesterday. Donna's phone call had come out of the blue. Her news was too important to wait for inclusion in the weekly letters the two girls had been exchanging since Donna's temporary move to Italy. Donna was fizzing with excitement, her words tumbling over each other so fast Julia could barely make sense of them. After Julia replaced the receiver, she had the strangest feeling that whatever happened next, the course of Donna's life had been irrevocably altered.

Over the coming months and years, Donna's letters had brought her relationship with Giovanni vividly to life: the midnight rides up in the hills, the spontaneous trips to the coast, the tattoo of their entwined initials Giovanni got a week after they met. Then came Donna's unexpected pregnancy and the sudden purchase of Bella Vista. And through all these years there were silly rows and passionate reconciliations.

Julia sometimes wondered what Donna made of her letters. Often the biggest drama in *her* week was a collapsed Victoria sponge. Of course, she did have the odd short-lived relationship: the mature student who read Thomas Hardy aloud to her and couldn't hide his disappointment when she confessed to a preference for Joanna Trollope; the tweed-wearing doctor who took her punting on the Cam (how her mother liked the sound of him!) and the political activist who made love to her on a Moroccan bedspread whilst Che Guevara stared disconcertingly down from a giant poster on the wall. They were interesting enough companions, but Julia had never experienced the all-consuming love that Donna felt for Giovanni. Occasionally she felt a little pang of envy but she was inclined to think that a relationship like Donna's sounded rather exhausting. Then, at last, when Julia was living and working at Bella Vista, accepting that love had passed her by, she'd met Luigi.

Luigi was a quiet, solid man. There were no dramatic declarations of love, no over-the-top bouquets or rose petals scattered across the sheets, though sometimes, on the way to his work at one of the farms, he would stop his van to pick Julia a few wildflowers, which he presented to her straight from his big, warm calloused hands. When he was not working she would likely find him fixing a broken window at Bianca's house, helping his cousins with the olive harvest or playing endless games of cards at Bar Beppe with the friends he had known all his life.

It would not cross Luigi's mind to run naked along a beach at midnight or tear off to the other side of the country on a whim. Luigi had never been further than Florence. She wasn't sure he had ever seen the sea. But when she thought of his loyalty, his steadfastness, and his kindness it was like being bathed in a soft light, like soaking in a warm bath, like coming home. She would not swap him for a thousand Giovannis.

Donna would never settle down with a man like Luigi. The charismatic Giovanni was her soul mate. Julia hoped fervently that they could put the past behind them and that he and Donna could be happy again.

Harriet hovered in the kitchen. She ran her finger absent-mindedly round the edge of the small glass bowl. 'Mmm, what's this?'

'White chocolate sauce for my orange bavarois – it's a kind of mousse.'

'Sounds amazing.'

'It's a bit fancier than the things I usually make, and I know having three desserts is a bit over the top, but tonight I want everything to be perfect.'

'Giovanni's pupils will be eating here, won't they,' Harriet said.

'I do hope there's going to be enough to go round.' Julia's forehead wrinkled.

Harriet surveyed the groaning kitchen counter. 'I think you could safely invite half of Siena. It's just a shame Daniela couldn't come back here tonight.'

'I've got a funny feeling there's going to be plenty more opportunities for Daniela to enjoy a family dinner.'

'Do you think Donna and Giovanni will definitely get back together?'

Julia glanced around as if fearing that one of them might pop out from behind the fridge at any moment. 'I don't want to tempt fate, but I would like to think so.'

'After all this time . . .' Harriet said.

'You can storm out of a marriage, but you take all that shared history with you.'

'Surely it's not that easy,' Harriet said.

'No, it's going to be difficult. He's going to have to

pull out all the stops to win her trust but when you love each other you can find a way.'

'I wouldn't know,' Harriet murmured.

'You're nearly thirty; you must have been in love. Sorry, that was really tactless of me . . .' Julia said.

'I was once . . .' Harriet paused. She could remember the summer before last so vividly: in Norfolk, with Peter walking by the sea; in Harrogate, dancing together at her best friend's wedding. Those once seemingly perfect days were now just tarnished memories. The man she had been in love with had gone back to his old girlfriend. He was sorry, Peter said. Not as sorry as Harriet was. After that, it had been easier to throw herself into her work rather than risk getting hurt again.

'There was someone, but it turned out he did not love me. I suppose one or two of my past boyfriends might have been in love with me. I enjoyed their company, but they were never The One – if there is such a thing.'

'Oh, there is.' Julia put her hand on Harriet's arm. 'I truly believe there's someone for everyone. It might even be someone you've already met. Remember, Luigi and I were friends for a long time. We didn't get together until a couple of years ago when I was nearly forty.'

'You're really happy with him aren't you.' Harriet could not mistake the way Julia's face lit up at the mention of Luigi's name. One day Harriet might feel that way about someone. She hoped she wouldn't have to wait until she was forty. Maybe she would find love again. Maybe it was time she moved on – but not now. She just wasn't ready.

The metallic ringing sound grew louder. Julia switched off the timer. 'I think everything's finally ready – for now. I'll just take these peppers out. Shall we join the others?

They should be out on the terrace.' Julia opened the oven door and bent down to retrieve a glass baking dish.

Harriet used the tail of her shirt to wipe the steam from her glasses. 'Did you see Giovanni's pupils? What are they like?'

'You're not nervous about meeting them, are you?'

'Maybe a little.'

The arrival of four new riders later in the week did not concern Harriet at all − they would all have something in common − but the thought of spending this evening with a group of wannabe writers who all knew each other already was a little bit daunting. She wished Jess was still there.

'Oh, I'm sure you'll get on with them all just fine. There are two girls about Marco's age, Candy and Allie, who look like they're going to be fun. The older guy, Nigel, seems a little intense but the other boy, Tom − he's rather interesting.' Julia grinned.

'Interesting? How?'

Julia lowered her voice. 'He's really rather gorgeous. About your age or maybe a year or so younger, not that that matters.'

'Really?' Harriet could not help laughing. Had Julia actually winked at her? The last thing she was looking for right now was a man. Even so, she could not help being rather intrigued.

'Go on, Harriet, go out and join them before I chase you out there with my rolling pin. I'll come out myself in a few minutes,' Julia said.

Harriet adjusted her glasses. She wandered onto the terrace. Everyone seemed to be talking at once.

'Aah, Harriet, I was wondering where you had got to.' Giovanni was propped up on the wicker lounger, his right foot now resting on an embroidered cushion. He had a glass of red wine in his hand and was radiating bonhomie. 'Candy and Allie have kindly raided the village shop. Would you like a glass?'

Harriet gladly took a sip from the long-stemmed wine glass that Candy – or was it Allie? – handed her. The wine had an unexpected sparkle, which made her nose tingle.

'Like it? I had no idea what I was buying.' The girl laughed, making her long black braids jiggle. 'I'm Candy by the way. This is Allie. We met at an evening class in creative writing and decided to come out here together.'

'I'm Harriet. I've been learning to ride, though I actually came out here thinking I was going on a yoga holiday.'

'You're kidding! How funny.' Allie started giggling.

'What a terribly unfortunate situation for you. I'm Nigel.'

Nigel spoke in a deep, rather posh voice, keeping eye contact for slightly too long. He shook Harriet's hand rather formally. It was an effort to keep a straight face. Out of the corner of her eye she could see Candy stuffing her knuckles into her mouth to stop herself from laughing.

'Tom will be here in a moment. He's just been to look at the horses,' Nigel said. 'Oh, here he comes . . .'

The boy from the train was walking towards her. Harriet stifled a gasp.

Tom was dressed casually in well-fitting light-blue jeans fastened with a worn belt with a slightly battered brass buckle. A simple T-shirt showed off his well-formed chest. The last of the day's sun glittered on the golden hairs on his lightly tanned, muscular arms. Harriet never imagined a pink T-shirt could look so utterly masculine. *You're right, Julia, he's absolutely gorgeous. As gorgeous as the day we met.*

'Hey, Harriet, are you okay?' Nigel said.

'Yes . . . umm, fine,' Harriet mumbled.

'Hello again,' the boy said.

'Again?' Candy said. 'Have you two met before?'

'We met on the train. This is so strange,' Harriet said.

'Strange but nice.' Tom smiled. The dimples appeared at the corners of his mouth just as Harriet remembered.

Harriet tried to think of something interesting to say but her mind was blank. She gulped down a mouthful of wine. Too quickly. A moment later she was coughing and spluttering.

'Steady there. I'll thump you on the back.' Tom banged her back a couple of times with the palm of his hand. He was so close she could feel the heat of his body. He smelt as though he had showered in a Norwegian pine forest.

'Here's a glass of water.' Julia had come to the rescue. Harriet took it thankfully, certain that her flaming cheeks now matched the colour of Tom's T-shirt.

'So you remembered me,' Tom said.

'Of course. You offered me a wet wipe.'

'You don't remember anything else?'

'Umm . . . you had a blue shirt?' Harriet ventured.

'Is that all?' Tom frowned slightly. He looked as though he might say something, but Donna was rounding everyone up to come and eat.

'Is everyone ready to eat? Please, come and sit over here. It's warm enough to eat out tonight. Help yourselves to the *antipasti*.' Donna waved her hand across the laden table. Candy and Allie took the seats either side of Harriet.

The hum and babble of chatter quietened. Giovanni's four pupils tucked in hungrily, as did Alfredo who was wolfing down the *crostini* as if he hadn't eaten for a month.

Donna took a spoonful of *peperonata*. The mixture of yellow and red peppers, onion and tomato tasted as good as it looked but it was hard to give the food her full attention when she could feel Giovanni's eyes on her. She looked up, expecting him to look away, but his caramel eyes did not leave her face. She could not help wondering what it would be like to sleep with him again. She felt her face flushing. She reached for her glass of iced water and looked away.

She turned her attention to the others, anything to avoid looking at Giovanni. Marco had stopped eating, mid forkful, to stare across the terrace. Donna had long since given up trying to fathom Marco out; there could be any number of thoughts and feelings that were playing on his mind. But why did Harriet keep looking at the rosemary bush? Donna followed Harriet's gaze. Aah, that explained it. It wasn't the rosemary bush that was attracting Harriet's attention, it was the person sitting nearest to it. It was Tom.

Donna caught Tom's eye. He smiled, his eyes crinkling and a dimple forming at each corner of his mouth. What a handsome young man he was. No wonder Harriet had taken a shine to him. And she was sure she had caught Tom looking at Harriet too. How strange it was that the two of them had met before on the train.

'I think we'll take a few minutes before I fetch the spaghetti,' Julia said. She stood up and began collecting up the plates. Donna picked up the *peperonata* dish. It was a shame it was empty; she loved eating it cold. She placed it in the sink to soak and slipped out the kitchen door. She stood by the chicken run and pulled out her mobile. She scrolled down to the number for Villa Susino. Vittoria answered on the third ring.

Chapter Nineteen

Harriet woke with a start. What a strange dream. She was asking Giovanni about the story he had written but he turned into a panther and chased her through the olive grove.

She laced up her trainers, crept quietly down the stairs and out through the boot room. All was quiet except the sound of the house martins chirping in their nest under the eaves. Lupo was snoozing on the back doorstep but when he saw Harriet he got to his feet, stretched and followed along behind her. Miu Miu was crouched down at the edge of the chicken run peering through the mesh at a big white hen, which was scratching around in a vain attempt to find some uneaten corn from the previous day.

'You've got no chance of catching that, you daft cat!' Harriet said.

Harriet rummaged in her pocket and found a couple of mints she could give to Coco. Someone was already in the stable yard leaning over Guido's door. Harriet could tell at a distance that it wasn't Alfredo and he did not have Giovanni and Marco's dark curly hair. There were no other men staying at Bella Vista. Harriet's heart began to beat faster. There was a broom leaning up against Coco's door but she did not imagine it would prove much use against this intruder. She gripped Lupo's collar tightly and began to back away slowly and quietly. Lupo had other ideas. He let out a string of loud barks.

The man swung round. It was Tom.

'Harriet! My God! You and that hound gave me quite a fright. Do you always creep around like a ninja?'

'I was worried you were a burglar. I didn't expect you guys to be here 'til after breakfast.'

'I'm armed with a carrot and a packet of Polos,' Tom joked. 'I thought I'd get up early and come and look at the horses. This grey one's beautiful, isn't he?' He held out a mint on the palm of his hand for Guido.

'Have you met Coco, the little pony? That's the one I've been riding.'

'That figures.'

Harriet didn't know if it was the way his eyes crinkled or the dimples at the corners of his mouth but Tom's smile had a very strange effect on her insides.

'He's faster than he looks,' she said in mock indignation.

'I'll believe you, but I bet he's not as fast as this one.' Tom stroked Caesar's dark forehead.

'Do you ride?' Harriet said.

'Not really. I've had a go a couple of times. I certainly wouldn't fancy my chances on this big chap.' He gave Caesar another pat. 'Will you join me for a coffee on the terrace? I happen to know Julia's put a pot on.'

'That sounds good.'

'Why don't you go and sit down whilst I fetch it?'

'Great, thanks.' Harriet wandered round to the terrace and flopped down in a chair with Lupo at her feet.

Tom reappeared a few minutes later.

'There you go,' he said. He handed her a cup.

'Mmm, smells delicious. So, was everyone else still asleep when you left?' she asked.

'I wouldn't know. I stayed here last night.'

Harriet was glad she hadn't known that. She wasn't sure

she would have slept so well knowing Tom was under the same roof.

'Apparently there was a mix-up down at the guest house. It was either stay here or share with Nigel.'

'You definitely made the right choice,' Harriet said. She hoped she didn't sound bitchy.

'Nigel's a nice enough bloke, just a bit odd. He's got a lot of talent though. Giovanni gets everyone to send him a piece of writing before they join his course. Nigel wrote about a local haunted chapel; it was pretty incredible.'

'So, what did you write about?'

'I'm not sure I can tell you. It's really a bit embarrassing.'

Harriet leant forward and looked into Tom's clear, hazel eyes. 'Whatever it is, I promise I won't laugh.'

'Okay, I'll tell you, but you might think it's a bit weird. You see, Harriet, I wrote about you.'

There was a strange silence in the air. The birds had ceased singing. Even Lupo had stopped scratching. It felt as though time had stopped. Harriet gazed at Tom, open-mouthed.

'You wrote a story about me?'

'We knew each other years ago. You really don't remember me, do you?' Tom said.

'No.' Harriet answered simply but her brain was whirring. Where on earth could she have met this boy before? More to the point, how could she have forgotten someone this attractive? And yet, now she was studying him intently (he had given her a lovely excuse to stare), there was something about him that triggered a long-forgotten memory.

'I suppose it was too much to hope.' Tom smiled, dimples forming at the corners of his mouth.

That's it. It's those dimples. Harriet had seen that smile somewhere before. It belonged to a small impish boy. An ordinary, very skinny, pale little lad, barely five foot tall. He had gone to her school but she had never spoken to him; there was no reason to – he had been in the year below her and his family had moved away at the end of the fifth form. Somehow a name came to her out of the blue: 'Little Tommy Williams? It can't be!'

'I didn't think you'd recognise me straight away. I guess I look a bit different from the way I looked at school and everybody calls me Tom, now.'

'You're so . . .' *handsome, desirable, hot.* Harriet wasn't interested in getting involved with anyone, but she couldn't deny how attractive Tom was.

'. . . much taller,' Tom supplied.

'Yes, much taller,' Harriet agreed, relieved.

'I reckon I was barely five foot back in those days. I finally started to grow after I left. By the time I started sixth form college I was six inches taller. I was shooting up so rapidly Mum actually dragged me to the doctor thinking I had some strange growing disease. Fortunately, I stopped once I hit six foot. It took me a long time to fill out, mind. I was gangly as anything.'

'I'm finding that hard to imagine,' Harriet said.

'I was so scrawny I was cast in the college Christmas panto as the beanstalk – in *Jack and the Beanstalk*, though I was so wooden they should have cast me as a telegraph pole.'

'Stop it! You're making me choke on my coffee.' Harriet spluttered.

'It's true, honest.' Tom gave her a grin that made her stomach flip over again. 'But that day on stage was the day that changed my life. When the curtains closed and the audience clapped I knew I couldn't act but I knew what I wanted to do. I wanted to be a playwright. It's just a dream but one day, who knows . . .'

'So, that's why you're taking Giovanni's writing course. You said this story was about me. What on earth did you write?' Harriet asked, although she was sure she already knew the answer.

'Giovanni told us to submit something inspired by a childhood memory. Nigel wrote this great piece about a toddler visiting a stately home; it was so scary it made our skin crawl. I could never write anything like that; comedy's more my style. I was stuck at first, then I remembered the funniest story from school. It was you and Zoe: the legendary pigeon smugglers. You remember that outing to Trafalgar Square . . .'

'Remember it? I thought I was going to get expelled,' Harriet said. The memory of standing outside the headmistress's office still made her shiver.

'It was the talk of our class for weeks. We couldn't believe it when we heard what you and Zoe had done. Please tell me it was all true.' Tom leant forward and rested his chin on his hand.

'It was a trip to the National Gallery. I remember loads of us going, I think it must have been the whole year. Miss McLain and Miss Taylor really had their hands full. We were all given these worksheets and had to go from room to room filling them in. Of course, Zoe, being Zoe, had somehow got hold of a copy of the answers so we disappeared into the loos to quickly fill our sheets in then we sneaked back out to Trafalgar Square.

'There was a man in a checked flat cap near the bottom of the steps. He reminded me of my grandad. He had a couple of pigeons perched on his arm. He told us you weren't supposed to feed the birds any more, but he gave us some little packets of seed and told us that if we saw a policeman we had to run away. Soon we had pigeons pecking out of our hands and standing on our shoulders. It was such fun we stayed there until we saw the others snaking two by two towards the tube station. We tagged along at the back. I remember the newspaper sellers shouting "Standard, Standard!" and the smell of roasting chestnuts.

'It was only when we were standing on the platform that I realised that Zoe had one of the birds under her coat. I don't know why it didn't flap around or make a noise. Zoe said it was because it liked her but now I realise it was probably terrified.

'The tube was so full we all had to stand. Somehow, we got wedged in right next to Miss McLain. I was looking down at the floor because I knew if I looked at her I'd start giggling. The tube stopped in a tunnel; everyone lurched forward. Zoe cannoned into Miss McLain. Then it happened: a big slimy white blob fell splat onto Miss McLain's shiny black shoes.'

Harriet paused. Tom's shoulders were shaking with laughter. 'Go on, Harriet, tell me what happened next.'

'Miss McLain went mad. Do you remember how she never shouted; she just put on this icy voice that terrified you? She made us go to the headmistress the next day. I couldn't sleep all night for worrying. We had to write out hundreds of lines and she wrote to our parents. Looking back now, Mum and Dad probably thought it was funny, but they had to pretend to be cross for a while.'

'So, it was all true! I wasn't sure, but it was such a good story I couldn't resist using it. You don't mind, do you?'

'I don't mind at all,' she said.

'Phew!' Tom wiped his brow in a jokey gesture.

Harriet felt like a weight had been lifted. The story in Giovanni's blue folder had been Tom's all along. Now she could look at Giovanni without the creepy sensation of wondering what else he knew about her.

'I'm just amazed you remember it after all these years.'

'I'd never forget Zoe. She was larger than life, wasn't she? And I couldn't forget you either. I must confess I had a little bit of a crush on you.'

'Really?' Harriet raised her eyebrows.

A red flush was spreading across Tom's neck. 'It was a long time ago,' he muttered.

'It was,' Harriet said. It was funny how life worked out. All those years ago she had barely noticed him. Now their roles were reversed. *She* certainly wasn't going to confess she had a bit of a crush on Tom *right now*.

Donna glanced at the bedside clock. She was in the same bed, in the same room but something felt different. She was lying naked in the semi-darkness. She reached out her hand to pull up the bedding; she must have kicked it off during the night.

She groped around for the corner of the duvet and tried to pull it back over her before realising it was firmly wrapped around Giovanni's sleeping body. His face was buried in the pillow. Only the back of his head and one smooth, brown shoulder were exposed.

Donna plucked her turquoise cotton kimono off the floor and wrapped it around her. Yesterday's blouse, bra and knickers were strewn across the bedside rug where Giovanni had tossed them as he undressed her. All her initial self-consciousness had evaporated in the heat of his obvious desire for her. And her body remembered him as if it had been only days not years since she had last lain in his arms. She did not regret last night but she feared it would now be much harder to hold on to her heart.

Very carefully, so as not to wake him, she fastened the sash on her kimono and crept to the window. She opened the rose-printed curtains just a few inches and peeked through the shutters. It was going to be a beautiful day. She could see Harriet and Tom out on the terrace. It looked as though they were laughing.

Giovanni stirred. He rolled over and looked at her. 'Hello, my love.'

'Hello to you.' Donna smiled. She bent over the bed and touched the rough stubble on his cheek.

'Why are you getting up? Come back to bed.' He gave her wrist a little tug. She let herself fall forward onto the bed, laughing. He rolled her onto her back and propped himself up on one elbow. Those caramel-coloured eyes locked onto hers.

'What are you looking at,' she asked.

'Everything I've been missing all these years. My beautiful wife. I love you.'

Donna smiled but she did not reply. She was nowhere near ready to say 'I love you' back.

Marco knocked on the door for the third time. Still no answer. Papa might not be too happy to get woken up but Marco wasn't going to stand around all morning clutching this cup of coffee. He pushed open the door.

The room was empty. His father had gone. His bed had not even been slept in. Marco slammed down the coffee cup sending hot liquid splashing all over the dressing table. He had been so convinced that his parents were going to get back together but he should have known Papa would do a runner.

Marco's legs felt heavy as he climbed the stairs. He dreaded breaking the news, but it was better for Mum to know sooner rather than later. He had been such a fool to lure Papa back to Bella Vista; it was inevitable his father would end up hurting his mother all over again.

Marco turned the door handle but the door did not budge. That was strange; his mum never locked her bedroom door. There was an odd noise coming from behind the door like a muffled cry. Then the distinctive sound of his father's voice.

Marco scuttled back down the stairs, his face burning. He hurried into the stable yard. Caesar was already kicking his door, demanding his breakfast. Marco busied himself stuffing the hay nets with sweet-smelling hay and emptying plastic buckets of horse and pony nuts into the corner mangers. He was going to be busy today; Mum had insisted that Alfredo take a much-needed day off. Marco fetched the wheelbarrow and long-handled fork. The horses were used to someone mucking out around them as they ate.

He was surprised how much he enjoyed the work even though after pushing half a dozen full barrows up the muck heap he was beginning to sweat. The physical activity was a good distraction. Over the years he had imagined his parents back together in all sorts of charming scenarios: chatting over candlelit dinners out on the terrace; strolling hand in hand through the olive grove; dancing along to the radio in the kitchen. But this morning's scene was one he really did not want to dwell on. His father was forty-seven, for heaven's sake! If anyone was creeping around in the night finding his way into some girl's bed it should be Marco. It was time he got himself a girlfriend. The trouble was the girl he wanted was hundreds of miles away.

Chapter Twenty

'Your English cup of tea and one for me.' Luigi handed Julia a huge earthenware mug.

'Thanks.' She wriggled up the bed and made herself comfortable against the pillows.

'One of your finest traditions and one of ours. Nothing beats a siesta.'

'Though I think you're supposed to sleep.' Julia playfully slapped his hand.

'But this is much nicer . . .'

'Mmm . . .' Julia closed her eyes as Luigi's hand worked its way towards the top of her thigh.

'More relaxed now?' he asked later as he wrapped his arms around her.

'Yes,' Julia said. *Though not as relaxed as you are.* Luigi was already snoring gently.

Julia pulled on her clothes and ran Luigi's hairbrush through her unruly hair before tying it back with her blue floral scarf.

'Don't go yet.' He reached for her.

'I thought you were asleep.'

'Just a catnap . . . You can spare another ten minutes, can't you.'

'Of course.' She settled herself on the edge of the eiderdown.

'Good. Because now you can tell me what's bothering you.'

'I'm fine.' Julia spoke rather more briskly than she intended.

'No.' Luigi fixed his coal-dark eyes on her. 'There is something, I know it. It's Giovanni, isn't it?'

Julia nodded. How well Luigi knew her – sometimes even better than she knew herself. Still, she hesitated; it was so hard to explain.

'It's just such a shock, that he's come back, I suppose.' She shrugged.

'For you, as well as for Donna.' Luigi took her hand in his.

'Donna's so happy. I'm thrilled for her, I really am, but I'm so worried that everything will go wrong again. Giovanni's buying all these gifts. He doesn't seem to realise that Donna just needs his trust – and his love.'

'Us men aren't always very good at expressing our emotions. But you know that I love you, I hope. And Giovanni loves Donna no matter how foolish he's been in the past.'

'I guess I'm just being silly; maybe I'm worrying over nothing.'

'It's never silly to feel the way you feel,' Luigi said simply. He drew her near and put his arms around her. Julia inhaled the comforting, slightly salty smell of his skin. She liked the way he did not mask his natural scent with aftershave or cologne.

'Everything will be okay, you'll see,' he murmured.

She put her arms around him. She hoped Luigi was right. Donna deserved to be happy after all those painful years.

Chapter Twenty-One

Alfredo stroked his wiry moustache as he pondered his three cards. It wasn't a bad hand, but he would need an awful lot of luck if he and Vincenzo were going to beat Luigi and Old Dante today. Dante stirred a second twist of sugar into his espresso and slurped it noisily. He gave a small belch of satisfaction and fixed his rheumy blue eyes on Alfredo. Alfredo placed the six of swords face upwards on the table.

Dante grinned, revealing his three remaining front teeth. He slowly flipped over a card: The King. He swept the remaining cards off the round metal table: Alfredo sighed. The game wasn't over yet but there was every likelihood that Alfredo and his partner were going to be paying for the coffee. Again.

Alfredo had been playing *scopa* with Old Dante since he was a teenager and Dante had a full set of teeth. Luigi had not even been born when the two of them had graduated from the playground to Bar Beppe in the days when Beppe's father, the original Beppe, had run the place. Alfredo had been losing eight games out of ten ever since. When Alfredo and Vincenzo joined forces to play in a four Alfredo's luck was no better.

Alfredo had not wanted to take today off and come to Bar Beppe, but Donna had insisted. Marco would take care of the horses today. Alfredo's body was desperately in need of a rest and the sun's warmth was doing a marvellous job of penetrating his aching bones but his head was clogged with worries.

The thought of Giovanni living at Bella Vista filled him with dread. Why would he want to keep an old man like Alfredo pottering around the place? Once Giovanni was up and about he would not fail to notice how a younger man like Marco ran up the muck heap as if he was pushing a doll's pram not a heavily laden barrow. And tomorrow Carla would arrive.

When Donna had first told Alfredo that Bianca's granddaughter, Carla, would be working at the stables during her university holidays Alfredo had been cynical. He had known the girl since she was born; she was a tiny little thing, not much taller than Harriet. Looking after horses was strong, physical work. What use would Carla be? Then Carla had come for a trial during her half-term holiday. What a revelation that had been! The girl was as strong as an ox. Alfredo's mouth had dropped open as he watched her move the heavy hay nets four at a time and carry a pair of full water buckets across the yard as easily as two cups of cappuccino.

Alfredo would look even older and slower once Carla arrived. The only solution was to work harder than ever. Tomorrow he would forgo his usual siesta. He would oil every bridle and polish all the metal fastenings in case Giovanni appeared. Then he would sweep and sweep and sweep until there was not a piece of hay nor a scrap of wood shavings to be seen.

But however hard he worked Giovanni was bound to blame Alfredo for his accident. Alfredo knew his days at Bella Vista were numbered. What would he do then? Bella Vista was his life.

'*Tocca a te!*' Luigi said loudly. 'Alfredo, *tocca a te!* It's your turn!'

Alfredo chewed his bottom lip and tried to think. He had completely lost track of the game. He pulled out his red spotted handkerchief and dabbed at his watery eyes to buy some time. He *ummed* and *aahed* then laid down his cards.

The tip of Dante's tongue flicked across his upper lip like a snake. He leant across the table and gathered up all the cards. Again. 'Next round.'

Alfredo nodded. He did not want to go home and sit in his empty cottage and think.

Luigi's hands were big and rough but he dealt the cards deftly. Dante examined his cards. His ice-blue eyes gave nothing away. Alfredo looked at his hand: he had the prized *settebello*, the seven of coins. Now he had a chance of winning. Luigi placed four cards face up on the table.

'Ready?' Dante said.

A shadow fell across their game.

'*Buongiorno.*' The rich honeyed tones were unmistakable.

Alfredo's heart sank; his good hand of cards no longer mattered. What was Giovanni doing here? He was supposed to be resting his ankle up at Bella Vista not gallivanting around the village.

'Giovanni. *Buongiorno.* It has been a long time,' Dante said. He made to rise from his seat.

'No, no, sit down.' Giovanni waved his hand. 'Beers, gentlemen? On me.'

'Well, if you insist,' Dante said. 'Hey, Beppe!' he bellowed in the direction of the doorway. 'Look who's here!'

Beppe lifted his head from his copy of *La Nazione* and brought five green bottles of beer over with uncharacteristic speed. He had heard the news of Giovanni's arrival and short-lived escape on horseback and was eager to glean any gossip.

The cool beer could not lift Alfredo's glum mood. He traced a pattern with his finger on the side of the bottle whilst his friends laughed at a funny story Giovanni was telling, their game of cards temporarily abandoned. Eventually Giovanni turned towards Alfredo to answer his unspoken question.

'Marco has just dropped me off. We went to the market to buy a few essentials. I don't mind wearing my son's shirts but sharing his underwear is a different matter.' Giovanni grimaced.

'Your ankle, it is better?' Alfredo asked.

'Still painful, but yes, much better. I could return to Siena tomorrow, but my pupils are in no hurry to go back. In fact, they are keen to stay at Villa Susino. They are finding the Tuscan countryside quite an inspiration for the challenge I have set them this afternoon. I left them creating their own Japanese *haiku*.'

Alfredo had not got a clue what Giovanni was talking about but if Giovanni wanted to talk about Japan, *haiku* or Timbuktu that was fine by him. He would gladly talk to him about anything except the staffing arrangements at Bella Vista.

Giovanni lowered his voice. 'I was hoping to have a quiet word.'

'With me?' Alfredo glanced over his shoulder, willing there to be someone else standing behind him.

'Indeed.' A small smile played across Giovanni's lips. He gestured at an unoccupied table for two under the shade of an almond tree. Alfredo felt himself shiver despite the warm sunshine.

'Hey, Beppe. You want to take Alfredo's place and team up with Vincenzo?' Dante swiped Alfredo's good hand of cards and handed them to Beppe.

'Sure, sure. My wife will look after the customers.' Beppe slid into Alfredo's seat.

Alfredo pulled back the chair opposite Giovanni. He wiped away the beads of perspiration bubbling on his forehead. So, this was the beginning of the end. He wished it were somewhere less public.

'So how are you, Alfredo? Glad of some time off, I expect. The last couple of days have been exhausting for all of us.'

Alfredo stared down at the table. He *was* tired, he *was* glad of a day off but he did not want to agree with Giovanni. He wished he had the energy to leap from his chair and dance a jig. Or, better still, wrestle Giovanni to the ground and show him that he, Alfredo, had the strength of a lion.

'Alfredo . . .' Giovanni repeated softly.

Reluctantly, Alfredo raised his head.

'Marco has managed to extend his holiday for a few days. He's happy to assist you until Bianca's granddaughter arrives. That will help won't it? But the reason I'm here is to talk to you about the other evening. If you hadn't left Caesar's old saddle lying around I wouldn't have ended up staying at Bella Vista.'

Alfredo took a long swallow of beer. He had left the saddle lying around but it was not his fault Giovanni had ridden off into the night. But he was going to suffer for it. It was so unfair.

Giovanni fished out an envelope from the inside pocket of his light-blue jacket and placed it on the table. 'I went to the bank before I came here. I wanted to give you something: a little present. A token of my esteem you might say.'

Alfredo eased the envelope open with trembling fingers. Euros, maybe a hundred or two. Severance pay. That wasn't going to last very long. 'I don't know what to say,' he muttered.

'*Grazie* will do.' Giovanni grinned.

Alfredo was not going to cry. A man like him didn't. So how could a tear be running down his cheek? He swiped it away angrily.

'When do you want me to go?' he managed at last.

'Go? Go where?' Giovanni's brow furrowed.

'Finish, leave – however you want to put it,' Alfredo mumbled.

'Leave? I don't understand you, Alfredo. Why do you want to leave?'

'I don't want to leave. Bella Vista . . . it is my life.'

'Well. I don't know anyone who wants you to leave either.' Giovanni frowned.

'I'm not getting any younger.' Alfredo's voice was barely a whisper.

'Pah! My grandfather rode a horse until he was ninety-five. Besides, how would Donna manage without you? How would any of us manage? You can look a horse in the eye and see that it's unwell long before it shows any signs of illness; you can feel the heat in its leg and know it's gone lame.'

'That's true. But . . . this . . .' Alfredo poked the envelope.

'A present. For you. To thank you for helping to bring me back to Bella Vista.' Giovanni fixed his golden eyes on Alfredo.

'For me? No. I did nothing. And besides I don't need any money. What would I spend it on? A new suit?' Alfredo laughed.

'I couldn't help noticing your doorframe is rotten. You should get that fixed whilst the weather is nice. Unless you are planning on moving away . . .'

179

'Now I know you are teasing me,' Alfredo said. 'But . . .'

'No buts. I insist. I am giving you a few euros, but you have helped give me something that money can't buy. A second chance with the woman I love. And maybe one day we will renew our vows and you'll need a new suit after all.'

Giovanni stood up and made his way gingerly towards the corner of the road where Marco was waiting by the van. Alfredo waited until they were out of sight before carefully counting the money.

The clock on the tower chiming four drowned out the sound of Luigi and Beppe celebrating their win at *scopa*. It should have been Alfredo's winning round. But he didn't care. He would suggest they play another game. He was feeling lucky.

It was surprising how quickly the day went when you played card game after card game then finished up with a couple of beers and a bowl of spaghetti rustled up by Beppe's wife. Alfredo fell into bed, tired but happy.

A few hours later he woke up with a start. The luminous hands on the alarm clock told him it was three in the morning. He cursed his bladder for rousing him from his comfortable bed. He had been sleeping like a baby tonight.

He slowly groped his way across the room and back. He could have switched the light on – after all he had no one to disturb these days – but old habits died hard. He pulled up the sheet and adjusted his thin, brown blanket; it wasn't cold enough to warrant anything more. He would never truly get used to lying here without Benedetta by his side; it was unnatural for a man to be alone. Now, he felt her presence in the room, as he so often did. He caught a waft of her favourite lily of the valley scent. *I told you everything would be okay, my darling*, she said. He reached out into the darkness, but she had gone.

★

'I can't believe how dark it is.' Harriet's brow was creased with the effort of walking carefully and steadily. There was a fine line between merrily tipsy and embarrassingly drunk, and she was just the right side of it. At least she hadn't succumbed to a bout of hiccups like Allie and Candy.

'A city girl like you probably can't imagine a place without streetlights,' Tom said.

'Too right! How on earth does anyone find their way around?'

'Looks like they're all tucked up in bed by now,' Tom said. He was right: all the little houses were in darkness. Behind them, Beppe's Bar was the only bright spot in the village. Nigel's booming voice drifted over as he walked arm in arm with Candy and Allie towards Villa Susino.

'I don't think the locals have ever met anyone quite like Nigel,' Tom said.

'I don't think *I've* met anyone quite like Nigel.' Harriet laughed.

'He's a mad genius, that's for sure.'

'I had such a good night. I don't know when I last laughed so much,' Harriet said.

'Candy and Allie are great fun aren't they?'

Harriet could not disagree, but she felt a little sick. Both of the girls were several years younger than she was, and Candy was particularly pretty – all big brown eyes and an hourglass figure to die for. Why would Tom look at her with those two around? Sure, Tom had admitted he had been interested in Harriet once, but as he said himself: it was a long time ago.

'Do you think we kept Beppe up? He started stacking the chairs the minute we left,' Harriet said, deliberately changing the subject. If Tom was interested in Candy or Allie she certainly did not want to hear about it.

'I did see Beppe sneaking a look at his watch after Alfredo left, but I guess he was happy the till kept ringing . . . Careful, it's a bit uneven here.'

'Too late!' Harriet grabbed a fence post to stop herself falling.

'Are you okay?' Tom's steadying hand on her arm felt curiously intimate.

'Yes, I'm fine.' She straightened up.

'Here, use my phone as a torch.' Tom fished it out from his jacket pocket.

'Don't you want to hold it?'

'No. I'm going to hold your arm and make sure you don't trip again.'

'Oh.'

Harriet kept the phone low down so as not to shine it in the windows of the houses and wake the village's sleeping inhabitants.

'Wait! Look!' Tom said.

Harriet followed his gaze. A firefly hovered nearby like a tiny glowing cigarette end; she could have reached out and touched it.

'Magical, isn't it,' Tom whispered.

'Beautiful,' Harriet said. She stopped herself from exclaiming *how romantic!*

A cloud moved, revealing a thin, silver sliver of moon, which illuminated the gnarled and twisted trunks of the old trees ahead of them. They were nearly at the olive grove. Tom's pace slowed.

'Let's take a walk through the trees. It's such a beautiful evening it's a shame to go straight back.'

'Sure.' Harriet's heart skipped a beat.

'There's something I meant to ask you earlier,' he said.

Harriet stopped. The fantasy she had been harbouring all evening was really happening. Despite her best intentions, it was impossible to deny she was falling for Tom. The dark, inky night; the moonlight; the fairy-tale setting of the olive grove. Could there be a more perfect moment than this?

'Ask me anything you like,' she said. She looked into his hazel eyes.

'I was just wondering . . .' Tom hesitated.

Harriet stood on tiptoe and turned towards him; she could smell his fresh pine forest scent. Her heart was racing. He was going to kiss her. She knew it. 'Go on . . .' she said softly.

'Do you think Donna would mind if I went riding with you guys tomorrow?'

Harriet's heart plummeted. 'Umm . . . err . . . sure,' she muttered.

Tom frowned. 'I guess it was a daft idea. I'll just slow everybody down. It's not like you're a beginner, yourself, any more.'

'No, no. I think it's a great idea,' Harriet said. Her voice sounded unnaturally bright.

'Are you sure? You don't sound terribly convinced.'

'No, honestly, I'd love you to come along. You took me by surprise that's all.'

Harriet was glad she had the darkness to cover her blushes; her face must be as bright as Bianca's balloon. Thank goodness she hadn't made the first move. Just imagine her embarrassment if she had reached up and kissed him. The thought of it made her shiver.

'You're cold.' Tom started to shrug off his jacket.

Harriet was about to protest but Tom was too quick. He slipped the jacket over her shoulders and knotted the sleeves together at the front. The hem reached nearly to her knees.

'You do look cute,' he said. The way he smiled still flipped her stomach over, but she now knew not to read anything into his comment.

'That's the way, isn't it?' she said briskly.

'Yes, I think I recognise that cottage at the bottom of the lane.' Tom took her hand in his. 'Can't have you falling over again.'

Why did he have to do that? He obviously couldn't know the effect he had on her. She wished Nigel was the one who was staying at Bella Vista. She wouldn't be wasting her time mooning over him.

Chapter Twenty-Two

'Duck!' Marco shouted.

Harriet leant right forward, pressing her body against Coco's neck. She had to put her trust in the little pony's ability to pick his way through the low-hanging branches. All Harriet could see was Coco's mane and the path beneath his four neat feet. It made a nice change from looking at the back of Tom's head.

Harriet had half hoped that Tom wouldn't be able to join their morning ride, but Donna had quickly come up with a programme to suit them all. Carla's timely arrival meant that she and Marco could ride with the four less experienced riders: Harriet, Tom and two new guests, Phil and Sarah. Donna could take the other new guests, Astrid and Freja, on a more demanding route. Both women were highly competent riders who had competed in dressage events in their native Sweden until the demands of work and family intervened. They would have no trouble enjoying the most challenging rides Bella Vista had to offer.

Donna was so pleased with her plan that Harriet had to feign enthusiasm as best she could. She was dreading spending the whole morning with Tom now that their easy conversation had been replaced by strained small talk and awkward silences. At least that was the way it seemed to Harriet. Tom didn't outwardly seem any different, and that wonderful smile of his was as frequent as ever, but he must have sensed a change in her since their walk back from Bar Beppe. What a relief it was when she and Coco were instructed to take their place behind Tom, with Marco leading the way and Phil and Sarah bringing up the rear. It was an even bigger relief when her mild hangover faded away. She wondered how Candy and Allie were feeling that morning.

Harriet soon forgot her awkwardness as the ride got under way. The sun was strong; Coco's neck was hot and damp with sweat. They rode down into the valley, stopping by a small stream to let the horses take a drink. The scent of wild herbs hung heavy in the air. By the time they returned to the farm Harriet's top was clinging to her back. She could smell the salt on her skin.

Harriet rinsed Coco's metal bit under the outside tap and hung his bridle from the hook in the tack room.

'*Grazie*,' Alfredo said. He took Coco's saddle from her and slid it back on the saddle rack. 'You want a sweet?' Alfredo handed her the battered tin. Harriet popped one in her mouth just to be polite. A sticky pink residue clung to the empty cellophane wrapper.

'Oh, there you are! I saw Tom and Marco come back.' Freja's voice came from the other side of the open doorway.

'Just coming!' Harriet attempted to reply but the words came out in a jumble. Her tongue seemed to be stuck to the roof of her mouth. '*Ciao*, Alfredo,' she tried to say, then seeing his puzzled expression waved goodbye instead.

'Are you okay?' Freja eyed her curiously.

'Alfredo . . . sweets,' Harriet finally managed to get some words out.

'Aah . . . he gave me one of his toffees before we set off this morning. I think part of it's still wedged in a back molar.' Freja laughed. 'Aren't you coming to sit out on the terrace? Marco's gone to sort out some iced tea and orange soda.'

'Sounds great.' Harriet was really quite thirsty. The drink might even help dissolve Alfredo's sweet, though she wasn't counting on it.

'I had such a great time on the ride this morning,' Freja enthused as they walked back towards the house. Her eyes shone brightly and her face had caught a touch of the sun. She looked a decade younger than her thirty-five years.

'So did I. We trotted through the olive grove and crossed over a little stream by a dilapidated old shed. Alfredo told me an old man from the village used to keep a couple of goats in there.'

'Alfredo's such a character, isn't he? Everybody here is so lovely,' Freja said. 'You too, Lupo, sweetheart,' she added as the dog came bounding over.

'Donna and Julia are great hostesses,' Harriet said.

'I was thinking of the other guests. Phil and Sarah seem so nice. And what about that Tom – he's rather handsome.' Freja gave Harriet a meaningful look.

Harriet bent down and gave Lupo a pat so Freja couldn't see her face. 'He's nice,' she said blandly.

'Nice? Is that all? I can tell he really likes you.'

Harriet started to walk a little more briskly; she didn't want to hang around the stable yard talking about Tom. 'No, you're mistaken. I happen to know he's not interested in me at all.'

The orange soda fizzed pleasantly on Harriet's tongue. Her legs had grown used to hours in the saddle but she still appreciated the chance to stretch out on the wicker lounger and look out across the valley. Despite her fear of making a fool of herself again, Harriet could not help feeling disappointed that Tom had gone inside to join Giovanni's writing class, leaving the rest of the riders to exchange stories about their morning.

Donna paused in the doorway of the kitchen. Julia was rapidly chopping her way through a stack of onions, cucumber and juicy, ripe tomatoes. Yesterday's stale bread was already soaking in her yellow ceramic dish, ready to be added to the mixture.

Julia looked up at Donna and smiled. 'I thought we'd have some *panzanella* tonight. I just need to add some basil.' She tore off a few leaves from the plant by the back door.

'Wonderful. And what's that bubbling on the stove?' Donna said. The scent of sage and garlic never failed to make her stomach rumble.

'I thought the smell of my *fagioli alla salvia* would bring you running,' Julia said. She was probably only half joking; she knew the white bean dish was one of Donna's favourites.

'I'm sorry you had to smoke me out. I haven't meant to be so elusive, but I don't seem to have had a spare moment lately,' Donna said. She felt bad for making such a weak excuse. She knew there had been plenty of spare moments. But she had chosen to spend them with Giovanni.

'Nonsense! I've been rushed off my feet with all these extra people staying. I wouldn't have had time to sit down for a chat anyway,' Julia said.

'Fancy a cup of tea? I'll make it for a change.' Donna opened a cupboard door and lifted down the smaller version of Julia's huge brown teapot. It took her a moment or two to create a space for it on the cluttered work surface.

Julia set the tapestry-topped stool in front of one of the armchairs in the corner of the kitchen. 'I'm not going to complain about the chance of putting my feet up,' she said.

Donna pulled the other armchair nearer. She blew on her tea to cool it a little.

'It seems very quiet all of a sudden. Where's everyone gone to?' Julia said.

'Giovanni's class are beavering away in the dining room and the new couple, Sarah and Phil, have gone down to Bar Beppe.'

'What about the Swedish ladies, Freja and Astrid? Didn't they want to go with them?'

'They're out on the terrace doing yoga with Harriet.'

Julia raised her eyebrows. 'I'm not sure I can quite picture that!'

'I think it took Harriet quite by surprise. She just casually mentioned she planned to practise a little yoga and they insisted she teach them a few positions. I suspect Harriet was just trying to get out of a trip down to Bar Beppe. I think she had a couple too many beers last night; she seemed a bit quiet this morning.'

'I think that might have something to do with young Tom. She could barely look at him over breakfast.'

'Really? I wonder why. Those two couldn't keep their eyes off each other when he first arrived,' Donna said.

'Which is why you got Vittoria to pretend there wasn't enough room at Villa Susino for all the writers,' Julia said.

'Guilty as charged! You really can see right through me, can't you,' Donna said. She put her empty mug down on the floor. 'Julia, tell me honestly: Giovanni's trying so hard to put things right; do you think I'd be mad to take him back?'

'You have to do what's right for you,' Julia said.

Donna sighed. If only it was as easy as Julia made it sound.

'Don't look so stressed. No one can see into the future and know for certain how things will work out.'

'I'm okay, really,' Donna said. Julia was right. Maybe it was time to banish the noise in her head and start listening to her heart.

Harriet's yoga practice wasn't turning out quite how she had planned it. She had visualised saluting the sun whilst looking out over the still, green valley, the scent of wild thyme in the air, the peace and silence interrupted only by the sound of birdsong or a *miaow* or hiss from Miu Miu. Some hope!

Her two surprise pupils made an odd couple. Astrid, in a symphony of shades of grey, managed to make jersey jogging bottoms look sophisticated. Curly-haired Freja's outfit had quite the opposite effect. Harriet wondered what had possessed her to pack a Prince William T-shirt and a voluminous pair of zebra-print harem pants – or even purchase them in the first place – but she had to admit that the woman's outfit looked supremely comfortable.

As she coached the two of them through a series of poses she realised she was enjoying sharing her knowledge with her enthusiastic pupils. Both women were managing the routine fairly easily; their balance had been honed by years in the saddle.

'We'll move on to some gentle floorwork,' Harriet said. She spread out the strips of old carpet that Julia had dug out from under the stairs.

'Well done. Are you feeling that stretch in the side plank? It really helps improve your core strength,' Harriet said. 'Let's take a rest in child's pose.'

Freja dropped to the mat with a comical sigh.

'Now we'll move into a downward-facing dog. Lift yourself up on your arms, tuck your head in and don't forget your breathing,' Harriet said.

Freja stretched out her arms, tucked in her head and tilted her well-upholstered rear end skywards. Miu Miu leapt from the edge of a terracotta planter and landed slap, bang in the centre of her zebra-printed bottom. Freja jumped up with a shriek. Miu Miu flew backwards, four feet flailing wildly before landing on the wicker lounger.

'Oh my! Is she okay?' Freja gasped.

'She looks fine,' said Astrid. The cat was washing her paws without a care in the world.

'I guess she mistook my backside for a nice plump cushion,' Freja said.

Harriet, whose shoulders were shaking with laughter, could not contain herself any longer; she let out an uncontrollable snort, which set Astrid off too. Miu Miu walked off as if disgusted by the lot of them.

When Julia walked past a few minutes later, she found the three women sprawled across the terrace heaving with laughter.

'We never tried those positions in my old yoga class,' Julia quipped.

Harriet wiped the tears from her eyes with the back of her hand. 'Just a few stretches and we're done,' she said.

Astrid straightened up. 'I thought I'd go and meet Sarah and Phil at Bar Beppe.'

'I'm tempted but if I don't update my blog now it'll never get done,' said Freja.

'You write a blog?' Harriet was intrigued.

'I used to blog about the dressage competitions we went to. Now I just write about whatever takes my fancy.'

'She's got quite a following,' Astrid said.

'No, no, just a few people. It's really just a bit of fun.' Freja looked bashful.

'What about you, Harriet? Are you on for Bar Beppe?'

'Maybe after dinner. I think I'll sit here and read my book,' Harriet said. She suspected Tom and the rest of the writing class would soon be heading to Beppe's place. She wasn't going to go there, have a few drinks and risk making a fool of herself again.

'No problem. I'll just go and get changed.' Astrid headed off to change into another elegant outfit; she seemed to have a bottomless suitcase.

Harriet curled up on the wicker lounger, glad of some time alone. She had borrowed a novel from the shelf on the landing. It was nice to escape into another world for a while – a world where there was more to life than never-ending spreadsheets and meetings. Maybe she would accept Candy's invitation to join her book-and-a-bottle-of-wine club; they only lived a couple of tube stops apart. She could not help wondering if Tom was a member too. It was hard to stop thinking about him. Half of her was glad that he was safely ensconced in the dining room with the rest of Giovanni's pupils; the other half of her wished they were sitting out on the terrace, side by side, sharing a bottle of wine, just the two of them.

She had never met anyone quite like Tom. He was so easy to get along with, so funny and so handsome too. They had so much in common and so much to talk about. She felt she had known him all her life. It was hard to believe he was the same little Tommy Williams she had barely noticed so long ago. But there was no point wasting her time thinking of what might have been. Tom had been a teenager when he had a crush on Harriet. That was all in the past. Besides, Giovanni and his writing class were going back to Siena tomorrow.

Harriet laid down her book. Perhaps she could go and have a chat with Julia; that would take her mind off Tom. Lupo had other ideas. He was padding across the terrace, one end of his leather lead clamped in his jaws, the other dragging on the ground. He opened his mouth, dropped the lead by Harriet's feet and gave two sharp barks. Harriet ruffled Lupo's silky hair. The dog gave another bark.

'Okay, okay. You win. We'll go for a walk.'

Harriet swung her legs off the lounger and stood up. She was still wearing her pink leggings and her hair was mussed up and sticky after the exertions of exercising in the heat. The dog didn't care what she looked like, but Harriet was going to make sure she did not go anywhere near Bar Beppe. She didn't want to bump into anyone else looking like this.

They made their way down the lane in a stop-start fashion. One moment Harriet was waiting patiently whilst Lupo sniffed around the verge, the next moment the dog was pulling on the leash so fiercely that Harriet was forced to break into a jog.

'Whoa! Lupo, slow down.' Harriet didn't like to yank on the dog's lead, but she wasn't going to be towed past Alfredo's cottage as though she was riding on jet skis. Lupo skidded to a halt. Harriet was impressed; perhaps she had an undiscovered talent for dog training. Then she spotted the half-eaten *panino* that was fast disappearing into Lupo's jaws.

'Drop that!' Harriet shouted as fiercely as she could. Lupo gave a huge gulp and the rest of the sandwich disappeared. He turned his big blue eyes on Harriet. He looked a picture of innocence.

The clock struck five as Harriet led Lupo towards the olive grove. She unclipped the lead and wrapped it around her wrist, allowing Lupo to run in and out of the trees with unabashed delight.

It was the same corner of the grove where she had met Francesco as he cycled towards Bella Vista on that strange and eventful evening. She would never forget that night:

dancing to the Spice Girls; Alfredo's dramatic appearance and Marco riding off into the night to search for Giovanni. That night could so easily have ended in tragedy. Instead it brought Donna and Giovanni back together. It was early days, but she hoped it would work out for them. And just two days later she and Tom had stopped in this very spot, here in the darkness, and for a moment she'd thought she was one step nearer to her own happy ending.

Harriet touched an old tree trunk. What stories these trees could tell. This olive grove had been here for decades, perhaps for hundreds of years. How many past friends and lovers had walked here? What confidences had been exchanged beneath these branches? What relationships had begun – and ended – amongst these silent witnesses?

Lupo began to bark. There was no bicycle coming along the path this time, just a man walking towards them. It was Tom. Giovanni's class must have finished, but why was he walking down into the olive grove instead of straight along the path through the village where the others were sure to be meeting at Bar Beppe?

'Hi, Harriet!' Tom raised a hand in greeting.

'Hi!' She couldn't help smiling despite herself.

'Wow! You really have caught the sun. Your face matches your leggings.'

Sweaty, matted hair, dodgy pink leggings and a sunburnt face. She really must look a sight.

'Just kidding! You're getting really nice and brown. You look really well – must be the healing powers of yoga,' he joked.

'You heard about that then?'

'Heard about it? I saw you.'

'Oh.' The thought of Tom watching her made her feel fuzzy all over.

'It was the funniest thing . . . Giovanni asked us to take a minute or two to think about our reactions to an essay Nigel had written. It was an amazing bit of description, real thought-provoking stuff. I was looking at Giovanni, wondering what was going through *his* mind, when three pairs of feet appeared in the window behind him. For a moment I was completely flummoxed then I remembered how you loved yoga, and I guessed you were with the two Swedish women. Those mad, multicolour toenails had to belong to Freja.

'Giovanni knew I was looking at something behind him but he had no idea what was going on. Of course, when he turned around your feet had all gone. By then I couldn't contain myself; I just burst out laughing. Giovanni gave me the most curious look but Nigel was thrilled. Apparently, I was the only one to appreciate the hidden humour in his essay. I didn't have the heart to put him right.'

'So, it wasn't me you were laughing at . . .'

'The sight of you in your yoga pants has quite a different effect on me.' Tom's eyes flashed with merriment. This time, Harriet's cheeks really did turn as pink as her leggings. She wished he wouldn't tease her like this. She tried and failed to conjure up a quick quip to dispel the awkward moment.

'Shall we walk?' Tom said. He put two fingers in his mouth and whistled. Lupo came bounding up.

'So that's how you get Lupo to come to heel.'

'Pure luck. It used to work with my gran's old pointer.'

'I wish I'd known that when I met Francesco the other night. If I hadn't been chasing after Lupo I could have run after Francesco's bicycle and stopped him from going up to the house. It would have saved a whole lot of trouble.'

'But if Giovanni hadn't ridden off like a madman and fallen off, he would have gone straight back home. We would be having our writing classes in Siena; we would never have come to Bella Vista.'

'That's true. It's been fun having you guys around. And Nigel tells me the countryside has really inspired everyone's creativity.'

'Except mine.' Tom looked serious for a moment.

'Oh?'

'Ever since I've got here, I've found it hard to concentrate.' Tom stopped and ran a hand through his honeybrown hair. Her heart gave a little skip even though she knew nothing would happen between them.

'Look, Harriet . . . I don't really know how to say this but there's something I've got to ask you.'

He was looking at her so intently anyone would think he was going to say something earth-shattering. But she had been here before, just yesterday. What was he going to ask her today? If Alfredo would show him how to clean a bridle? If Julia would share her recipes for *crostini* toppings? The silence between them grew.

'You know we're going back to Siena tomorrow morning, straight after breakfast? Giovanni's okay to drive now, and Marco's going to run the rest of us down there in the van.'

'Yes . . .'

'Giovanni wants us to have our last few classes there. It will give us the chance to look around the city. Explore a bit. Nigel's really keen to see the famous frescoes in the Palazzo Pubblico, and Candy and Allie want to sample the nightlife. Candy says there's only so many evenings she wants to spend in Bar Beppe.'

'And you . . .'

'I could happily spend every night down at Bar Beppe if I got to eat dinner at Bella Vista first.'

'You're really going to miss Julia's cooking.' Harriet smiled. Tom's face lit up like a little boy's whenever Julia placed a new dish in front of him.

'That, and a lot more . . .'

'Siena's beautiful. You're going to have a wonderful time,' Harriet said quickly.

'You went there for a day, but you didn't see everything, did you?'

'No. I ended up walking off the beaten track following a strange man with a folder full of stories!' Harriet laughed.

'I'm really looking forward to exploring the city, but I don't want to wander around with the others.'

Harriet was confused. Tom always seemed so sociable; she thought he got on really well with Candy and Allie, and he and Nigel had bonded despite seeming like chalk and cheese. 'Oh, why not?' she said.

'Because I'd rather be with you. Come to Siena with me . . .'

Harriet didn't reply; she didn't know what to say. Surely it was better to say goodbye after breakfast than drag things out by spending a day in Siena together and promising to stay friends.

Tom looked down at the ground. 'It was a silly idea . . .'

'No, Tom, I . . .' she began.

'So stupid . . .' He turned and walked away, Lupo following at his heels. Then he broke into a jog. Lupo circled around him, looping in and out of the tree trunks.

Harriet had done the right thing. She wasn't going to make a fool of herself the way she had last night when only the darkness of the olive grove had disguised her blushes. But Tom seemed genuinely disappointed. His nervous demeanour; his hesitant speech; the slouched shoulders as he strode away. Could she be wrong after all?

'Tom!' she called. He was getting further away. She started to run. Despite the shade from the trees, her forehead was soon damp with sweat, her slip-on canvas shoes were rubbing on the backs of her heels, her glasses were slipping down her nose. 'Tom!' Still, he didn't turn around. There was only one thing for it: she put two fingers in her mouth and whistled.

Lupo reached her first, jumping up and leaving two smears of mud on the front of her pink leggings. Harriet pushed him away.

'Tom!' Before she had time to think she flung her arms around him.

'I wasn't sure if you were just whistling for Lupo,' he said. 'When I asked you to come to Siena I thought I'd misjudged things . . .'

'You took me by surprise, that's all. The other night in the olive grove . . . I thought you just wanted to be friends.'

'You don't know how much I wanted to kiss you then, but I didn't want you to kiss me back just because you'd had a couple of drinks then regret it the next morning. Anyway, what makes you think I want to be more than friends?'

'That huge grin on your face . . .'

'And the way I've still got my arms around you.'

'That as well. Though I have to say I'm still not a hundred per cent sure.'

'I can think of a good way to show you.' He bent down and tilted her chin towards his. His lips touched hers gently. Then he kissed her as though he had been waiting for that moment for a long, long time.

'Harriet . . . just in case you're wondering. I don't kiss my friends like this,' he murmured.

'I believe you. But perhaps we should do it again – just to be sure.' Harriet brushed her lips against his. This was her magic moment. Who needed fireflies and moonlight?

Chapter Twenty-Three

'Go on. Don't keep everyone waiting,' Harriet said.

She kissed Tom on the cheek. She wished she could kiss him the way they had kissed last night in the olive grove, but Candy and Allie and Nigel had walked up from Villa Susino and were already crammed into the van with all their luggage. Marco blasted the van's horn loudly.

'Come on, Tom. We're all waiting,' he shouted.

'Remember to text and let me know when you get on the train tomorrow,' Tom said.

'Of course, I will!' Harriet said.

'Don't forget about my book club!' Candy shouted through the open window.

'I won't. Send me the date.' Harriet mimed sending a text.

'See you tomorrow!' Tom said. He climbed into the front passenger seat. Harriet waved until the van disappeared down the lane and Lupo gave up chasing after it.

'You're going to miss him too, are you, boy?' The dog put one paw on Harriet's knee and looked up at her with big, sad eyes. 'Sit here whilst I finish my coffee, but you are *not* getting on my lap. You're built like a sheepdog not a chihuahua!'

Harriet drained the last of her coffee and made her way to the stable yard. Today was her last chance to ride Coco. Tomorrow morning she would be catching the train to Siena to spend her final day with Tom. She was as nervous and skittish as a new-born kitten. She couldn't stop thinking of the wonderful time they would have together. She must stop getting carried away. It was only a casual sightseeing trip. But it felt like a lot, lot more.

Carla had Coco tacked up and ready to go so Harriet only needed to check her girth as Marco had taught her and hop into the saddle. This time Donna and Caesar led the ride out through the back gate by the schooling ring, away from the village.

'We'll have a canter when we get level with that row of three trees up ahead,' Donna said. Harriet had guessed as much by the way Coco was jig-jogging and letting out little snorts of excitement.

The horses quickened. Harriet crouched forward in the saddle, taking the weight off Coco's back, as she followed the two Swedish riders. She could hear Phil and Sarah cantering along behind her. She felt a frisson of fear. Coco was only small but he was still a lot stronger than she was. Would she be able to stop?

To Harriet's relief, when Donna made a hand signal to indicate that they should reduce their speed she had no trouble complying; the path's gentle incline naturally slowed the horses' pace as they reached the brow of the hill. The views across the valley were stupendous.

They rode on through the woods to a clearing where Alfredo had parked the van and spread out their picnic on a blue checked cloth surrounded by cheerful mismatched cushions. He produced a small fold-out stool to sit on himself.

'This is just heavenly!' Astrid flopped onto a cushion and gratefully accepted the glass of rosé that Donna handed her.

'We don't produce a lot of rosé in Tuscany, but it's nice for a change. This is from San Gimignano,' said Donna.

'Lovely, but I'd better stick to one glass, I don't want to fall off my horse!'

Harriet smiled. She couldn't imagine Astrid falling off even after downing a whole bottle. She was a natural rider with beautiful posture, and she looked as elegant as always in an apricot silk shirt neatly tucked into belted, ivory jodhpurs. Freja, on the other hand, looked as though she had just rolled out of bed. Her checked shirt was rumpled – a sleeve appeared to have completely missed the iron – and one of her short leather riding boots was fastened with two tatty laces that had been knotted together.

Phil offered around the last of the spinach and onion flan.

'Maybe a small slice,' Sarah said. 'I've never eaten so much in my life. It must be the country air. Or maybe I'm just greedy.' She laughed.

'I couldn't eat another thing.' Freja patted her soft, round belly.

'Neither could I,' Harriet said. She wished she hadn't had second helpings of just about everything else. Poor Coco was going to be carrying a heavier load on the way home.

Carla helped Alfredo load up the van whilst Donna helped everyone saddle up and refasten their horses' girths, which had been loosened whilst they stopped for lunch. The afternoon sun was beating down on Harriet's back as they set off. She was glad of every patch of shade along the route. But the horses walked briskly, knowing that they were heading home. Even Coco did not seem at all tired thanks to his rest under the chestnut trees.

As soon as they were back, Harriet jumped off and led Coco back into his stable. The pony plunged his head straight into the water bucket by the door, took a long draught, shook his head and showered Harriet with droplets of water.

'Ugh! Thanks, pal,' Harriet said. She dug in her pocket and gave the pony a mint. She wiped Coco's slobber off her hands onto her jodhpurs and wondered again how Astrid managed to look so immaculate.

'Good ride?' Marco popped his head over the stable door and rested his broom against the wall.

'Yes, fantastic. How was your journey?' Harriet held Coco's reins in one hand as she slipped the bridle over his head and removed his saddle.

'I couldn't believe how little traffic there was. I must have got to Siena and back in record time. I thought I'd give Alfredo a hand. I guessed he might be a bit behind, what with Carla having gone out on the ride with you. And I thought I'd be safe out here.'

'Safe?' Harriet frowned.

'Yeah . . . I can't seem to go anywhere around here without bumping into another pair of lovebirds.' Marco scowled. 'Luigi's hanging around the kitchen with Julia – he shod a couple of horses straight after breakfast. And last night I caught Mum and Papa kissing on the terrace. Talk about embarrassing! At least there's no chance of catching Alfredo and Carla canoodling in the tack room.'

Harriet couldn't help laughing at his disgusted expression. 'Julia must be putting something in the *ribollita*!'

'Well it's not working for me,' Marco muttered.

'Candy was nice . . .' Harriet ventured.

'Candy is gorgeous, but she's not the girl for me.' Marco picked up the broom again and began to sweep vigorously, stirring up a cloud of dust and stray strands of hay.

'So, who is the girl for you then?' Harriet wasn't sure how much Marco wanted to share; she half expected him to tell her to mind her own business.

'Someone who's never going to be interested in me.'

'Have you told her how you feel?'

Marco shook his head. 'It doesn't matter anyway. She's hundreds of miles away.'

'That's a shame. But you never know who you're going to meet. Just look at me and Tom.'

'I won't meet anyone else like her. Goddesses like Jess don't grow on trees.'

'You like Jess?' Harriet stared at him.

'What man wouldn't? That beautiful, wild red hair; those endless legs – and a great personality too. I've got to face it, Harriet, she's out of my league.'

So, Marco liked Jess. Harriet would never have guessed; he wasn't the easiest person to read. But Jess liking Marco? That was a definite possibility.

'I think she might be keen on you too.'

'No, you're wrong. I just imagined there might be something between us. I tried to stop her leaving but she didn't want to listen. She seemed to hate me all of a sudden. She even accused me of flirting with you.'

'Me! Why would she think that?' Then she remembered Jess standing by the persimmon tree. Harriet couldn't help laughing at the absurdity of it all.

'See, even you think it's funny.' Marco's eyes darkened.

'No, it's not that. I just remembered: Jess was watching us after I almost fell off Coco. She must have put two and two together and made five. I'm sure if you just explained . . .'

'What does it matter.' He sighed. 'She's gone, Harriet. And I don't suppose she'll ever come back.'

Marco picked up the broom and began sweeping even more vigorously than before. Harriet's nose filled with dust. She sneezed twice. She racked her brain for something positive to say but she could only think of corny clichés.

Marco swapped his broom for a long-handled fork and disappeared into Caesar's stable. The conversation was over.

Harriet walked through the back door, humming to herself.

'Someone's happy.' Julia turned to face Harriet and wiped the chestnut flour from her hands onto her striped apron.

'Mmm . . .' Harriet said.

'Something to do with Tom?'

Harriet grinned. 'Yep. How did you guess? I'm going to meet him in Siena tomorrow. Just the two of us. I can't think of a nicer way to spend my last day in Italy but it's a shame I won't get to ride Coco again. I don't suppose Donna will mind as long as I tell her this evening.'

'Oh, I'm certain she won't mind at all.'

'Are you sure there's nothing I can help you with?' Harriet said. She was surprised how much she enjoyed hanging around in the kitchen with Julia. Perhaps she would finally dust off Gran's old cookery book when she got back to London; there were only so many years you could survive on jacket potatoes and toast.

'For once everything is completely under control,' Julia said with a grin. 'Now get back out and soak up that sunshine before it goes.'

'Guess I should go and be sociable. Everyone's bound to be sitting out on the terrace.'

'Oh, you could do one little thing for me. Could you stick these jars in the recycling? Do you know where I mean?' Julia said.

Harriet lifted the rather awkward lid of the recycling bin. The crate for glass smelt like the aftermath of a student party. It was jammed full of empty bottles; she recognised the label of the expensive *Brunello di Montalcino* Giovanni had brought on that eventful night. She wiggled the jars into a space between two empty pots of Marco's favourite chocolate-hazelnut spread.

As she closed the lid something in the adjoining recycling crate caught her eye: a bundle of neatly typed papers. *The Rabbit by Nigel Strathberry*, Harriet read. These must be the stories that Giovanni's class had been working on. She couldn't resist having a peek.

Harriet took the papers and sat cross-legged in a patch of sun by the chicken run where she could read in peace. Miu Miu wandered over to join her and chose the most inconvenient place to sit. Harriet tugged the first sheet of Nigel's story out from under the cat's furry bottom. It would be interesting to see if he really was as talented as Tom and the girls made out.

There was no doubting Nigel's skill. It was incredible how his choice of words could turn a few neat lines of type into a living, breathing, three-dimensional creature. But for all Nigel's talents, Harriet had to stop reading halfway down the first page. The images he used to describe the pet were so unsettling. Harriet's childhood rabbit had been a cute, cuddly, pompom-tailed creature. The rabbit of Nigel's imagination was more like a fluffy Hannibal Lecter. She shivered despite the sunshine.

She hoped Tom had written something more suited to chilling out in the last of the day's sun. She flipped through the papers. *The Garden*. There was no name on this one, but it must have been Candy or Allie's; the notes in the margin were written with a curvy, girlish hand. She put that one aside. *HARRIET – My True Feelings*: this was Tom's. He had written about her – again! How sweet that was. And this time she wasn't just an anonymous childhood memory. This was how he felt right now.

Harriet hesitated. Should she really be reading this? Shouldn't she wait for Tom to tell her how he felt, face to face? But if Tom was happy to share his feelings with Giovanni and the rest of the class surely it was only right that she should read this too. Even so, her hand trembled as she scanned the page.

. . . *peering myopically through greasy lenses* . . . That wasn't what she was expecting. Harriet's stomach tightened as she read on . . . *scrawny midget* . . . *hideous pink leggings* . . . Even her *squeaky voice* – she had never even thought about her voice – grated on him. And the way she smelt . . .

Harriet couldn't read on. She flung down the essay. So, these were Tom's true feelings. What sort of sick joke had he been playing on her? Was his feigned interest in her some sort of revenge for something that happened long ago? Try as she might she could not think of anything she could have said or done to him at school. She barely remembered him. Maybe that was the problem. The outwardly confident, charming Tom must be harbouring an ancient grudge, brooding on some imagined childhood slight, like a gun-toting teenager in a Californian basement. That first night in the olive grove she had made it so obvious she was keen on him. It had been so easy for him to manipulate her feelings, it was laughable.

Harriet rubbed angrily at her eyes. She stormed back to the recycling bin, dropped the essays back in and slammed the lid shut. Good riddance to bad rubbish. It was a pity there wasn't a shredder, or better still, a bonfire to throw them on.

She hesitated, unsure what to do next. She did not want to sit by the chicken run any longer, with only the haughty Miu Miu for company, and she certainly didn't feel like joining the other riders out on the terrace. She could not bear to tell anyone what had happened. She would never mention Tom's betrayal to anyone, not even to Julia – and she was the easiest person in the world to confide in. She still had her pride. How stupid she had been to let Tom ruin her holiday. She shouldn't have got involved with another man. Some people weren't good at relationships. She had to accept she was one of them.

She walked across the stable yard. The stables were now empty though the smell of their occupants lingered in the air. The horses were enjoying a few well-deserved hours in the grass paddocks at the far end of the property. She would see if Alfredo was around; he wouldn't ask her any questions. She could help clean the tack again. Working the waxy yellow saddle soap into the leather bridles would keep her hands occupied whilst her mind was racing.

The door to the tack room was padlocked shut. That was the end of that little plan. Something nudged the back of her leg.

'Lupo!'

The dog rolled onto his back.

'I know what you want!' Harriet rubbed Lupo's hairy stomach. The dog wriggled with evident pleasure. If only human beings could be so easily satisfied. Lupo didn't think about tomorrow; he had already forgotten yesterday. 'I'd swap places with you right now,' Harriet murmured. She wiped away a tear. Lupo's big blue eyes stared up at her.

Marco leant over the stable door and stroked Coco's nose. Coco breathed his minty breath over him. Marco gave him another treat. Ponies were so much less complicated than people. Harriet thought Jess was interested in him, but Harriet had not seen the look on Jess's face as she pushed him away at the train station.

Coco nudged Marco's shoulder.

'Sorry, pal. No more mints.'

Marco entered the house through the boot room. He did not want to walk through the kitchen; he wasn't in the mood for Julia's friendly chat. He tossed his gilet onto the peg rail, which was groaning with discarded clothing. He moved a brown paper package off the narrow bench and sat down to pull off his boots. The package was addressed but not stamped. He would ask Mum if she wanted him to take it to the post office in the morning.

He glanced idly at the address. Birmingham, England. He ran his forefinger under the seal. Jess's sketchbook – she must have left it behind in her haste to depart. He flicked through the pictures of Harriet, Miu Miu and Alfredo until he came to his own portrait. She had drawn it on her first visit. He remembered how her summery top had slid off one shoulder as she leant over her sketchbook. There were a few freckles on the bridge of her nose where she had caught the sun. How pretty she had looked. Why hadn't he told her?

He tucked the sketchbook under his arm and climbed the stairs to his old bedroom. He needed to be alone. He sat cross-legged on the bed and flicked through the rest of the pages. There he was again: another portrait and another. He had not posed for all of these. She must have drawn these from photographs. Hope surged through him. It looked as though she really did like him after all, and if Harriet was right, she had been upset with him over nothing.

The sound of Giovanni's voice floated up from the hall. Marco knew what he had to do. He wasn't going to be like his papa – kept apart from the woman he loved by some stupid misunderstanding and his own foolish pride. His hands were sweaty as he scrolled down his phone to find her number.

Jess answered at once. Marco talked rapidly, afraid of what might happen if Jess spoke before he finished saying everything he needed to say. Eventually, the torrent of words dried up. 'So will you see me again?' he said.

The seconds before she answered felt like an hour.

'I've been trying to say "yes" for the last twenty minutes but you haven't let me get a word in edgeways.' Jess laughed. It was a happy laugh, the sort that you couldn't help catching.

Harriet rested her forearms on the fold-out plastic tray in front of her. The woman in the middle seat ripped open a packet of crinkle crisps and started munching noisily. Harriet turned away. She looked out of the smeared glass window at the pale blue sky. Miles and miles of nothing.

The woman tipped the remnants of the crisps straight from the packet into her open mouth then leant back, hogging both armrests. Harriet shifted in her seat. Yesterday they had ridden all day, stopping only for a picnic on the banks of a stream, and her thighs were still protesting. But it was worth every minute of her subsequent discomfort. The thrill of cantering along a path that ran through a meadow of wildflowers – she had stood up in the stirrups like a jockey! – was unforgettable. It was only once they were walking back through the village, with loose reins so that the horses might stretch their necks, that thoughts of Tom had marred her happy day.

Tom had sent her a dozen texts and there was a string of missed calls on her phone. He had even left a message at the house, with Julia, whilst they were out. Part of her wished she had gone to Siena to confront him about the essay she had found, but she didn't want to give him the satisfaction of knowing she had read his hurtful words.

Meeting up with him in order to be hurt and humiliated all over again would have been a horrible way to spend the last day of her holiday. She was so glad she had gone riding instead. She'd had such a wonderful time with the other riders. It had been sad to say goodbye.

'Please fasten your seat belts.'

The stewardess's voice made Harriet jump. She stole a glance through the window. The English countryside was spread out below them, a patchwork of greens and browns. The plane began to descend.

Tomorrow she would be back at work. She would throw herself into Savita's new project. She would still get in early but she was no longer going to stay late every night. She would go along to Candy's book-and-a-bottle-of-wine club, and catch up with some of the friends she had neglected for so long. She would find somewhere to go horse riding at the weekends. Heck, she might even give those tap-dancing classes a whirl. She would be far too busy to think about Tom.

She took out her phone and deleted his messages. Then she took a deep breath and blocked his number.

Chapter Twenty-Four

Donna flipped over the calendar and hung it back up on the dining room wall. September, already. The autumn was her favourite time of year. The swifts and swallows were on their way to their winter homes but the house martins, pied wagtails and sparrows still charmed her with their song. Soon it would be too cool to sit out on the terrace in the evening though it was still balmy during the day.

She loved the busy summer months when Bella Vista was full of guests. The long, laughter-filled evenings around the dining table; the bright mornings when the riders set off to explore the hills and valleys and returned buzzing with the excitement of new places seen and new friendships forged. But Donna wasn't sad when autumn arrived and the number of visitors inevitably dwindled. She enjoyed having more time to herself to walk or ride in the countryside or to sit in the corner of the kitchen with Julia, cradling big mugs of tea and talking for hours.

Once winter came everything would be harder. The horses would spend more time in their stables: that meant more hay nets to fill; more heavy water buckets to carry across the yard; more laden barrows to push up to the top of the muck heap. Every year Julia and Donna would help Alfredo as much as they could but this time they would take on an extra member of staff to join them once

Carla went back to university. It was no longer fair to expect Alfredo to shoulder all the responsibility for the horses' daily care.

That wasn't going to be the only difference this year. Giovanni was back. He had not officially moved back to Bella Vista, but now he spent almost all his time there, writing at the wooden desk in the tiny upstairs bedroom where Marco had once laboured over his homework.

Nothing could truly make up for the years they had wasted but Giovanni had worked so hard to win her back. On one occasion he had even managed to persuade Daniela to take the day off so that she and Marco could accompany the riders whilst Donna and Giovanni spent the day in Florence revisiting the places where they had first fallen in love.

Now that he was back in her life, Donna found it hard to believe they had ever been apart. He was as generous, fascinating, and exciting as ever. The craziness and spontaneity that thrilled and frustrated her in equal measure were still in evidence, though now the wild gallops and midnight picnics were replaced by quiet rides over to Il Carciofo where they ate lunch in the garden beneath the shade of the pergola. When they got the chance they still talked for hours, the way they had in the beginning. And later when she got undressed, those captivating, caramel eyes lit up as though the years hadn't changed her at all.

Giovanni had been in Siena last night and she had missed him. She checked her watch. He would not be back for a couple of hours and her new guests were not due until the afternoon. She went to the stables and saddled Pinocchio. It was a lovely morning to go for a ride.

★

'I missed you,' Giovanni said.

'You've only been away one night.' Donna finished unlacing her riding boots. She stood up and kissed him.

'Now close your eyes, and no cheating,' Giovanni said. He put one palm over Donna's face and used the other hand to guide her across the hallway. He pushed open the door to the sitting room. A beautiful fragrance filled the air. 'You can look now.'

'Wow! They're gorgeous!' Big blowsy creamy-white roses: she had carried them on her wedding day.

'Our anniversary. You didn't think I'd forgotten, did you?'

'No. But I wasn't expecting this. I only bought you a card.'

'The only present I need is you. How beautiful you are.' He gathered her hair in one hand and held it away from her face. 'More beautiful than ever.'

Donna stepped forward to kiss him. Something crunched under her shoe.

'Wait a moment, I've stood on something.'

Donna moved her foot to reveal a small sliver of white china. 'What is it?' she asked but as she turned the fragment over to reveal a blue and white pattern, she already knew. Her beloved willow-pattern vase had chipped. But it looked like a clean break; Alfredo would probably be able to mend it.

'Aah, yes. I have a small confession to make. When I tipped away the old flower water that vase slipped out of my hands. I thought I'd swept it all up but it looks like I missed a bit.'

'Oh.' Donna's voice sounded very small.

'It was lucky I bought you this lovely new vase from the florist. It looks great, doesn't it.'

Donna looked at Giovanni then back at the roses. The flowers were beautiful but the huge vase holding them couldn't have looked more incongruous. The shiny, chrome cube looked more suited to a law firm's reception desk than the old oak table it was sitting on.

'I'm amazed you were still hanging on to that vase. Didn't we find it in a box of old junk when we first moved in?'

Donna nodded. She had loved that vase – and not just because of its pretty pattern. It held so many memories of those heady days.

'Hey, you're not cross with me, are you?' Giovanni's eyes widened.

'No, not at all. How could I be when you've bought me these beautiful flowers,' she said quickly.

'I was worried there, for a minute.' He gave her a huge grin.

Donna managed a weak smile.

Giovanni wrapped his arms around her. 'We have a lot of guests staying this week, but we shall still celebrate tonight, you and I. After everyone has turned in for the night, we can have a drink together on the terrace, under the stars. And afterwards, we can think of other ways to celebrate. What do you say?'

Donna smiled up at him. 'That sounds wonderful.'

Giovanni was still so romantic after all these years. How lucky she was to have him back in her life. Most men weren't interested in lamps and cushions and jugs and throws. Why would he remember how much that old vase meant to her? To him, it was just a piece of old junk. It was silly to get upset over nothing.

Chapter Twenty-Five

'Is that the phone? Who's ringing at this time of the morning?' Giovanni said.

'I do hope it's not Carla phoning in sick or something. We really can't manage without her this week,' Donna said.

'Why don't you just answer it, Mum? Or shall I?' Marco said.

'No, it's fine, darling. I'll get it. Could you just give Julia a hand to bring in the rest of the breakfast things before all the guests come down?'

Donna picked up the receiver and leant back against the dresser. '*Pronto* . . .! Oh, it's you, Daniela. Is everything okay? Sorry, darling, I can't work out what you're saying; you'll have to slow down.'

'Is she okay?' Marco hissed. He placed the breadboard and a jar of chocolate-hazelnut spread on the table.

Donna shrugged. 'I didn't quite catch that, Daniela. You say Papa's got a virus? But he's fine. He's sitting right here drinking his coffee.'

'Give me the phone, Mum.'

'Okay.' Donna passed the handset to Marco. She hoped Daniela was all right; it was most unlike her quiet, sensible daughter to ring this early, talking nineteen to the dozen, and not making any sense.

'Are you joking? That's incredible! I'll tell him straight away . . . Okay, don't be late for work. *Ciao!*' Marco placed the phone back in its cradle and turned towards Donna and Giovanni, his eyes shining.

'What is it?' Donna demanded.

'Papa's gone viral.'

'I've gone what?' Giovanni finally looked up from yesterday's newspaper. 'Has Julia put on any more coffee?'

'More coffee? How can you ask at a time like this?' Marco gestured wildly.

'Seven thirty in the morning. What could be so important it keeps a man from his coffee.' Giovanni scowled.

'Would you mind checking on the coffee and bringing in that bowl of cherries if we've still got some left?' said Donna.

'What is it with you two? Don't you understand? Papa's gone viral. It's your new book, Papa, it's trending all over Twitter!' Marco shouted.

Julia appeared in the doorway holding the coffee pot and the huge brown teapot. 'Have you heard the news?'

'Apparently I'm trending, whatever they mean by that,' Giovanni said. He held out his coffee cup.

'It's Addolorata Di Marzio,' Julia said. She poured some coffee into Giovanni's cup.

'Addolorata? Now where do I know that name from?' Donna frowned.

'She was on that reality show, the girl with the big hair. There was some talk about her hitting the big time, playing Ingrid Bergman's role in a remake of *Casablanca*. Then she got embroiled in a punch-up on live TV and checked into rehab. "Exhaustion", her agent said. Apparently, someone sent her a copy of Papa's book and it changed her life. The story "opened her eyes about the essential truths of human nature" apparently.'

'So that's what all this fuss is about? Some C-list celebrity with a drug problem is talking about my book? It's not exactly the sort of publicity I'm looking for.' Giovanni stirred a teaspoon of sugar into his coffee and took a generous swig.

'It's really good news, Papa. Addolorata has got thousands of followers. This could be the start of something big. You could be world-famous.'

'Sure, Marco. When donkeys fly.' Giovanni threw back his head and drained the last of his coffee. 'Have a good ride. I'm going for a stroll before I start writing. I'd better get out of here before all the guests come downstairs. I don't want to be mobbed for my autograph.' He gave a sharp little laugh.

'Could you drop a half-dozen eggs round at Bianca's if you're going that way? I did ask Carla to take some down for her, but you know what young people are like for forgetting.'

'No problem. I'd be delighted.' Giovanni bent his head and kissed Donna's cheek.

'Come, sit. Don't mind little Pif.' Bianca shooed the cat off her front bench to make way for Giovanni.

'You're looking well, Bianca.' Giovanni plucked some cat hair off a knitted cushion and made himself comfortable; he knew he wouldn't get away for quite some time.

'Carla's got me wearing lipstick again. At my age! I must look like a vain old woman.' Bianca chuckled. Her eyes crinkled in her deeply wrinkled face.

'You don't look a day over seventy.'

'Enough of your nonsense. Now tell me, how is the famous author?'

'Famous? I don't think so, Bianca.'

'Did I not read that Bella Pellegrino was photographed with your book just yesterday.'

'Bella Pellegrino?'

'Come now, you must know who I mean. The girl who has just launched her own fashion line. She was caught up in that scandalous love triangle with the two players from Inter Milan.'

'How on earth do you know about these people, Bianca?' Giovanni tutted.

'I read it on my iPad. There's quite a good signal behind my cherry tree. Just because I'm over eighty doesn't mean I get my news by carrier pigeon you know. Are you sure you're okay, Giovanni? You're looking a bit peaky. Why don't you go in and put some coffee on? You know where everything is. That kitchen tap is working a lot better since you fixed it for me.'

'It was nothing,' Giovanni said. He waited until he was in the kitchen before he rubbed his sore wrist.

He scooped several heaped spoonfuls of coffee into the stove-top pot; Bianca liked her espresso even stronger than he did. He brewed up a couple of cups and settled down next to her on the front bench.

Giovanni leant back with the sun on his face as Bianca chatted away. By the time he made his excuses and left he was well versed in all the latest goings-on in the village, not to mention Bella Pellegrino's exotic love life. He was looking forward to a quiet half-hour down at Bar Beppe.

'Hey! Look who it is. Where are the paparazzi?' Beppe slapped Giovanni on the shoulder.

'Not you too, Beppe!'

'You should be pleased, my friend. Take a seat – sun or shade? Now what can I get you?'

'Maybe a small beer.' It was a bit early, but he could not face another coffee. He was still buzzing from Bianca's fearsome brew.

'Here you go. Nice and cold.' Beppe put the beer and a glass down on the small aluminium table.

'Thanks,' Giovanni said.

'Everything okay up at the house? Donna and Julia are well?'

'Yes, both fine. The riding centre is doing very well right now but for me, ugh, there are just too many people. There are so many guests and when Marco visits, I have to wait for him to get up before I can get into his old room to write. Though of course, it's great to see him.'

'Family is the most important thing,' Beppe said. He picked up a cloth and began wiping down the tabletops.

'That's something I had almost forgotten,' Giovanni said.

'So why aren't you happy?'

'All these years I have written my books, I have longed for a big success and now . . .'

'This is not what you want?' Beppe frowned.

'These so-called celebrities, I suppose it is nice they are parading around with my new book, but I am a serious writer, Beppe.'

'Wait right here.' Beppe raised a finger. He disappeared into the back of the bar.

Giovanni poured his beer.

'This serious enough for you?' Beppe spread today's *La Nazione* across the table.

'Looks a bit like the finance minister.' Giovanni reached into his jacket pocket and took out his glasses case. 'That's better. Yes, it is him.'

'Read it!' Beppe said.

'*The opposition accused the finance minister of bringing the government into disrepute when he was caught reading a novel on his mobile phone during a crucial parliamentary debate on taxation. The minister apologised but said Giovanni Ginistrelli's book was "impossible to put down".*'

Giovanni flung down the newspaper. 'This is incredible!'

'There's more.' Beppe said. '*It is rumoured that a certain ex-president of the United States has also been devouring this "book of the moment" whilst relaxing at his luxury rented villa in Tuscany.* Giovanni, I think you've finally cracked it.'

'I can hardly believe it!' Giovanni was smiling so widely his mouth actually hurt. 'Beppe, have you got any more of that favourite wine of mine out the back?'

'I'm certain I can find a bottle somewhere.'

'A bottle? You'd better track down a couple of cases. I'm throwing a party here tonight. The drinks are on me and the whole village is invited.'

Chapter Twenty-Six

Donna looked out of the kitchen window. Giovanni was standing stock-still, staring at the chicken run with apparent fascination. It seemed a strange place to find literary inspiration.

'What on earth do you think he's doing?'

'No idea,' Julia said. She put a shiny red pepper on her olive-wood board and began chopping.

'Wonderful morning!' Giovanni stepped into the kitchen. He yanked open a drawer by the side of the sink and started scrabbling around. Corkscrews, scissors, the old kitchen timer that had been waiting years to be mended, an unravelling ball of string and a bunch of curly-edged instruction booklets were soon piled up on the draining board.

Julia stopped chopping. 'What are you looking for?'

'Ah! Here it is.' He held up a metal tape measure. 'May I borrow Donna for a few minutes? Darling, would you come outside?'

'Of course.' Donna followed him.

'If you could just stand still here and hold the end of the tape.'

'You're measuring the chicken run?' Donna could hear the incredulity in her voice.

'We need to measure out this whole area. This tape's not long enough but if I make marks like this, I can add up the measurements.' He scratched on the ground with the toe of his new brown suede loafer.

Donna moved around the back of the house, standing here and there as Giovanni instructed. Giovanni narrowed his eyes, peering at the measuring tape.

'Should have brought my reading glasses out with me. Can you see this number?'

Donna let go of her end of the tape and went over to peer at the tiny figures. She could only just make them out. At this rate she would be needing reading glasses herself. 'Two hundred and twenty centimetres I think.'

'All done!' Giovanni was beaming. His golden eyes were sparkling. It was the most animated Donna had seen him in weeks.

'Now, are you going to tell me what this is all about?' Donna said.

'This morning I heard from my agent. Those crazy rumours were true. That American actor – whatshisname, multi-millionaire, four wives, lots of plastic surgery . . . it's no use, the name's completely gone out of my head . . .'

'Never mind his name. What's happened?'

'He's bought the film rights to my last book – that's what's happened. A million dollars. Man must be stark-raving mad.'

'A million dollars?' Donna echoed. It was marvellous news, but her stomach clenched.

'More than enough to upgrade this place.'

'The bedrooms could do with some new curtains,' Donna said. Her fingers tightened around the tape measure.

'Curtains? No, no. This will be a total transformation. Look at the wasted space out here. We can build some extra accommodation. Three luxury rooms with their own private decking. Or perhaps one large suite, with

huge floor-to-ceiling windows. Can't you just imagine it?'
Giovanni made a sweeping gesture.

Donna could imagine it all too well. What she couldn't
imagine was people like Jess or Freja wanting to stay in a
contemporary glass box. She looked at the hens pecking
at their grain, Lupo stretched out by the back doorstep.
How restful it felt. Apart from a lick of paint on the stable
doors she wouldn't change a thing.

Giovanni was smiling at her.

'What about the chickens?' she said, at last.

'Chickens? Pff! Once we've done this place up, our
guests aren't going to be the sort of people who'll want to
look at chickens! I thought we could construct a pergola
in that corner over there with climbing roses. It would be
the perfect place for making vows.'

'What do you mean?'

'It's time you and I renewed our wedding vows, don't
you think?'

Donna looked at him, dumbfounded. She had only just
accepted him back into her life and he was talking about
wedding vows. It was far too early for that.

Giovanni did not seem to notice her silence. He strode
off, whistling as he went.

Chapter Twenty-Seven

Donna pushed open the kitchen door. 'Morning!'

'You're up early,' Julia said.

'Couldn't sleep.' Donna glanced at the kitchen clock. It wasn't even seven. 'However early I'm up you always beat me to it.'

'I like this time of the day. It's so peaceful. I don't even switch the radio on, then I can hear the birds singing. Listen . . .'

'I think you've spoken too soon,' Donna said.

'What a racket! That will be Caesar wanting his breakfast. Alfredo must be late this morning.'

'That's not like him. I hope he's okay,' Donna said.

A flicker of alarm crossed Julia's features. 'When he didn't want to stay for supper last night, I tried to send him home with a dish of *pappa al pomodoro*. He said he'd pick it up on his way out but when I was tidying up the kitchen last night, I noticed the dish was still sitting on the side. I popped it in the fridge; I thought it would do for his lunch today.'

'I didn't notice him leave yesterday. Oh, God, Julia. You don't think . . .' Donna was enveloped by a cold feeling of dread.

'Shall I go and see?'

'No, you stay here. We don't want the guests to miss their breakfast. I'll check the yard but I expect Alfredo's just at home, sound asleep. He looked a bit tired yesterday, though he said he was fine when I asked him.'

'If he hasn't shown up by the time Carla gets here we'll go down the lane and knock on his front door,' Julia said.

'Yes. We'll go together.'

Donna walked briskly through the stable yard, resisting the temptation to break into a run. The door to the tack room was ajar. The padlock hanging uselessly. Donna's heart was racing. She yanked the door back and kicked the broken brick into place to secure it. The familiar scent of leather and saddle soap hung in the air.

Her eyes took a second to adjust to the dim light. Thank heavens! There was Alfredo in his usual chair, a pile of tack and the open tub of saddle soap beside him. A light breeze from the open door rustled the empty sweet wrappers scattered across the table. He must have arrived early and nodded off.

'Alfredo!' Donna called softly, but he did not stir.

Now she noticed that his eyes were open.

'Alfredo!' she repeated more loudly. The tremble in her voice seemed to fill the room. Still he did not move.

She stepped towards him. Slowly she reached out and shook him gently by the shoulders. She touched his cool cheek.

The loud sob seemed to come from someone else but there was no one else there, just her and Alfredo. Her hands began to shake.

'Alfredo. No . . . no. Please no.'

She sunk to her knees by Alfredo's side. She put her head in her hands. She couldn't understand why her palms felt wet. Then she touched her own cheeks and realised they were damp with tears.

Shaking, she clambered to her feet. She felt his pulse. She already knew there was nothing to feel. Remembering what she had seen on an old television show, she rooted around in the desk drawer and pulled out his magnifying glass. She held the mirrored side in front of his face but no breath clouded the glass. He was gone.

She gently closed his eyelids and raised his chin so his mouth was no longer hanging open. Now he looked as though he was sleeping, dreaming a peaceful, happy dream.

Somehow, Donna managed to hold it together through the church service. She even managed to stand at the graveside, dry-eyed, whilst Alfredo's coffin was lowered into the ground. The funeral had been uplifting, a celebration of his life and the speeches had demonstrated that many of the villagers felt Alfredo's loss as keenly as she did.

Afterwards, Bar Beppe was packed out with mourners. Donna moved from person to person in a daze, accepting condolences and listening to people's memories. It could not be real. Yet it was.

'Don't be sad, Donna. Alfredo will be with his beloved Benedetta now,' Bianca said.

'Thank you,' Donna said. This wasn't the first time she wished she shared her neighbour's deep faith. She hoped Bianca was right, but it was hard to imagine Alfredo floating on a heavenly cloud with Benedetta when she still expected to see him carrying the water buckets through the yard each morning.

'It's time to go, Mum.' Daniela slipped her arm through Donna's.

'Where's Marco?' Donna glanced around.

'He's out with Papa, having a word with the priest.'

'Thank you again for everything, Beppe,' Donna said.

'I am just glad that it all went well. As well as can be expected in the circumstances.' Beppe touched Donna on the shoulder, his eyes full of concern. He began to clear away the empty plates as the last stragglers drifted away. Donna let Daniela lead her away from the wake and take her back home.

Julia already had the kettle on.

'Do you remember that night when Giovanni galloped off and Alfredo drank that cup of tea?' Donna's voice cracked.

'His face was such a picture,' Daniela said. She laughed then flushed bright pink.

'It's not wrong to laugh,' Julia said gently. 'Alfredo would want us to remember the good times.'

Marco took a mug of tea from Julia and settled himself next to Donna on the sofa.

'He had a good life, Mum. He loved it here and we're never going to forget him.'

Chapter Twenty-Eight

'Flowers every week. I'm so lucky,' Donna said. She did not admit that she had seen enough flowers at Alfredo's funeral to last her a lifetime.

Giovanni tweaked a stem of hydrangea. 'I think these need a woman's touch. I am not so good at arranging these things.'

'Perhaps if we move these to the front and space out the foliage.' Donna stood back. The floral display was stunning, but the modern metal vase still jarred her senses. The flowers would look so much prettier in the old willow-pattern vase that Giovanni had broken.

'That's much better. Perhaps you should have been a florist. But something is still not right.' Giovanni frowned. 'Aah, now I know what is wrong. It's not the flowers, it's that vase. It's been bugging me ever since I bought it for you. It doesn't look right sitting on that old table.'

'That vase is very modern,' Donna said. She kept her tone light; she did not want to sound critical. 'This table is more of a farmhouse-style. It would look better with something more rustic: a glazed earthenware pot or one of those hand-painted styles they sell in Siena.'

'Then we must put that right. Now I've had this windfall we can get you a brand-new table. It's high time we got rid of that old one.'

'I remember the day we brought that home.' Donna's

voice sounded very quiet, but Giovanni didn't seem to notice.

'How could I forget? I thought we would never get it through the door. We had to pull and push like mad, didn't we? I can still see you now, bright red in the face, your hair all mussed up.' Giovanni laughed.

So, he did remember. She reached up and kissed him. His cheek was rough. He hadn't shaved that morning, but a hint of stubble suited him. How had she ended up with someone so attractive? Why did she care about an old table when the man she loved had come back?

'And I've brought you this as well. What do you think?' Giovanni thrust a thick brochure into Donna's hand.

Donna flipped it open, the pages were super-glossy and smelt of some unidentified chemical. Giovanni had turned down the corner of a page to mark his place. She stared at the photograph and diagrams on the double-page spread.

'A conservatory?' she said.

'More than that. A complete extension. Come here and let me show you what I mean.'

Giovanni led her out onto the terrace, put his hands on her shoulders and turned her around to face towards the house.

'Imagine knocking down this part of the outside wall and extending onto the terrace. We could have a wonderful big dining room with huge glass sliding doors leading out to more outside seating out here.'

'But why would we need that? What would we do with the old dining room? We could turn it into more bedrooms, I suppose, but unless we get a lot more horses in we're never going to need those, especially if we build those new rooms on the back that you suggested,' Donna said.

'Not everyone who stays here needs to be a rider. Once this first draft of mine is finished I'm planning to offer some more writing courses. I won't even have to advertise; Silvia says she's inundated with enquiries. It seems daft for me to trek back into Siena to teach; I may as well move the whole operation here. I could turn the old dining room into a study space. My pupils would love it. Remember when my writing group came here? They said they'd never been so inspired. Imagine the wonderful conversations we'll have over dinner. Of course, Julia might need some extra help . . .'

Donna stared at her husband. His words were rushing out in a torrent, his gestures even more flamboyant than usual; his golden eyes were sparkling. Why was he so obsessed with changing things? She couldn't deny the place could benefit from a little money being spent on it. It would be nice to refresh some of the tired decor, maybe make some small upgrades to the bathrooms; the pink suite in the downstairs cloakroom had been there so long it was threatening to come back into fashion. She could even go along with building a couple of extra bedrooms onto the back of the house providing the chickens could be rehoused by the paddocks. But this was a step too far. No, a thousand steps too far. And it wasn't just the thought of the building work that was making her heart sink.

'I know it's a lot to take in. Why don't you relax out here with a nice cup of tea and take a good look through the pictures? You might like another design better than the one I've picked out.' Giovanni smiled at her.

Donna suddenly needed to get away. 'I was thinking of walking down to Villa Susino to visit Vittoria,' she said.

'Wonderful idea. Go and enjoy yourself. I'm going to try and write a few words before lunch.' Giovanni dropped a kiss on her forehead.

★

Donna knocked on the door of Villa Susino.

'It's so good to see you!' Vittoria greeted her with a hug and led her through to the kitchen. The smell of baking bread wafted from the old iron range. Vittoria moved a pile of bank statements and bills out of the way and placed the coffee pot on the kitchen table.

'I'm not interrupting you, am I?' Donna said.

'No, of course not. I have been meaning to ask you over for ages, but you know . . .' Vittoria waved a hand in the direction of her sturdy oak dresser where the pile of paper-work was now perched precariously on a mountain of ironing.

'We have some news,' Vincenzo, Vittoria's husband, said.

'Some wonderful news. Our daughter is expecting at last.' Vittoria held out a creased sheet of paper with a blurry black and white image. It had clearly been folded and unfolded numerous times.

'Is that what I think it is?' Donna said.

Vittoria's smile lit up her whole face. 'Twins. We are so excited!'

Vincenzo nodded. He was a man of few words but his shy smile said everything. 'I will leave you ladies to chat. I promised to meet Old Dante down at Bar Beppe for a game of cards.' He sidled out the door.

Vittoria gestured to one of the kitchen chairs. 'Please, do sit down.'

'I am so pleased for you,' Donna said.

'We thought we'd never get the chance to be grand-parents. But now, after all these years our prayers are answered. Two babies at once.' Vittoria dabbed her eyes with an embroidered cotton handkerchief.

'When did you find out?' Donna asked.

'Two weeks ago. I have been longing to say something but it seemed wrong to share our good news so soon after your loss.'

Donna nodded. She blinked away a tear. Time healed, she knew that, but right now everything still felt terribly raw. 'I'm so happy for you both. I really am.'

'I can hardly wait. But . . .'

'Your daughter, she is okay, isn't she?' Donna had a strong feeling that Vittoria was holding something back.

'Yes, she is very well and the twins are perfect. But still it's a worrying time. Her husband lost his job at the factory in Turin last month. He has excellent references but he is finding it hard to secure something suitable. He is having to stack shelves at the local *supermercato*.'

'That must be hard.'

'It is, so Vincenzo and I have made a decision. We are putting Villa Susino on the market and moving to Turin. If we pool our resources and all pull together things will work out. And of course we will be able to see our new grandchildren every day and that will be a blessing.'

'You're moving away for good?' Donna said. Vittoria and Vincenzo were her oldest friends in the village. She would miss them so much.

'We will miss it here but in the end family is what matters most.'

Donna nodded and smiled as Vittoria expanded on their plans. There was no point letting Vittoria see how upset she felt. It couldn't have been an easy decision for her friend, despite the brave face she was putting on.

'I wish you all the luck in the world,' Donna said. She stood on the doorstep, hugging Vittoria tight. She wanted to melt into her friend's soft, motherly body; she smelt so comforting, like vanilla *biscotti*.

Donna's footsteps slowed as she walked back through the village. It was a beautiful September day but the weather didn't matter. Even the sight of a pied wagtail dancing daintily on the roof of Bianca's house failed to lift her spirits.

She trudged back up the lane and flopped on the wicker lounger on the terrace. There was a hole in the wicker that needed mending, the sort of job that Alfredo would have done. Now Alfredo, her rock and confidant, was gone. Daniela and Marco were busy leading their own lives in Siena and Vittoria and Vincenzo were moving away. Giovanni was devising plans to transform Bella Vista into a place she would not recognise. She felt the gulf opening up between them.

Lupo put his paw up on the edge of the lounger. He seemed to sense something was wrong. Donna stroked the fluffy tuft of hair under the dog's chin.

'Oh, Lupo!' Donna murmured.

The dog rested his head on Donna's thigh. Donna stretched out and stared up at the sky. She had a hundred and one things to do but all she wanted to do was lie here and do nothing.

Chapter Twenty-Nine

'You'd better shut down now, or you'll be late,' Savita said. She had a horrible habit of popping up out of nowhere.

'I really can't make yoga tonight. I still haven't finished this spreadsheet,' Harriet said.

'I thought you'd stopped working late.' Savita tutted.

'I have, but you said if I didn't get this presentation finalised you were going to kill me.'

'True enough, but I've every confidence you'll be in early tomorrow.'

'Of course.' Harriet's hand hovered over the mouse.

'Come on, Harriet. You know I never take no for an answer.'

Harriet sighed. She closed down the spreadsheet and reached into her bottom desk drawer for her leggings. She had left on time every other day this week but there was never any point trying to argue with her boss. Savita's favourite motto was *there's no such thing as can't*. She deployed it even more often than *work-life balance*.

'Hurry up!' Savita rapped her long, painted nails on the edge of Harriet's desk. They were iridescent purple this week.

'Oh, I haven't got my kit.' Despite her protestations, Harriet had been looking forward to tonight's class.

Savita held up her shiny, white sports bag. 'Lucky I have a spare set, then.' Of course she did.

Harriet's screen went dark. 'Thanks. I'll nip to the loo and get changed.'

Savita handed her a neatly folded, ironed T-shirt and hoody. They smelt of fabric conditioner. 'And of course, you'll need these . . .'

'Zebra-print leggings?'

'Cool, aren't they.' Savita grinned.

Harriet suppressed a giggle. At least she wouldn't have to worry about a cat landing on her bottom whilst she was doing the downward-facing dog in the boardroom. She'd had such a wonderful time at Bella Vista until she'd found out the truth about Tom. She was going to put him out of her mind, once and for all. She couldn't let him spoil those happy memories.

How cosy the dining room felt tonight with the lamps glowing softly and the shutters closed tight.

The table was laden and the local red wine was flowing. Tonight's guests were a couple from Rome stopping off for three days in the countryside before they celebrated their wedding anniversary in Florence, as well as three women from Denmark.

Giovanni wasn't there tonight. He had excused himself to go down to Bar Beppe where Old Dante had arranged a game of *briscola*, which would last into the small hours. Donna was shocked to realise how much more relaxed she was now that Giovanni was out of the house.

Julia was dishing up second portions of *coniglio con peperoni* from the huge, metal cooking pot. So what if a little sauce splashed on the checked table cloth or Lupo lay across someone's shoes hoping for some scraps to fall to the floor. This was the Bella Vista Donna loved, and her guests loved it too. Look at the wife from Rome: on her first morning she had appeared at breakfast with coiffed hair and vermilion lipstick. Now she was sitting down for supper in tracksuit bottoms and a giant pair of pink, furry slippers, chatting with the Danish ladies about their ride through the hills.

All this would change if Donna went along with Giovanni's plans. And not for the better. Donna didn't want to turn this cosy room into a classroom and take her meals in a trendy glass-fronted box. She didn't want to step carefully around designer furniture with spindly legs, afraid to put down a mug. And much as she loved books, she didn't want her guests to feel alienated by the intense discussions of modern literature or, heaven forbid, obscure poetry that some of Giovanni's pupils loved to indulge in. She wanted to sit down to dinner with a group of guests brought together by their common love of horses, bonding over their shared experiences and looking forward to what tomorrow's ride would bring. People who arrived as strangers and left as friends.

Maybe she was being selfish, but Bella Vista was so much more than just a house and a business. She needed to share it with people who loved it like she did, just the way it was. She loved Giovanni but she could not let him threaten all she held dear. She and Giovanni no longer wanted the same things. Maybe they were just too different to make it work.

Donna waved as the Danish ladies drove away in their little green hire car. They'd wanted to set off early, so Julia had packaged up some *cornetti* and yogurts in lieu of breakfast. This morning Donna would lead the Roman couple on their final ride. She would probably take them through the chestnut woods. It might be the last chance she had to ride that way this year. Once the weather turned, the carpet of fallen leaves would be too slippery and the horses risked pulling off a shoe in the boggy ground.

Bookings over the next week were sparse but Donna didn't mind. It would give her time to catch up on the million and one practical tasks that always needed doing. If she had a proper sort-out, she was bound to come across Jess's sketchbook. She had wrapped it up and left it in the boot room after Jess had gone, but by the time she had got round to taking it down to the post office it had disappeared.

She would even force herself to tidy up the tack room and go through Alfredo's things. Carla had offered to do it herself one weekend and although Donna was sorely tempted to let the young girl carry out the unenviable task, she knew it wouldn't be fair on her. And perhaps tackling the task herself would help bring her some sense of closure.

The aroma of Julia's freshly baked *cornetti* was wafting into the hallway. Donna slipped out via the boot room to enjoy a few moments alone before breakfast. Lupo was in his usual spot toying with a rubber bone, Miu Miu was washing herself by the chicken run and the new groom was heading for Caesar's stable, a bulging hay net hoisted over each shoulder. So far, so familiar.

What Donna didn't expect to see was Giovanni up and about, strolling towards her, whistling the tune of 'Volare'. She double-checked her watch. He had never been a morning person. If she didn't know better she might think he had come straight from Beppe's card game – except for the scruffy old clothes he was wearing. How dishevelled he looked; he certainly wouldn't have gone down the village in that old T-shirt. The logo across the front advertised a local feed merchant that had gone out of business more than a decade ago. It had ridden up, exposing an inch of brown midriff.

As he got nearer, she realised he was covered in a fine layer of dust. There was a great smudge of dirt across one cheek. She reached out and picked something out of his hair. It was soft and grey and crumbled in her fingers: an old cobweb.

Giovanni pushed his unruly curls away from his face and flicked away a strand of hay.

'What on earth . . .' she said.

'I decided to clear out the tack room. It's about time, don't you think?'

'I can't believe it was so dirty,' Donna said. She must have been going in and out of there in a daze not to notice. Alfredo would be horrified. He always kept things clean and tidy.

'It is – up on that shelf where the old jute rugs are.' He smiled ruefully.

'You climbed up there?'

'Yes, I borrowed an extra-long ladder from Beppe last night. It seemed a good idea after a few drinks. It looks much better in there. Be prepared to be amazed,' he joked.

Donna followed Giovanni into the tack room. It did look brighter and cleaner than it had done for a long time. She couldn't blame the new groom; he had been working flat out to cope without Alfredo. Now everything was neat and tidy, though Caesar's old saddle was still lying on top of the chest.

'You didn't find a new place for Caesar's old saddle?' Donna said.

'Luigi is going to pick it up and take it to a friend of his to mend.'

'You have been organised.'

'Yep. I even cleaned out Alfredo's old desk.'

'Oh, where did you put his things?'

Giovanni kicked the base of a black plastic sack. 'There was nothing worth keeping so I chucked it all in there.'

Donna felt a sudden need to sit down. She put her hand on the back of Alfredo's chair to steady herself. She stared at Giovanni.

'Those drawers needed a good scrub.' He spread out his hands. The nails were black with grime. 'That top drawer was the worst. There was a great blob of something sticky stuck in it. I had to prise it off with an old hoof pick. I dread to think what it was.'

'Toffee,' Donna whispered.

'I bet you're glad I've got it all done. I'd better go and get washed and changed before breakfast. Shall we go in? Don't worry about the rubbish. I'll put that bag out for the bin men tomorrow.'

'No, you go. I've got a few bits to do,' Donna said quickly.

Giovanni touched her cheek and bent to kiss her. The moment he was gone she wiped her mouth with the back of her hand.

Donna pulled open Alfredo's desk drawer. It was dark and empty. The battered old tin of sweets was gone, the last lingering scent of toffees and strawberry bonbons obliterated by the harsh smell of cleaning products.

She shut the tack room door and walked round to the terrace. She stood there for a while looking out over the valley. The seasons were still changing; the world was still turning. She wished, once more, that she shared Bianca's deep faith. If only she could believe that Alfredo was grooming a horse's flanks somewhere with his dear Benedetta by his side. That would surely compensate for the grief she felt. But faith couldn't be magicked up on demand. She needed a sign.

A generous display of orange roses greeted her as she entered the hall. Giovanni's modern steel vase now stood on a glass-topped hexagonal brass table that he had bought the week before. Donna had already banged her leg on it twice.

The flowers no longer thrilled her. These days they seemed more like a habit than a romantic gesture. She considered asking Giovanni to cancel his standing order at the florist, but the weekly bouquets were such good quality that she passed them on to Bianca once the next delivery arrived. Bianca was delighted, so Donna said nothing and the weekly flowers continued unabated.

Giovanni did not seem to understand that candlelit meals and rose petals scattered across the bed meant nothing if he did not appreciate the places she loved and the people she loved, like dear Alfredo. Had they always been so different? Had she been blinded by his flamboyance, his intellect, his charm – and those mesmerising caramel eyes? Had she ever really known him at all?

Julia walked past Donna, carrying a laden tray. 'Breakfast!' she called.

Donna inhaled through her nose and breathed out through her mouth slowly, three times. She had to put on a happy face for her guests.

As she crossed the hall, she saw something caught in the fringing on the Persian rug, something sparkling in a shaft of autumn sunlight. She bent down and picked it up. She held the small rectangle of crumpled cellophane between her fingers. As she smoothed it with her thumb a strong artificial strawberry scent hit her nostrils. Tears filled her eyes. It was the sweetest thing she had ever smelt.

Chapter Thirty

Donna's hands were clammy; her throat was dry. She felt as though she was about to be sick. Asking Giovanni to leave was the hardest thing she would ever do. Despite all his faults, she could not deny she still loved him. She would never stop loving him. But she had to accept she had been in love with a dream: *The handsome prince returns, and they live Happily Ever After.*

Giovanni wasn't a fairy-tale prince though he was as good-looking as any storybook hero. Her stomach still lurched with excitement when he entered the room. And he only had to undo one button on her shirt – or his – to make her quiver with lust. But she couldn't build a life based on physical attraction, not after she had seen the real Giovanni. His impulsiveness now seemed like thoughtlessness. His confidence now looked like arrogance. What right did he have to try to change Bella Vista with his grand schemes and plans? Many of their guests returned year after year. She knew all their quirks and foibles; how could he begin to know what drew them back time after time?

Worst of all, she could not forget the cruel way Giovanni had thrown Alfredo's belongings into an old bin bag, ready to be tossed away like a barrow-full of soiled straw destined for the muck heap.

As soon as the words were out of her mouth, Donna longed to take them back. She had been prepared for

Giovanni to rant and rave or to beg her to change her mind. But he just stood and stared at her as if she were speaking a different language. Then he turned and walked up the stairs. She stood rooted in the hallway, listening to the sounds of drawers and cupboards being opened and closed.

He dragged two bags down the stairs behind him. He stopped in the middle of the Persian rug and looked at her. 'Just tell me: why?'

She tried to explain but the words did not make sense even to her own ears. He did not wait for her to finish. He picked up his bags and brushed past her. The car door slammed. Giovanni drove away. He did not look back.

Donna sank down onto the bottom step of the stairs, too numb to cry. The romantic roses in the corner of the hallway seemed to mock her. The flowers were barely three days old, but Donna knew that if she did not take them down to Bianca's straight away, she would not have the strength to deal with them. She couldn't face watching them wilting on the hexagonal glass-topped table until the petals curled and the water turned cloudy and green.

She snatched up the flowers and set off down to the village, water dripping on the front of her jeans.

Bianca's face lit up then clouded as Donna approached.

'So, he is gone. And you have come to tell me why. But first you will have some strong coffee and a piece of my homemade chestnut cake. I insist. You will need all your strength to deal with whatever has happened.'

Donna gulped down the coffee and cake; it tasted like cardboard but it was easier than arguing with Bianca.

'Now, tell me.' Bianca fixed her dark eyes on Donna.

The old lady listened in silence then she took Donna's hands, clasped them in her own and urged her to reconsider.

'Love isn't easy, Donna. Sometimes it is hard. There will be days when you could throttle the man you love. But love is the most important thing. It is so easy to lose, so hard to find. The only things in my life I regret are the times I let love slip away.' Bianca shook her head and looked down at her lap.

Donna walked back through the village feeling quite unsettled. *So easy to lose, so hard to find.* She could not afford to dwell on Bianca's words. Bianca was just a sentimental old lady living in the past. Donna knew she had done the right thing. So why did it feel so wrong?

Donna scrolled through the photographs: Coco trotting through the olive grove; beautiful, grey Guido cantering across a meadow of wildflowers; Freja and Astrid in the woods – that one was a little dark but their smiles made up for it. There were more than a hundred images on the screen. How could she possibly whittle them down to less than a dozen?

And everyone in the pictures looked so damn happy. She knew nobody was happy all the time, but the smiling faces displayed before her were so at odds with her current mood it made the task of choosing even more difficult.

'Mum?' Marco was looking at her with concern.

'I just can't decide,' she said.

'We don't have to do this today. We can wait until Daniela comes over next week.' Marco spoke slowly, clearly trying to hide his irritation.

Donna felt a pang of guilt. She had been nagging Marco for ages to help sort out the website and now she was the one dragging her heels over the finishing touches. She just didn't have the enthusiasm.

'Mum?'

'Yes, let's wait for Daniela. She's got a good eye for these sorts of things.' Donna knew she was procrastinating but Daniela had such good taste; she was sure to pick just the right images.

'Okay. We'll leave the pictures for now. I'm going to go and help in the yard, but let's work on the words for the home page this afternoon. We don't need to write a lot, just a few lines that sum up the spirit of Bella Vista. I'll make some tea about four o'clock and then you and I can have a brainstorming session.'

'Brainstorming?'

'That's what they call it at the radio station.' Marco laughed.

'Brainstorming it is then,' Donna said. She forced herself to smile.

Donna slumped in her chair, staring at the screen. Her mind hadn't stopped churning these last few weeks but *brain fog* was a more accurate description of her mental state than *brain storm*. Since making the momentous decision to ask Giovanni to leave she had found it impossible to make any others. It was as though the effort involved had used up every cell in her brain and body. She no longer knew what was right and what was wrong. She couldn't see a way forward.

Harriet bent down and picked up her key – again. Each time she tried to insert it into the lock it slipped from her fingers. She straightened up slowly holding on to the doorframe to steady herself. The front door seemed to tilt towards her. Somehow, this time, she managed to open it.

She stumbled inside, dropping her shoulder bag on the floor with a thump. The hallway smelt of Chinese food. Vikki and Matt's takeaway boxes were strewn across the coffee table. There was no sign of her flatmates; they must be in bed already.

Harriet grabbed the takeaway boxes and shoved them into the kitchen swing-bin. The clock on the oven said 03.06. It was well over twelve hours since she had last eaten. Ravenous, she opened the fridge. The chilli she had made two days ago had all gone; she only had a wilting bag of salad and a pack of yogurts left.

The labels on the yogurt pots were swimming before her eyes. She wiped her glasses on the edge of her rumpled white shirt and put them back on. She could just make out the fuzzy words *fruits of the forest*. She ripped off the foil lid and began ladling the yogurt into her mouth with a dessert spoon. Yum. She opened another.

What a great night it had been. All the girls from work had been out celebrating Savita's pregnancy. Their boss had insisted on treating them all to drinks in the new fancy bar near their office. The cocktails were lethal so they were all feeling a little drunk by the time Savita had finished her second Virgin Mary and discreetly slipped away. But Savita had responsibilities; Harriet didn't.

The rest of the evening – the cab to the cool new club in the East End; the stomach-churning mixing of Prosecco and craft beers; the crazy dancing to the retro 80s music – was all a bit hazy. Harriet hadn't had such a good evening for a long time. She was going to feel like hell once she sobered up. Next time she wouldn't drink on an empty stomach. And there would be a next time. Why had she wasted time moping over Tom? She had almost forgotten how to enjoy herself. Being single was the best fun ever. Who needed men, and all the trouble they caused?

Six hours later Harriet wasn't feeling too good. She slugged down another glass of water and poured the kettle over her teabag. She added the last dregs of milk and tossed the carton away. There was nothing left to eat in the house except dry cereal, but she wasn't too bothered; the thought of food made her feel quite nauseous.

She carried her mug out of the kitchen and flopped on the green velveteen couch. At least it was Saturday; she would never have made it into the office. Judging by the messages pinging on her phone a couple of her pals at work were feeling equally dodgy.

What a waste of a beautiful autumn day. But there was nothing that could be done about it. She would just have to lie here bingeing on a boxset and scrolling through her emails. At least the room had stopped spinning and she would be fine tomorrow for her weekly horse-riding lesson. They were going to practise trotting over some poles. One day soon she might jump a small fence. She couldn't wait to give that a try.

She picked up her phone and scrolled down her emails: more spam and special offers. Who or what was *marco-giovanniginistrelli3@gmail.com*? Harriet stopped herself pressing *delete* just in time. Marco, from Bella Vista! She hoped it wasn't a problem with Jess. Harriet had been so thrilled to hear that the two of them had got together after all, but she couldn't think of any other reason he would message her. She clicked open the mail.

Ciao Harriet,
I hope you don't mind me contacting you. I found your email address in Mum's paperwork. I know it's a bit of a cheek to write to you out of the blue, but I'm hoping you can help. It's Mum.

So, this was about Donna. That was odd. Of course, she would try to help if Donna was in trouble, but she couldn't imagine what use she would be, here in London.

Things haven't worked out the way I hoped since Papa came back. Mum seemed so happy at first; I thought everything would be perfect. Well, as perfect as two people can be. I know Papa can be difficult and maybe Mum has got used to doing things her way. But when Mum told me she'd asked Papa to leave I could hardly believe it. Neither of them will tell me what happened. I'm not sure they know themselves.

Papa seems bewildered by the whole thing but he's deep into his next book and when he's not writing he's teaching. He's never been in so much demand. It's Mum I'm worried about. She hasn't been the same since Alfredo died.

Tea sloshed over the edge of Harriet's mug and splattered on her lap. Alfredo: dead. What a kind, lovely man he had been. No wonder Donna was devastated. Harriet would do whatever she could to help, short of flying out to Bella Vista.

Julia thinks Alfredo's death might have something to do with Mum and Papa's split but there must be more to it than that. My contract at the radio station has finished so I'm back home for a while, helping Mum sort out the website. But I'm supposed to be going travelling soon. I don't think I should leave her, but she won't hear of me cancelling my plans.

Mum needs to focus on the future, but I know all she's doing is dwelling on the past even though she insists she's done the right thing. I've been trying to persuade her to find a new yoga teacher and start up those yoga weeks again.

So, that was where Harriet fitted in.

She needs to do something to attract the visitors again once the winter comes or she'll end up moping around. She says she'll start speaking to people about it but she never gets round to it.

I know it's a long shot but if you came out for a few days you might help drum up her enthusiasm. It might even give her the impetus to bring someone in for a trial lesson. If she had your input I'm sure she'd feel more confident about the whole project. And it's perfect weather for riding out now it's a bit cooler. I could give you a couple of private lessons too — if that doesn't put you off coming!

Please think about it.

Marco x

P.S.: Coco misses you, and Julia's cooking is better than ever — if that's possible!

Harriet put down her phone. Return to Bella Vista: why would she want to do that? When she'd caught the train to Pisa airport she had never even considered the possibility of going back. But the more she thought about it, the more it started to make sense. She had fallen in love with the old farmhouse, the beautiful countryside and little Coco. If it hadn't been for that idiot, Tom, she could have happily stayed there forever.

The promise of cantering up the side of the vineyard, walking Lupo through the village and curling up with the latest selection from Candy's book club with Miu Miu on her lap was just what she needed. Even though she could barely stomach a handful of dry cereal right now, the thought of Julia's cooking made her mouth water. And helping Donna plan a yoga week would keep her too busy to think about Tom's unfathomable behaviour. Returning to Bella Vista was a wonderful idea.

Harriet still had plenty of holiday allowance left over. It was almost worth going back to Italy just to see Savita's face when she went into her office and voluntarily asked for some time off. She would sign off Harriet's holiday form before you could say *work-life balance*.

Chapter Thirty-One

Julia bit into the slice of *panforte*. It was so nice to eat something that she had not made herself. It was a rare treat to take a walk down to Bar Beppe and linger over a cappuccino and a slice of Beppe's wife's baking. And today she could not wait to get away from Bella Vista.

It had been foolish to think that everything would slot back into place once Giovanni had gone. His presence lingered everywhere. The hexagonal glass-topped table was now squeezed into the corner of Julia's bedroom so that Donna did not have to look at it. Once Julia had arranged her hairbrush, mirror, rarely used bottle of scent and even more rarely used powder compact on it, she had to admit it was a pretty piece of furniture though completely unsuited to the rustic style of the house. She rather liked it, but she couldn't help feeling that there was something wrong about Giovanni's carefully chosen gift ending up in her bedroom.

It wasn't the only thing making her feel uncomfortable. Donna's breezy insistence that she was absolutely fine wasn't fooling anyone. The new groom wasn't too affected – he could busy himself in the stable yard all day – but Julia spent almost all her time in the house where the atmosphere hung heavy.

Julia had spoken to Giovanni on the telephone but he could throw no light on what had gone so terribly wrong. Julia was in no doubt that he still loved Donna very much. And that Donna loved him.

Perhaps Donna's expectations were too high. No relationship was perfect. Julia had long given up hoping that Luigi would get down on one knee and present her with a diamond ring. But she knew that although she and Luigi were totally different, they belonged together, side by side, like salt and pepper. Just like Donna and Giovanni did.

'*Come stai*? You are okay?' Beppe was looking at her with concern.

'*Si, bene.*' Julia smiled. She was not going to burden Beppe with her problems.

He picked up a thin brochure that was lying on the table. 'Here, let me clear that out of your way. *Luxury Tuscan Properties*. I can't think why my wife picks these things up. She must imagine she is married to a wealthy man.' Beppe chortled.

'Actually, I might take a look at that,' Julia said. She had been hoping to read Beppe's copy of the local paper but it had been commandeered by Old Dante who had nodded off with it wedged under his elbow.

'As you wish.'

Julia scanned the first page. *Six-bedroom villa with pool outside Florence*. Very nice. But even if Luigi won the lottery Julia could not imagine him leaving the village, and Julia could not leave Bella Vista now that Donna needed her more than ever. Nevertheless, it was nice to look at the pictures and imagine who lived in these beautiful places.

She took a sip of coffee and turned the page. That property halfway down looked familiar. Of course! Why hadn't she thought of it before? It could be the answer to all her problems.

'Beppe!'

He put down the cup he was wiping up. 'You need more coffee?'

'No, this is perfect. I was wondering . . . would it be okay to take this?' She held up the brochure.

'Of course. I was going to throw it out.'

'Thanks, Beppe, that's very kind.'

'I'll tell Luigi to start saving.' Beppe chuckled.

Julia turned her attention to the local paper, which was lying on the table Dante had now vacated. She started to read the front page but her mind was occupied by the rolled-up property brochure stashed in her tote bag. She couldn't wait to see Luigi tomorrow. She was dying to tell him her plans.

It was hard to concentrate that evening. Chopping and stirring usually calmed her mind but tonight she was all geed up. She was thankful that she had prepared the *ragù* the day before. It always tasted better when it had been in the fridge overnight.

Donna ate with gusto; she had hardly eaten anything these last few weeks but the steaming plate of *pici* pasta seemed to have rekindled her appetite.

'This is wonderful, Julia,' she said.

Julia lifted the metal lid. The smell of meat and garlic tickled her nostrils. 'Donna, any seconds?'

'Maybe a little,' Donna said.

Julia brought in the hazelnut *semifreddo*. There was silence as they tucked into the delicious ice-cream dessert.

Donna ate a whole dishful; she couldn't believe she had only been picking at Julia's wonderful food since Giovanni left. It was time she stopped wallowing in self-pity. She was so lucky to live and work alongside her best friend. Things hadn't been easy lately, but Donna knew that everything would turn out all right. As long as she had Julia by her side.

Chapter Thirty-Two

Giovanni leant against the white countertop and picked up his coffee. Strong and slightly bitter: just how he liked it. Antonio had been running the café in Siena for as long as Giovanni could remember – juggling the coffee maker, the under-the-counter dishwasher, and the wiping down of tables without missing a beat. Giovanni's espresso was ready on the counter each morning the moment he walked through the door.

'Look!' Antonio said. He was pointing at a stainless steel contraption attached to a giant jar of chocolate-hazelnut spread.

'What is it?' Giovanni said.

'My new toy. See, I take this ordinary *cornetto vuoto* . . .' Antonio pushed a flaky brown croissant onto the dispenser's protruding metal spout and pressed a lever on the top. 'Now it is filled with chocolate-hazelnut paste. For you! No, don't worry. I am just kidding. I have your usual breakfast *crostata* right here.'

Giovanni frowned. When had he become so predictable? 'No, I'll try that chocolate one.'

Antonio raised an eyebrow. 'Okay, I will put it in a napkin for you. If you don't like it, I will swap it.'

Giovanni took a bite, conscious that Antonio was watching him as if it were feeding time at the zoo. It was on the third bite that he reached the gooey chocolate filling. His back molars sang in protest. He finished the pastry, taking a second paper napkin from the metal dispenser to wipe off the viscous chocolate coating from his fingers. He opened his mouth to ask for another coffee to counteract the sickly concoction, but Antonio had already placed a small, steaming cup in front of him.

'Very good,' Giovanni said.

'But perhaps, tomorrow you have your usual.'

Giovanni nodded. He ran his tongue over his teeth; they still felt sticky. He wasn't going to touch one of those again, though Marco would love it. He would have to tell Beppe to order one of those machines for his bar. Then he remembered: Marco would be off on his travels next week and there was no earthly reason why Giovanni would set foot in Bar Beppe ever again.

Antonio's café was clean and smart. It had suited Giovanni well for many years, but he missed Beppe's place. He missed wandering down into the village and reading the paper; he missed arguing about local politics at the bar; and he missed playing *scopa* even though Old Dante relieved him of his money with painful regularity. He missed the life he had begun to rebuild.

He even missed his trips to the florist near Il Carciofo. It would have been easy enough for him to set up a standing order for Donna's bouquets, but he liked to choose the colour combinations himself and help the owner to pick out the prettiest blooms. And he insisted that she only used the freshest flowers knowing that Bianca would enjoy them once Donna's next delivery arrived. Flowers weren't enough to show Donna how much she meant to him, so he had searched out little gifts to please her: that stunning modern metal vase, the pretty hexagonal table.

When Hollywood came knocking he had been thrilled. At last he could treat Donna to anything her heart desired.

He could transform Bella Vista. He had done everything he could think of to make his relationship with Donna work but it had still gone wrong. Some days he convinced himself that Donna hadn't really wanted him to go. When he had asked her to explain, she hadn't made sense. She had muttered some nonsense about the old oak table. After all they had been through, he couldn't believe they could be splitting up over furniture. Maybe it had something to do with Alfredo's death. Donna hadn't been the same since. That would pass. It must do. It was the only thread of hope he could cling to.

Giovanni remembered the stress he had gone through himself when his parents died. The memory of going through his mother's belongings still brought a tear to his eye years after the event. He couldn't bear to think of Donna going through that same pain so, after a decent interval, he had forced himself to deal with the sad task of sorting Alfredo's things. He had hesitated before throwing out Alfredo's well-worn jacket, but it was full of holes; he knew Alfredo was too proud to want to be remembered by something so tatty. Giovanni had almost spared the battered tin in which the old man kept his sweets, but the sight of the empty tin was just too poignant. He knew it would break Donna's heart to see it sitting in the tack room. It was a shame there were no other personal things, but he knew Donna didn't need to keep a pile of old junk to honour Alfredo's memory.

'*Buongiorno!*'

Giovanni turned his head.

'Would you mind signing this for me.' A young man was shifting from foot to foot, holding out a well-thumbed copy of Giovanni's first novel.

Giovanni reached into his jacket for his expensive new fountain pen. He signed his name inside the front cover. The man scuttled off, his face beetroot red.

'Fame!' Antonio said with a grin.

Giovanni shrugged.

'Your new book has been shortlisted for some sort of prize, hasn't it?' Antonio added.

'Mmm.' Giovanni's response discouraged further conversation.

He opened his soft calf-leather wallet and put a ten-euro bill on the saucer. He replaced the wallet in the pocket of his new nine-hundred-dollar linen jacket. He had bought himself a whole new wardrobe of designer clothes but without Donna to admire them, they meant nothing. He turned to leave without waiting for his change.

He opened the door of his office. Silvia had put some post on his polished mahogany desk. Among the bills and circulars was a small envelope addressed in an italic hand. He slid his paperknife under the flap: a thick, gilt-edged card confirmed his invitation to a literary dinner in Milan. He was to be the guest of honour. It was the ultimate affirmation of his success. But how could he be a success when he had failed at the only thing that mattered?

It was only later that he spotted the familiar writing on a large buff-coloured envelope. Julia's handwriting. He ripped open the envelope, his heart racing. He quickly scanned the letter and the other papers she had enclosed. Property details: that was interesting, but he could not foresee how they would help him win Donna back. He tossed them to one side with a sigh.

Chapter Thirty-Three

What a lovely surprise to hear from you. No need to apologise for the short notice. Julia and I look forward to seeing you next week – and so does Coco! Could you bring your yoga kit when you come – I'll explain when you get here. Donna x

Donna closed the lid of her laptop. What a stroke of luck! Just when she had been fretting about restarting the yoga holidays, Harriet had emailed out of the blue. Now she could run her plans past Harriet. It would make her feel more confident about the whole endeavour.

Sorting out the yoga week would be one step forward – like the first piece of a jigsaw puzzle slotting into place. Then, slowly, slowly, she could start to put her life back together.

Marco was already outside the railway station, leaning against the van. The tattoos on his upper arms were visible below his sleeveless white T-shirt. He was nut-brown after a summer of sunshine.

He slid open the door of the van. Harriet lobbed her holdall into the back; it smelt of leather and wet dog. She gave Lupo a pat then clambered into the passenger seat. The dog stuck his nose between the front seats as they drove along.

Marco's hair had grown since she last saw him. His curls bounced in the breeze through the open window. She examined his profile out of the corner of her eye. That wild hair, that strong Roman nose: his resemblance to his father was striking. Only his dark brown eyes differed from Giovanni's melting, amber gaze.

'Thanks for coming, Harriet. It was really good of you.'

Harriet looked out of the van's window; there wasn't a cloud in the sky. Returning to Tuscany wasn't exactly a hardship. 'I'm really glad to be back and I'll be more than happy to help Donna. She asked me to bring my yoga kit, by the way.'

'Mum was thrilled to hear from you. She's got no idea I contacted you. You won't tell her, will you?'

'No, of course not. How's she doing?'

'High and low. Sometimes she walks into a room and stands there staring into space as if she has no idea why she's there.'

'Losing Alfredo must have been hard for her. And for you too, of course.'

'Mum relied on him so much. I just wish he were still around now that Papa's gone.'

'Why did your father leave?'

Marco didn't answer. He kept his eyes fixed on the road ahead. Harriet grew hot with embarrassment. She turned her head away from Marco and looked out of the side window.

'Sorry, I shouldn't have asked,' she muttered.

'No, it's okay. I'm just trying to work out whether that idiot in the pickup truck is going to turn right.'

The truck cut across in front of them at the last possible moment. Marco blasted his horn. 'Italian drivers!' he joked. 'But to answer your question: I have no idea what went wrong with Mum and Papa. Maybe some people just aren't supposed to be together.' He stared straight ahead.

Harriet took the hint and changed the subject. 'How's things with Jess?'

Marco beamed. 'Going really well. We talk and text almost every day.'

'I'm so glad.'

'Not as glad as I am.'

Marco turned into the road that led to the village. They continued up the dusty lane to the farmhouse. Marco jumped out and opened the five-bar gate. Bella Vista looked as welcoming as ever. It was good to be back.

It was strange to wake up early and wander into the stable yard now that Alfredo was no longer there, but the horses were still looking out of their boxes as though nothing had changed. The hens were pecking around their enclosure and Lupo was nosing around. Harriet pushed open the door to the tack room where Marco was sorting out the saddles and bridles.

'We're going to have a lesson in the schooling ring this morning. Mum knows you've been doing a bit of riding back home but she'd rather you had a lesson here before you hack out. She's got a full day's ride planned for you tomorrow.'

'Great,' Harriet said.

'Want to tack him up?' Marco took Coco's brown leather saddle from the rack.

'Sure,' Harriet said.

Marco handed her the saddle and laid the pony's bridle on top. Harriet's arms buckled slightly; the tack was heavier than she remembered.

'Don't look so serious. I'll check everything is okay before we start.'

Harriet slid back the bolt on Coco's door.

'Do you remember me?' she murmured. The pony pushed his nose against her arm, as if in answer. Harriet slipped the bridle over Coco's head and did up the throat lash. She tried not to fumble, conscious that Marco was leaning on the door watching her.

'Good. Don't do up the nose band too tightly.'

Harriet gently slid Coco's saddle into position and fastened the girth. She scratched the pony behind his ears and led him towards the mounting block. Coco walked willingly towards the schooling ring.

Marco stood in the centre calling out instructions to walk on, to speed up, to slow down and to halt. Harriet furrowed her brow in concentration.

'Remember what I told you before: hold those reins like two little birds,' Marco said.

Harriet took a deep breath and exhaled slowly, relaxing into the rocking motion of Coco's walk.

'Great, I can see you've improved but try and keep your heels down . . . that's better. Now shorten up your reins and next time you draw level with the persimmon tree squeeze your legs and take up a nice steady trot.'

After a few bumpy strides Harriet began to rise and lower herself into the saddle in time with the pony's rhythm. A sparrow was chirping in the hedgerow; the sun was warm on her back. Her mouth almost hurt from smiling so much.

'You did well, Harriet,' Marco said as she led Coco back into his stable.

'You're a good teacher.' Harriet smiled.

'Hmm, what do you want?' Marco joked.

'Nothing. I'm just pleased to be here. I can't wait to ride out in the countryside tomorrow.'

'Mum will have planned a nice route for you, something that's not too tricky. That couple she's taken out today are leaving this afternoon. There's no one else staying for the next couple of days so you'll be getting a private ride.'

'Aren't you coming too?' Harriet said. She undid the buckles on Coco's bridle and lifted the headpiece over the pony's ears.

'No. I've got to get sorted for my trip. It's less than a week 'til I go and I haven't got a thing organised – apart from my tickets – and that's only thanks to Mum.'

'Where are you starting off? Germany, wasn't it?'

'I've had a bit of a change of plan since you were last here. I'm heading in the opposite direction. I'll be taking the train to Paris then heading for Scotland.'

'Scotland?' Harriet tried not to sound too surprised.

'Francesco has invited me to stay with him and his husband Alasdair for a few days, then I'll see Edinburgh and Glasgow before travelling down to England.'

'To see Jess in Birmingham?'

'Of course. I've got a parcel to deliver.'

Harriet had never seen Marco blush before. 'Jess's sketchbook, of course!'

'At least she should be happy to see that even if she changes her mind about wanting to see me,' he joked.

'Believe me, when you turn up on her doorstep, she won't give that sketchbook a second thought.'

'Thanks, Harriet. Now give me that saddle and bridle. I'll put them away if you fetch a couple of cans from the fridge – that is, if you fancy a drink on the terrace.'

'That's just what I needed.' Harriet took a long slug of her orangeade. She gave a little hiccup and put her can down by the side of the wicker lounger.

'I reckon it won't be long 'til lunch. Mum and the other riders are stopping off at Il Carciofo on their way home so Julia's sorting out something for us to eat here.'

'Then it's lounging around out here for me and packing for you.' Harriet shot him a grin.

'Yeah. I want to get some of it sorted out today so I can meet Papa in Siena tomorrow.'

'Do you see much of him . . . sorry, you don't have to answer that.'

'We met up a couple of times a week when I was still working at the radio station, but I haven't managed to see him since I moved back here. I think it'll do him the world of good to have a break from his work tomorrow. He's halfway through the second draft of his new book. Apparently, the plot is so fiendish it's driving him demented. And when he's not working on that he's teaching.'

'I'm surprised he's still doing that,' Harriet said.

'So was I, at first. But Papa gets a lot out of it and he's taken so many classes over the years it's not too taxing. He uses the same old exercises time after time: *Plot in Reverse, My True Feelings* . . .'

A cold feeling crept over Harriet. '*My True Feelings*? I've heard that somewhere before.'

'It's quite a clever idea. You describe something or someone you love and twist it into something hateful. Papa says it really gets people thinking about their use of language. You remember Nigel? He wrote a brilliant piece about his childhood rabbit; it was seriously creepy . . . Hey, are you okay, Harriet? You don't look at all good.'

Harriet shook her head. Marco's eyes were full of concern. 'You're worrying me now, Harriet. What the hell is it?'

'It's Tom, Marco . . . I've made the most terrible mistake.'

263

'He didn't . . . he didn't write . . .'

'Yep. *My True Feelings*. All about me. I found it when I put something in the recycling bin for Julia.'

'It's okay, Harriet.' Marco put his hand on her arm. 'You can contact Tom, tell him what happened . . .'

'It's too late, Marco. I cut him off without giving him a chance to explain. He tried to contact me and I blocked his number. And now I'm here, he's back in England and he's probably with someone else.' Harriet's voice shook. She tried to blink back the tears but it was too late; they were running down her face. She gave a big gulp and pulled a crunched-up old tissue from the pocket of her jodhpurs.

'I would have thought living with Nigel would put most girls off,' Marco said.

'Tom and Nigel are living together? No way!' Harriet couldn't help laughing despite her tears.

'Yep, Tom's sharing a flat with Nigel. And you're going to go and see him.'

'I suppose I could try and look him up when I get back to England. But it's probably hopeless.' Harriet scuffed the toe of her boot on the ground.

'There's no need to go that far. Nigel's writing a novel set in sixteenth-century Tuscany and Tom's studying Italian and helping Papa with some research on his next book. Tom's here in Italy, living in Siena.'

Chapter Thirty-Four

Giovanni drummed his fingers on the desk. Four blank faces stared up at him. It was moments like this when he questioned the wisdom of continuing with his writing courses. He no longer needed the money, and he barely had the spare time what with all the invitations he received to attend this and that. But he enjoyed watching his pupils grow in ability and confidence. So, much to his secretary Silvia's surprise, he preferred to turn down invitations to appear on radio shows and the like in order to carry on with his teaching.

The occasional weeks that he reserved for pupils from England helped keep up his fluency in English, now that he no longer had Donna to talk to. Giovanni recognised that not every writer or wannabe writer found it easy to express themselves in the classroom; writing was a profession that attracted more than its fair share of introverts – but never had he experienced a group as quiet as this one. Getting them to speak up was like pulling teeth.

'So, no one has any idea? No one can think of a person they would like to describe.' Giovanni's voice rose. 'Very well. I will decide for you. We will describe me. Yes, me. Okay, everyone. Tara, you first.' He fixed his eyes on a girl with a thick black fringe covering half her face, who had barely said a word since she arrived.

Tara gazed back at him with big, doe eyes; a blush suffused her cheeks. 'Handsome?' she ventured.

Good grief. Funny how students never had a crush on him before he was famous. He hated it. But he only had to look in the mirror to know he wasn't bad-looking, so it was as good a start as any. He picked up a thick, blue marker pen. *Handsome* he wrote at the top of the whiteboard. 'Okay. Now you, Sebastian.'

Sebastian hesitated. His prominent Adam's apple moved up and down his skinny, white neck. 'Hair like an ageing Botticelli cherub.'

'Now we're getting somewhere!' Giovanni slapped the palm of his hand on his desk. 'Good!' 'Better!' 'Fantastic!' Giovanni shouted as Piers, a chubby guy in Bermuda shorts; Enid a bony woman with blue-veined hands and Sebastian competed to impress him. Even Tara began to show the promise Giovanni had seen in her pre-course assignment.

It was funny how a lesson could turn from dire to inspiring. It was like turning the ignition key in a rusty old banger, hearing a spluttering sound then, suddenly, *whoosh* you were off and the next thing you knew you were in danger of breaking the speed limit.

'I think we've exhausted physical attributes, so let's move on to character,' Giovanni said.

'But we only met you yesterday evening,' Piers said.

'You must have formed some impressions. I've certainly formed some impressions of you.' Giovanni gave a little laugh.

Sebastian shrank back in his chair. Giovanni raised an eyebrow; surely the boy couldn't find him that intimidating.

'Tara?'

'Interesting?' Tara gave him a beaming smile. Giovanni wrote *interesting* on the whiteboard.

'Impetuous,' Piers suggested. Giovanni nodded. That was quite perceptive of Piers.

'Like a boy on Christmas Eve,' Tara blurted out. At last, she was coming out of her shell. Giovanni was surprised. He thought he did a good job of concealing his impatience. He felt Enid's sharp little eyes on him. He had an uncomfortable feeling she was going to contribute something unflattering. Why in heaven's name had he used himself as an example?

'Like an elephant in a summer's meadow,' Enid said. She looked him right in the eye.

Giovanni's nostrils flared. An elephant? What the hell did she mean by that? He hesitated, then picked up the pen and scrawled across the board.

'Anyone like to expand on that?' he said.

An uncomfortable silence filled the room. Sebastian sank even further into his chair; Tara was chewing the end of her pen.

'Don't worry. I am not easily offended,' Giovanni said. He forced himself to smile. And smile some more as his class untied their tongues. The list on the whiteboard grew longer. The descriptions were ones he would never have expected. How had he had spent a lifetime blissfully unaware of half the negative character traits this disparate group of writers had uncovered after knowing him for just a few hours? Was there an element of truth in what they said? Did he really trample through life like an elephant in a summer's meadow? He had tried to make Donna the happiest woman in the world. But had he ever stopped to stand in her shoes, to consider what she wanted?

Giovanni banged one fist against his chest. The room fell silent. Piers and Enid exchanged glances.

'You are right! I am an impossible man!' he roared. 'Would you live with a man like me?'

'Certainly not,' Enid said.

'Tara, would you live with a man like me?'

'Well, umm . . .' Tara began. She was silenced by a look from Enid.

'Time for lunch. There's a café around the corner. Tell Antonio I sent you. I'll pick up the bill.' Giovanni marched across the room. The door slammed shut behind him.

He flung open the door to his secretary's room. Papers fluttered on Silvia's desk. She peered at him over the top of her spectacles. Giovanni began rummaging through her neatly stacked piles of work. He fanned out a pile of folders, sending her metal hole puncher flying. Hundreds of little white spheres scattered across the parquet flooring.

'Where is it?' he said.

'If you tell me what you are looking for, I imagine I'll find it,' Silvia said. She flicked a minuscule piece of fluff from her purple silk blouse. Silvia was always calm; three years working for Giovanni had given her plenty of practice.

'That big, brown envelope. I asked you to put it in the recycling pile a couple of days ago.'

'I guess that's where it is then,' Silvia replied.

Giovanni looked at her sharply but there wasn't a trace of sarcasm in her voice. Silvia calmly handed him the envelope and continued tapping away at her keyboard.

'There has been an emergency,' Giovanni said.

Silvia looked up.

'When the class returns from Antonio's you will need to tell them that this course is cancelled. Everyone can continue to stay in their accommodation for the week but they will receive a full refund. They'll be back soon; I know Antonio is closing up early today. Oh, and tell Tom I won't need him for the next couple of days.'

Giovanni could see a question form on Silvia's lips, but she just nodded and continued typing. He leant across the desk and kissed his secretary on both cheeks.

'What would I do without you?'

'What indeed? Good luck with Donna.'

Giovanni gave a wry smile. Silvia knew him too well.

Giovanni set off, the envelope with Julia's handwriting on the front tucked under his arm. He tried to walk briskly but his progress was constantly halted by his fellow citizens. Where were they all going and why did they have to walk so slowly? Now the pavement was blocked by two young women both with double buggies. One of them was holding up a newly manicured hand with long electric-blue fingernails for the other girl's approval.

Giovanni stepped off the pavement into the road, muttering under his breath. A scooter swerved; the long-haired rider treated him to an obscene gesture. Giovanni remounted the pavement, feeling slightly shaken. Getting himself killed wasn't going to help anyone. He took a deep breath, but he did not feel any calmer. He crossed into the next piazza. A flea market had been set up, with stalls on all sides. Giovanni ran a hand through his hair. He felt like pulling it out. He nipped down a side street. It was even busier with people swarming into the town and more stalls of bric-a-brac. He dodged here and there, trying to keep his frustration from boiling over.

An elderly woman stepped right in front of him. She gave him such a genuine smile that he swallowed the curse he was about to utter.

'After you, *signora*.' Giovanni stepped aside.

'*Molto gentile*, very kind,' the old lady murmured. Her brown eyes were warm and friendly. She reminded him of Bianca.

As he stopped to let her pass, Giovanni's eyes roamed over the nearest market stall. A turquoise glass cat with strange orange eyes and a pair of china spaniels flanking a carriage clock mounted on a lustrous green-glazed base sat amongst tottering piles of crockery. Amongst the floral patterns, one tureen stood out: a tureen decorated with a blue and white pattern.

The stallholder was onto him quick as a flash. 'Like that, do you? It's a lovely piece; shame the lid's missing. Only ten euros.'

'No. No, thank you.' Giovanni didn't have time for all this. He went to move away but a small crowd had gathered around the adjacent stallholder who was offering free samples of her lemon-scented *ricciarelli*.

The women with the tureen rummaged in the pocket of her tatty apron.

'For you eight euros? I've got change.'

'No, really. It's the pattern. It reminded me of something, that's all,' Giovanni said.

'I've got some other pieces.' She reached into a wooden crate and produced a lumpy newspaper package.

'Really, I'm not . . .' Giovanni began. Then he stopped.

'Beautiful, isn't it? Just a little chipped. Twenty euros,' the woman said.

Giovanni was already reaching inside his jacket pocket. 'I'll take it.'

The woman's eyes widened. She had clearly expected him to barter her down to half that price, but Giovanni wasn't in the mood to play games. The woman smoothed out the crumpled newspaper wrapping and refastened it with a piece of sticky tape that she tore off the roll with her few remaining front teeth. She stuffed the twenty-euro note into her pocket and put the parcel into a cheap, striped plastic bag.

Giovanni hurried down the street, dodging the shoppers as best he could. He was tempted to run but he did not want to arrive at his destination hot and dishevelled. The crowds thinned out as he turned into Via di Città; the market was a bigger attraction today. He hurried past the boutiques. He wasn't interested in leather shoes, or the latest shirts. He had something far more important in mind.

He flung open the door to the estate agent. The bell jangled. The woman behind the desk looked up and eyed Giovanni warily. She clearly wasn't impressed by this strange man with his wild hair, a brown envelope under his arm and an odd newspaper-wrapped parcel sticking out of his cheap carrier bag.

Her face softened once she noticed his elegant silvery grey jacket and caught a waft of his expensive woody cologne. She gestured to the empty chair on the other side of her desk.

'How may I help?'

Giovanni placed the brown envelope on her immaculate wood-effect desk. He pulled out a sheaf of papers. He shifted in the uncomfortable seat. He hardly dared ask a question in case the answer was *no*. The silence grew. The woman smiled encouragingly.

He forced himself to speak: 'This property, is it still for sale?'

'Let me see.' The woman moved her computer mouse across the desk. Giovanni swallowed hard. The seconds ticked by. 'Yes, it is,' she said.

He wanted to punch the air.

Chapter Thirty-Five

'I can't just turn up on Tom's doorstep,' Harriet said.

She was still trying to process what Marco had told her. Everything she believed had been turned upside down. The essay she had read was just some daft writing exercise Giovanni had dreamt up for his pupils; it was her own insecurities and negative thoughts that had made her so quick to believe that Tom was insincere. Tom's feelings for her were genuine. He didn't hate her after all. How rejected he must have felt when she had inexplicably failed to meet him in Siena then refused to answer his texts and calls. Would he, could he, ever forgive her?

'I'm not suggesting you go and ring his doorbell. Anyhow I'd need to ask Papa for his address,' Marco said.

'No, please don't.' If Tom was going to blank her – and why wouldn't he after the way she had treated him – Harriet did not want anyone else to be party to her humiliation, least of all Giovanni.

'You don't need to go to Nigel and Tom's flat. Tom takes his laptop to Bar Antonio, near Papa's office, every afternoon. He sits in the corner doing Papa's research whilst Nigel gets some peace and quiet to write. All you have to do when you get to Siena is walk into Bar Antonio and order yourself a drink and take it from there.'

'Oh no!' Harriet clapped her hands over her eyes. 'I can't do it.'

Marco lifted Harriet's hand away from her face. 'Yes you can.'

'But won't Donna think it's incredibly rude of me to disappear off like this?' Harriet was clutching at straws.

'Mum won't mind what you do this afternoon as long as you're here for supper. My sister Daniela is joining us tonight so Julia has a real feast planned. Besides, wondering how you're getting on with Tom will certainly help take her mind off Papa.'

'Glad to be of service,' Harriet quipped.

'So, you'll go to Siena if I drop you at the railway station after lunch?'

'Do I have a choice?'

'Absolutely not!' Marco grinned.

The waiter placed a glass of white wine and a tiny dish of light-green olives on the table with such exaggerated ceremony that Harriet had to stifle a nervous giggle. He looked curiously at her before leaning over to flick a couple of barely visible crumbs from the gleaming metal tabletop then vanished back inside leaving a cloud of aftershave hanging in the air.

One glass only: just a little Dutch courage before she set off to find Bar Antonio. Harriet wiped her hands on the front of her jeans and took a large mouthful of the lemon-scented wine.

On the table next to her an elderly American woman was reading aloud from her guidebook whilst her male companion nodded and drank his beer. A couple of teenage girls walked arm in arm in front of the café, giggling and tossing their hair. How carefree they looked.

Harriet opened the pocket map that Marco kept in the glove compartment of the van. Bar Antonio was just around the corner from Giovanni's office on the square with the panther fountain. It would not take long to walk there.

She sipped her wine and speared an olive with a small wooden pick: tart and juicy – delicious. She knew she was procrastinating. The clock tower told her it was already gone four o'clock. She should set off right now. Or maybe she could forget the whole crazy idea, order another glass of wine, then go and explore Siena.

The American couple were now standing up, holding their mobile phones in outstretched hands to capture a tiny figure waving to them from the top of the Torre del Mangia. Harriet could climb up the tower herself or visit the Gothic Palazzo Pubblico to see the famous Frescoes of Good and Bad Government. She would go sightseeing – that was the sensible thing to do. She could tell Marco she hadn't found Tom.

She waved over the waiter and handed him the small metal saucer with the bill and some cash, which he put in the pocket of his apron. She hovered by the fountain at the top of The Campo. A pigeon was sitting on the carved head of a she-wolf, leaning forward to drink from the stream of water spurting from its mouth. It would be so easy to pretend to be another tourist. But she needed to do the right thing. If Tom didn't want anything to do with her, she would have to accept that. But she owed him an apology. Face to face.

She hurried across the sweeping bowl of The Campo and down Via di Città, her ponytail bouncing comically in the reflection from the shop windows. She didn't look too bad today. Her favourite white, puff-sleeved shirt showed off the remnants of her tan and the tiny pink rosebuds were pretty and feminine. She didn't look too try-hard after she had added a shell necklace from her last beach holiday, mid-blue denim jeans and flat leather sandals. She had long given up wearing heels; even stilettos only elevated her to a less than stately five foot three.

Bar Antonio was just where Marco had marked it on the map. Harriet stared at the notice taped to the glass door but she didn't need to understand a word of Italian to realise her trip had been in vain. The upturned chairs, the lack of customers and the empty glass domes on the long white counter told her all she needed to know.

She took off her glasses and polished them on the edge of her shirt and put them back on again as if taking a clearer look would somehow bring the café to life. Then she rummaged in her bag for her phone, but her fingers failed to find the slim, leather case. She knelt in the doorway of the café and tipped the whole bag upside down. The contents scattered across the stone step. Still no phone. She felt like crying.

'Marco!' Donna popped her head out of the front door. Her son was sitting on the terrace with his feet resting on a terracotta pot filled with rosemary, basking in the last of the afternoon's sun.

Marco scrambled to his feet, looking guilty. 'Oh hi, Mum. Do you want me to run that couple down to the station?'

'No, I'll do that, darling. I just wanted to let you know I'm about to drive down there now. You stay here and keep Harriet company. Oh, where is Harriet? Is she in the stable yard?'

'No, she's not here.'

'Not here? Has she taken Lupo for a walk?'

'She's gone a bit further than that. I dropped her at the railway station after lunch whilst you were out riding. She's gone to Siena.'

'Gone to Siena? Whatever for? She only arrived here last night.'

'She's gone to see Tom; they had a big misunderstanding and she's gone to try and sort it out. I told her she'd find him at Bar Antonio, that place around the corner from Papa's office.'

'Oh.' It was all Donna could manage to say.

'You don't sound very pleased, Mum. I thought you'd be thrilled at the idea of Tom and Harriet getting back together.'

'I am, which is why I've invited Tom here. He's on his way. He's joining us for dinner tonight.'

Marco stared back at her. 'Does he know Harriet's staying here?'

'Umm.' Donna felt herself flush. 'Not exactly. But I thought if he and Harriet didn't hit it off again then maybe he and Daniela . . .'

'Mum! Daniela would kill you if she heard that. You know she's perfectly happy as she is.'

'I know, I know, but sometimes I can't help worrying about her.' Donna sighed. She knew she shouldn't interfere. She'd made a mess of her own life. There was no reason she'd do any better trying to matchmake anyone else.

'Mum, haven't you forgotten something?'

'Oh, my goodness. That couple: they're still waiting for me to give them a lift. You'd better text Harriet. I guess there's no point keeping Tom's arrival a surprise any longer.'

'I would, but there's one problem. When I got back from the station, I found Harriet's phone in the footwell of the van. It must have dropped out of her bag.'

Harriet stared out the window disconsolately as the train chugged slowly through the Tuscan countryside. The journey back seemed interminable. She wished she had never gone to Siena. She should have spent the afternoon drinking wine on the terrace, not going on a wild goose chase. She'd come to Italy for a relaxing holiday, not to dig up old memories of Tom. It was all for nothing. She had to accept it wasn't meant to be.

They pulled into another barely used station. The platform was much shorter than the dozen carriages that made up the train. Harriet supposed those at the back would have to walk through the train to alight but the only people she could see getting on or off were a mother and two children who squeezed into the seats opposite her. Their dog, a scruffy white mongrel with a bandaged front leg and a plastic cone around its head, was wedged in between them; its tail thumped up and down on Harriet's sandals. The younger child, clutching an orange fabric teddy, wriggled in his mother's arms grabbing at her long straggly hair with chubby fingers. She began to sing: '*farfallina bella bianca* . . .'

At last Harriet stepped down from the train. The heat had gone out of the day. She couldn't wait to get back to Bella Vista and sink into an armchair with Miu Miu on her lap. She would go on long rides and help Donna devise her yoga holidays. She was determined to make the most of her stay. But first, she needed to find someone who could help her find her way back to the farmhouse. She wished she had bothered to learn a few words of Italian instead of relying on the language app on her missing phone.

The station foyer was almost empty, even the newspaper kiosk was closed up for the night. The clerk behind the window did not glance in Harriet's direction; she was too engrossed in conversation with her friend. Harriet shivered in her thin top. She did not fancy walking two or three miles to Bella Vista even if she could work out which way to go.

Harriet stepped outside the station. Marco was parked on the opposite side of the road. She wanted to run across and hug him.

'Marco!' she called.

He looked up as she crossed the road.

'I am so glad to see you. How on earth did you guess which train I was going to be on?'

'I didn't. Mum sent me here to meet . . .'

'Marco!' Tom's voice came from across the street.

Harriet gasped. She shrank back against the van. It was too late to duck behind it.

'Marco!' Tom called again. He waved with difficulty; he was clutching a bottle of wine in one hand and a bunch of flowers in the other.

Harriet's stomach flipped over. That honey-coloured hair, the dimples when he smiled. Apart from a deeper tan, he hadn't changed a bit.

'Harriet?' Tom stopped in the middle of the road. The smile had left his face. 'Marco, what the hell is Harriet doing here? Is this some kind of joke?'

A car sped past, blasting its horn. Marco grabbed Tom's arm and yanked him onto the narrow pavement. 'Better hop in the front before you get killed. Come on, Harriet, get in the back with Lupo.'

Tom climbed into the front seat without saying a word. Harriet clambered into the back. At least Lupo was glad to see her, burying his big head in Harriet's lap. Harriet ruffled the dog's fur, but Lupo could sense something was wrong. He stared up at Harriet with mournful eyes.

Harriet kept quiet. Tom was angry with her; she could tell from the stiff way he held his head and stared straight ahead. Marco turned on the radio to drown out the silence. He drummed his fingers on the steering wheel in time to the beat as he drove along. Finally, they took the fork in the road that led towards the village. Marco wrenched the steering wheel to the right. The van mounted the verge. He slammed on the brakes. Harriet lurched forward. She grabbed the door handle, glad she had bothered to fasten her seat belt. Lupo let out a whimper.

'Right. If you two aren't going to talk I will,' Marco said.

'Go ahead,' Tom said flatly.

Harriet shifted uncomfortably; the seat squeaked.

'I've had enough angst and drama with Mum and Papa to last a lifetime. I don't need any more with the two of you. I don't know what went wrong with my parents or why Mum asked Papa to leave but I'm sure as anything that if they'd sat down and talked, really talked, they could have worked it out. Tom, Harriet's got something to say to you and when she's spoken it's your turn. When you've both had your say I'll put the van back on the road and we can head home and open a bottle of wine. And if you're still not talking then at least I'll know I've tried.'

Harriet did not want to talk but she couldn't stand the awkward silence any longer. And once she found her voice the whole sorry tale about the story in the recycling bin came tumbling out.

'I am so sorry,' she said. 'I should have had more faith in you. I should have given you a chance to explain. I know you're angry with me and you've every right.' There was so much more she wanted to say but she didn't trust herself to continue.

At last, Tom twisted around to look at her but she could not meet his eyes. She stared down at her sandals.

'I was angry with you, but I should have known you wouldn't have cut me off without a good reason,' he said slowly. 'I should have had more faith in you too. I could have tried harder to speak to you. Heck, I could have hopped on a plane and waited outside your office – I knew where you worked. Meeting you after all those years and falling in love with you all over again was so wonderful, I was always afraid it was too good to be true.'

Falling in love with you. Harriet held her breath. Had he really said that? Yes, he really had. She looked up into Tom's eyes.

'It *was* true,' she said.

'And it still is,' Tom said. He stretched one arm back through the gap between the front seats and reached for Harriet's hand. He linked his fingers through hers.

'Looks like I can drive on,' Marco said. He restarted the engine.

Chapter Thirty-Six

Donna kissed Tom on both cheeks. 'What beautiful flowers, thank you.' She lifted up the bouquet and inhaled its heady scent.

'Harriet was on the same train as Tom,' Marco said.

'That was lucky,' Donna said.

'Very lucky.' Tom grinned.

Donna smiled. How right she had been to invite Tom tonight. He and Harriet seemed to have reunited before they had even got through the front door.

'Please come through and sit down,' Donna said. She pushed open the sitting room door.

'Tom, this is my daughter, Daniela. Daniela, this is Tom, and of course, you've met Harriet before. Please sit anywhere you like; make yourselves comfortable.'

'Sorry, Miu Miu.' Daniela pushed the cat off the couch so that Harriet and Tom could sit together.

'I'll fetch a couple of bottles of wine and persuade Julia to come out of the kitchen and join us,' Donna said.

'No, I'll get the wine. It's time you sat down,' Marco said.

'And I'll fetch the glasses,' said Daniela.

'Thanks,' Donna sat down gratefully. Her marriage had failed but at least she could be proud of the way her children had turned out.

'Here you are, Mum.' Marco handed her a glass of Chianti.

'Everything's under control in the kitchen, so I guess it won't do any harm to sit down for a bit,' Julia said. She undid the tie at the back of her apron and draped it over the edge of her chair.

'We should have a toast,' Donna said.

'To Marco's travels,' Julia said. She raised her glass.

'To the new exhibition Daniela's been working on. I hear it's in line for an award,' Marco said.

'Thanks,' Daniela murmured. She lowered her eyes and smoothed an imaginary wrinkle out of her skirt.

'Well done,' Donna said. Even now she was still surprised at how different her children were: impulsive Marco who could never sit still; quiet sensible Daniela, with her calf-length skirts and neat, ironed blouses, content with her job at the museum.

'To all our future adventures, big and small,' Tom said.

Everyone raised their glasses. Donna took a big draught of the wine. It began to work its magic: she felt her shoulders drop and her limbs relax.

'It's so wonderful to have you all here,' she said. It was true: her best friend, her children and her guests were Donna's family now. She was lucky, in so many ways. But that didn't stop her missing the one person whose absence she still felt so keenly.

'Another glass, anyone?' Marco said.

'Not for me, I need to go and check on the sauce.' Julia stood up.

'I can hear something. It sounds like a car,' Daniela said.

The familiar sound of the engine, the impatient slam of the car door. Three raps on the front door. It could only be one person. Donna froze.

'I'll go,' Marco said.

Donna could hear Marco opening the front door, the sound of Giovanni's voice in the hall. She stood up.

'It's okay, Mum,' Daniela said softly.

The door opened. Marco and Giovanni walked in. Donna wished she had stayed sitting down. Her legs felt weak and her heart was turning somersaults.

Giovanni put down the striped plastic bag he was carrying. He looked around the room. 'I wasn't expecting such an audience. Tom, what are you doing here? And Harriet – I didn't think I'd be seeing you again, though I am delighted of course . . .'

'I was just going to help Julia in the kitchen. She, umm, needs to get something down from a high shelf,' Tom said.

Donna could not help smiling at his awkward improvisation.

'Harriet and I are going to help Marco with his packing. That's right isn't it, Marco,' Daniela said, scrambling to her feet.

'Yep, I can't decide which shirts to take,' Marco said.

The door swung shut behind them. Giovanni stood awkwardly in the middle of the room.

'You'd better sit down,' Donna said.

He sat, stiff-backed on the couch. Donna perched on the other end. It was so hard to sit next to him. She scooped Miu Miu up off the floor and plonked the cat beside her like a furry, feline shield.

'Oh, before I forget, Vittoria and Vincenzo send their love,' Giovanni said.

'When did you see them?' Donna asked.

'Just now. I called in at Villa Susino on my way here.'

'Oh, right,' Donna said. This wasn't what she expected at all. She did not think she could bear it if Giovanni's visit to Bella Vista was just another social call. She would rather he left right now than make stilted small talk as though she were just another old neighbour.

Giovanni reached and took her hand. 'Donna, we can't go on like this. Please give me one more chance.'

So, he did want her back. But she had vowed to forget him.

'Donna . . .'

The sound of his voice saying her name tugged at her heart. The look in his caramel eyes told her that he still loved her. Her reserve was melting like a bowl of ice-cream under the rays of a summer sun. But she had to be strong. Nothing had changed. If she let Giovanni back into her life everything would be wonderful for a day or two. Then it would all go wrong. And this time, she wouldn't have the strength to ask him to leave. She looked away.

'Giovanni, I can't . . .' Donna's voice cracked.

'No, Donna, don't say anything more. Please hear me out,' Giovanni said.

'Okay,' Donna said quietly. She had nothing to lose. She would hear what Giovanni had to say. Then she would summon up all her strength and ask him to leave.

'Donna, please look at me. Something happened in my class today, something that made me look at myself and see a person I hardly recognised. I held up a mirror and saw all my faults staring back at me. Donna, I am an impossible man. I am impossible to live with. All my plans for this place were foolish and unthinking. I never even asked myself if those changes would make you happy. I never asked you what you wanted to do with Alfredo's things. I cleared everything away to make it easier for you, not thinking that you might need to keep something, however small. I did not put myself in your shoes. I never thought about what you wanted. I thought flowers and gifts would be enough to win you back.'

284

'I didn't need presents, Giovanni. I just needed you to be there for me.'

'I was too foolish to realise. I always thought I knew best. You were right to tell me to go. I could not see a way forward until I remembered a letter Julia had written to me. In my arrogant way, I dismissed her suggestion but today it all began to make sense.

'I have spent the last two hours with Vittoria and Vincenzo because I have agreed to buy Villa Susino, but only if I have your blessing. I'm planning to modernise the place; to indulge all my crazy schemes and plans. I might even put one of those modern glass extensions on the side. I'll have plenty of room to host my writing workshops there and the rest of the time I can write in splendid solitude.'

'You're planning to live at Villa Susino?' Donna said.

'Yes. I shall live and work there. We will be neighbours and, I trust, friends. I'm hoping I might be able to come to Bella Vista for dinner. Not every night – no woman could put up with me every night – but as often as you want. If we got to know each other again we could understand each other better. Then maybe, I hope and pray one day we will be together again, on your terms whatever they may be.'

Donna turned towards Giovanni. She let go of Miu Miu. The cat jumped off the couch and walked off with her tail in the air. For the first time in weeks Donna felt a small stirring of hope. Giovanni's plan might work out. It really, really might. At least, it must be worth a try.

'Perhaps we should both have done things differently,' she said. 'Maybe I should have made my feelings clearer instead of expecting you to read my mind.'

'No, I am certain the fault is entirely mine. And now I must do something I have been longing to do.'

Giovanni traced his forefinger across her cheek. He leant forward as if he was going to kiss her.

'Wait! I almost forgot. I bought you something.' He took a newspaper-wrapped parcel from his striped carrier bag. 'Careful, it's breakable.'

Donna unravelled the layers of newspaper.

The vase was a little taller than the one Giovanni had broken and instead of having straight sides it flared out at the neck.

'There is a chip on the rim and a small crack down one side, but I thought you would like it all the same,' Giovanni said.

Donna traced the pattern of weeping willow trees, pagodas and deer drinking from wavy blue brooks with her fingertip. It was beautiful.

'The things you love don't have to be perfect,' she said.

'I wasn't expecting to have such an eventful evening.' Tom grinned. It was dark out on the terrace, but his eyes gleamed in the light cast by the lantern above the doorway.

Harriet put her wine glass down by the side of the wicker lounger. 'You really had no idea I was staying here when Donna invited you over?'

'None at all. I thought she might want to ask me about Giovanni. Whether he was missing her or something like that.'

'Looks like he was.' Harriet laughed.

'And I was missing you,' Tom said. 'And this . . .' He pulled Harriet closer and kissed her softly.

'I wish I was going to be in Italy for more than four days.' Harriet sighed.

'I'm glad you're not staying much longer,' Tom said.

Harriet tensed. Surely she couldn't have misread the situation. Not this time.

'I'll be back in England next week, myself.'

Harriet's body relaxed. 'I thought you were working for Giovanni in Siena.'

'He's letting me go. For my own good.'

'Oh, I'm sorry.' Harriet fiddled with the stem of her wine glass.

'Don't be. It's good news. Fantastic news, actually. Giovanni's given me the chance to adapt one of his old short stories for the stage. It looks like a small theatre company in North London is interested in putting it on. If I do a good job . . .'

'I'm sure you will. That's wonderful news. So, you're moving back home to Sussex?'

'To my folks? No, I'm planning on renting a room in London but it's a long time since I've lived there. I might need someone to show me around.'

Harriet smiled. 'I think I know just the right person.'

Epilogue

Julia washed up the last of the utensils and left them on the draining board. Every surface of the kitchen was covered with bowls and dishes and the fridge was full to bursting. Giovanni had offered to pay for someone to come in and help but Julia had insisted on taking sole charge of the buffet and Giovanni knew better than to try to dissuade her.

Daniela was laying the tables outside on the terrace, Beppe was uncorking the wine and Carla had gone to fetch Bianca. Bianca did not get out much these days, but she said she would not miss today for the world. Nearly everyone in the village was coming.

It was a pity that Marco would not be there, but Donna was insistent that she did not want him to cut short his trip to Australia; he and Jess were planning to work their way around the world.

Julia opened the back door. It was a beautiful June day. The only sound came from the chirping of the house martins who had once again made their nest under the eaves. She stepped over Lupo who was lounging in his usual place by the doorstep beneath the shade of the pretty hanging basket that Tom and Harriet had sent.

She walked past the chicken run, through the stable yard, past the cherry tree sapling they had planted in memory of Alfredo and down to the paddocks where the horses were grazing.

Bianca's nephew had finished off the pergola beautifully and the trailing roses had opened up their blowsy, pink petals right on cue. Giovanni's plans for Bella Vista had filled Julia with horror, but he had been right about one thing: the pergola was the perfect place for him and Donna to renew their vows.

Giovanni had stayed at Villa Susino last night; he said it was more romantic that way. Although the guest house was officially his home and the place where he held his writing courses he spent less and less time there nowadays. The project had certainly kept him busy but now the refurbishment was nearing completion. Julia had to admit the new decor was very stylish, even though it wasn't what she would have chosen herself. As for the glass extension on the side – the less said about that the better.

Soon the guests would be arriving. She had nothing left to do. She walked back to the house, hung her apron on the back of the kitchen door and went upstairs to get changed. Her new polka-dot dress was lying on the bed. How pretty it looked! Everyone was making a special effort today; even Luigi had dusted off his one and only suit.

Julia brushed her hair and sprayed on a little scent from the glass bottle on top of the chest of drawers. She rather missed the hexagonal, glass-topped table now that it was back downstairs. Donna's willow-pattern vase had pride of place on it. The two objects did not really go together but nobody cared.

Julia fastened her delicate dew-drop necklace and checked her appearance in the mirror. There was one thing missing. She opened the top drawer of the chest and took out a small, dark blue box. She flipped open the lid. The two tiny diamonds either side of the antique amethyst sparkled in the light.

She slipped the ring on her finger and turned her hand this way and that. Then she put the ring back in the box and closed the drawer. She and Luigi would share their good news another time. Today belonged to Donna and Giovanni.

THE END

Acknowledgements

Firstly, thank you to the people of Tuscany and to the late Kenneth and Marjorie Russell who made our many family trips there even more memorable. Thank you to Jenny Bawtree and the team at Rendola Riding for introducing me to the joy of riding through the Tuscan countryside and whose farmhouse is as warm and welcoming as Donna's 'Bella Vista'.

Thank you to my agent Camilla Shestopal of Shesto Literary, always a calm port in a storm, and to the team at Orion, particularly my editor Rhea Kurien, for helping to steer *A Farmhouse in Tuscany* in the right direction, Helena Newton for her copy editing and the cover design team for another evocative image.

A big mention to the Romantic Novelists' Association and all its friendly members who have been a wonderful source of support, especially during the dreaded lockdowns. Thanks to Tina Page, Nicola 'Sham' Geller, Nina Lewis and my husband, Robert Wasey, for their early feedback. Finally, last but not least, to all my readers: thank you for choosing my book.

www.ingramcontent.com/pod-product-compliance
Ingram Content Group UK Ltd.
Pitfield, Milton Keynes, MK11 3LW, UK
UKHW022318280225
455674UK00004B/356